TAKING
RELIGION
SERIOUSLY
ACROSS THE
CURRICULUM

WARREN A. NORD · CHARLES C. HAYNES

Association for Supervision and Curriculum Development
Alexandria, Virginia USA

Nashville, Tennessee USA

Association for Supervision and Curriculum Development
1703 N. Beauregard St. • Alexandria, VA 22311-1714 USA
Telephone: 800-933-2723 or 703-578-9600 • Fax: 703-575-5400
Web site: http://www.ascd.org • E-mail: member@ascd.org

First Amendment Center
1207 18th Avenue South
Nashville, TN 37212
Telephone: 615-321-9588 • Fax: 615-321-9599
Web site: www.freedomforum.org • E-mail: info@fac.org

Printed in the United States of America.

August 1998 member book (p). ASCD Premium, Comprehensive, and Regular members periodically receive ASCD books as part of their membership benefits. No. FY98-9.

ASCD Stock No.: 198190
ASCD member price: $15.95   nonmember price: $18.95

Library of Congress Cataloging-in-Publication Data
Nord, Warren A.
    Taking religion seriously across the curriculum / Warren A. Nord, Charles C. Haynes.
       p.   cm.
    Includes bibliographical references.
    ISBN 0-87120-318-9
    1. Religion in the public schools—United States. 2. Education—United States—Curricula. 3. Interdisciplinary approach in education—United States. I. Haynes, Charles C. II. Title.
LC111.N675 1998
379.2'8'0973—dc21

98-8560
CIP

02 01 00 99 98   5 4 3 2 1

Contents

95903

Preface

ONE MIGHT EXPECT THERE TO BE A VAST SCHOLARLY LITERA-
ture that deals with the role of religion in the public school curriculum. After all, the public square is often filled with smoke from battles
over religion and schooling; our subject would appear to be both
timely and important. And yet, with only a very few exceptions, scholars and schools of education have ignored our subject. So it should
not be surprising that the proper role of religion in the K–12 curriculum is poorly understood, and the importance of what is at stake is
not sufficiently appreciated, among educators.

We will argue that public education is deeply flawed by its failure to take religion seriously, and we will argue on what we regard as
powerful civic, constitutional, and educational grounds that the
study of religion must be much more fully integrated into the curriculum than is now the case.

We have written a short book—given the complexity of our subject and the controversy surrounding it—and many of our issues require a longer and more sophisticated discussion than we can provide
here. Indeed, we have addressed many of these issues more fully in
other contexts and refer our unconvinced readers to those sources.
Warren A. Nord's *Religion and American Education: Rethinking a
National Dilemma* (1995) is a comprehensive study of the role of religion in education (historically, philosophically, constitutionally, and
pedagogically) that provides context for, and elaboration on, many of
the claims and arguments we make here. *Finding Common Ground: A
First Amendment Guide to Religion and Public Education,* written by
Charles C. Haynes and Oliver Thomas (1994, 1996), includes a wealth
of documents and commentary dealing with the civic and constitu-

tional dimensions of our argument. Haynes's *Religion in American History: What to Teach and How* (1990) further develops our argument in Chapter 4, and provides primary source material that will be of considerable help to history teachers.

We would like to thank a number of individuals who read all or significant portions of the manuscript and improved it by their suggestions: E. M. Adams, Marcia Beauchamp, Martha Dill, John Dixon, Carl Ernst, Mark Gerzon, Sidney Rittenberg, and Oliver Thomas. We are especially grateful for the valuable assistance of John Ferguson, Religious Freedom Analyst at the First Amendment Center.

We thank the Lilly Endowment and the College of Arts and Sciences at the University of North Carolina at Chapel Hill for funding academic leave that enabled Warren Nord to research and write much of his portion of the book. We also thank the Freedom Forum First Amendment Center for supporting the participation of Charles Haynes in this project.

Introduction

IT IS ALL BUT INEVITABLE THAT OUR SUBJECT CALLS TO MIND the rhetoric and images of a culture war. Much of the public debate is framed in terms of the combat between two polarized groups: those religious conservatives who would restore prayer to school activities, add creationism to the curriculum, and drop sex education from it; and those liberals who would keep prayer out of schools, keep religion out of the curriculum, and keep sex education in it. Battles in this culture war are fought regularly in courtrooms, direct-mail campaigns, local school board elections, and national politics. Journalistic dispatches from the front typically frame the conflict in its most dramatic and polarized terms.

We intend in this book to provide a more nuanced account of what is at issue, articulate a set of civic and educational principles that we might use for adjudicating our differences, and stake out common ground on which we might stand together in discussing the role of religion in the curriculum. Indeed, although our differences are deep, we believe that our subject need not be nearly so controversial as it now appears to be.

The Problem

The United States is a religious nation. About 90 percent of Americans claim to believe in God, and almost 80 percent say that religion is an important part of their lives. Seventy percent of Americans pray and 40 percent attend religious services and read the Bible each week. No doubt much belief is nominal and much religious practice is perfunctory. Still, for a great many Americans, religion makes a pro-

1

found difference in how they live their lives and how they think about the world. After all, religious traditions carry with them implications for all of life; they shape our most fundamental beliefs and values. Indeed, a vast religious literature, contemporary as well as historical, deals with economics, psychology, sexuality, nature, history, morality, politics, and the arts—in every subject in the curriculum.

This being the case, it is striking that, apart from history courses (and some historical literature read in English courses), the curriculum all but ignores religion. The conventional wisdom of educators appears to be that students can learn everything they need to know about whatever they study (other than history or historical literature) without learning anything about religion. If religion was once pervasive, it now appears to be irrelevant.

In our deeply religious culture this development has not gone unnoticed. Indeed, many religious conservatives are outraged by it; they take the absence of religion to imply a hostility to religion. This has fueled our culture wars and has driven many to private schools and to support the voucher movement.

No doubt most educators have come to take the growing political power of the "Religious Right" seriously. Unhappily, most discussion of the role of religion in public education has focused almost exclusively on politics rather than on the underlying educational and intellectual issues. We will argue that questions about the role of religion in the curriculum are much more important, and cut much deeper, than conventional educational wisdom would have it.

What Is Religion?

We often assume that religion must be defined in terms of God. But, of course, what counts as God (Nirvana, Brahman, the Tao, the Transcendent) differs considerably from religion to religion. Indeed, some religions—the oldest forms of Buddhism, for example—make no claims about any god, and much religion places rather more emphasis on tradition, community, and how we live, than on belief in God.

In defining religion for the purposes of determining whether an applicant for conscientious objector status was religious, Supreme Court Justice Tom Clark noted that

> over 250 sects inhabit our land. Some believe in a purely
> personal God, some in a supernatural deity; others think

> of religion as a way of life envisioning, as its ultimate goal, the day when all men can live together in perfect understanding and peace. There are those who think of God as the depth of our being; others, such as the Buddhists, strive for a state of lasting rest through self-denial and inner purification.

After citing a host of theologians, Clark rather tentatively suggested that religion is grounded in a "power or being, or upon a faith, to which all else is subordinate or upon which all else is dependent."[1] That is, it makes sense constitutionally to talk about religion apart from God.

Paul Tillich was one of the theologians whom Justice Clark cited. In his very influential interpretation of religion, Tillich argued that the object of faith is what *concerns us ultimately* (1957, pp. 1–29). Historically, the great religions have nurtured and shaped people's ultimate concerns and commitments but, he argued, people can and sometimes do direct their faith—their religious commitments—toward what is not *truly* ultimate but idolatrous. For Tillich, living in Germany in the 1920s and 1930s, Nazism was an all too common form of "religious" idolatry.

Similarly, social scientists have often discussed *functional religions*—those comprehensive ideologies and symbol systems that (although they needn't involve God) define ultimate reality in ways that give meaning and direction to people's lives: nationalism, communism, psychoanalysis, humanism, even, perhaps, science (or scientism). Like traditional religions, they too can define people's ultimate hopes, values, and convictions and be grounded in a faith to which all else is subordinated.

And then there is *spirituality*, an awareness of the presence of the divine in nature and in our lives that isn't linked to particular religions, orthodox doctrines, or institutional structures. Because it is "nonsectarian," educators sometimes believe that it isn't religion and encourage spiritual practices (such as meditation and visualization exercises) in the classroom. Not surprisingly, many religious conservatives object to such practices, seeing in them the practice of a New Age Religion that conflicts with their own.

In the end, we suggest, no hard and fast lines can be drawn between spirituality, traditional religion, and those functional "secular"

---

[1]United States v. Seeger 380 US 163, 174, 176 (1965).

religions that shape the thinking and lives of so many people. As we proceed we will see, from time to time, that the conventional sharp dichotomy between the sacred and the secular gets in the way of our ability to think clearly about religion. It isn't always clear when religious claims are being made, and we must keep in mind the richness and relevance of a spectrum of possibilities. Ordinarily, however, when we talk about religion in the chapters that follow, we mean the traditional major world religions—Judaism, Christianity, Islam, Hinduism, Buddhism, and Taoism, for example.

We will not attempt any further effort at defining religion here—other than to suggest three generalizations about these major world religions that will be relevant to our discussion.

1. Each of them discerns a *richer reality* than does modern science. Ultimate Reality (be it God or Brahman or Nirvana or the Tao) can't be grasped in scientific categories, expressed in scientific language, or analyzed in scientific laboratories.

2. From within each tradition, religion can't be *compartmentalized*; it isn't simply a matter of what one affirms or does on Friday evening or Sunday morning. The implications of God's existence extend to all of life—to how we act the rest of the week, and to how we make sense of the world.

3. And, of course, religion is *important*. Religions deal, as Tillich argued, with matters of ultimate concern. People are not free to ignore God. Religion is a matter of concern not just to scholars and antiquarians.

Religion and America's Culture Wars

Historically, religion has played three somewhat different roles in America's culture wars.

In the 17th century the most fundamental conflicts in America and Western Europe were between different religions—particularly Catholicism and Protestantism. Of course, the hostility among Protestants could be fairly intense without bringing "Papists" into the picture: the Massachusetts Puritans found it necessary to hang a few Quakers, for example. Religious discrimination has not disappeared in America, and these conflicts continue to be violent elsewhere in the world where, tragically, Catholics and Protestants, Muslims and Jews, Hindus and Sikhs, continue to kill one another.

By the end of the 18th century the first skirmishes in a new culture war had been fought—this one between theologians and the growing number of secular intellectuals committed to the Enlightenment and modern science. Over the last century many of the major battles in this war have been fought over evolution, but continuing conflicts between secular and religious interpretations of the world take place in all domains of our cultural and intellectual life (and, as we shall see, in all areas of the curriculum).

By the end of the 19th century deep divisions had appeared within Christianity and Judaism between "conservatives" who wished to maintain theological orthodoxies grounded in Scripture or tradition, and "liberals" who believed that religion could be progressive as theologians used modern scholarship to rethink and reform their own traditions. So, for example, the liberal theologians who shaped the mainline Protestant denominations and Reform Judaism came rather quickly to accept evolution and historical criticism of the Bible. Many conservatives, in response, reasserted their belief in the inerrancy of Scripture and the authority of tradition, and their opposition to evolution.

In his very influential book *Culture Wars* (1991), James Davison Hunter argued that battles of this third culture war are most prominent in contemporary America. On most moral, political, and educational questions a wide measure of agreement links liberal Jews, Catholics, and Protestants on the one hand—as it does their conservative counterparts on the other. These distinctions can be overdrawn; there is an evangelical Left, for example, and some religious liberals are political and moral conservatives. Still, the culture war between conservatives and liberals has submerged denominational differences to a striking extent.

Consequently, in our discussions of neutrality and liberal education we must keep in mind three distinct sets of tensions—tensions between religious and secular interpretations of reality, among different religions, and tensions between liberals and conservatives within each of those religions.

Why Is Religion Absent from the Curriculum?

Three (ultimately inadequate) reasons are often given to this question. First, some educators continue to believe that the constitutional "separation of church and state" means that the curriculum cannot include religion. True, it *is* unconstitutional to *practice* religion in public schools; it is unconstitutional to *proselytize* or *indoctrinate* students. But it is *not* unconstitutional to *teach students about religion*—if it is done properly. No Supreme Court justice has ever held that students can't study the Bible or be taught about religion. Of course, what it means to teach about religion *properly* is not always clear or uncontroversial.

Second, many educators and textbook publishers believe that including religion in textbooks and the curriculum is too controversial. But, of course, it is also controversial to leave religion out of the curriculum. Indeed, textbooks and the curriculum already include much that is controversial—sex education, multiculturalism, feminism, and evolution, for example. Why not religion?

We will argue that religion need not be nearly so controversial as is often thought. In fact, there now exists widespread agreement—what we will call the New Consensus—about the role of religion in the curriculum among representatives of most major religious and educational organizations at the national level. (More about this shortly.) Unfortunately, word of this consensus has yet to reach many of the combatants in the trenches.

Third, religious conservatives often argue that public education has been taken over by intellectuals promoting the "religion" of secular humanism. What secular humanism is, and whether it might function as a religion, are matters of some complexity and controversy. Although much more needs to be said in response to this charge, we note two things. It is clear that the great majority of educators do not *intend* to undermine religion, and surely no "conspiracy" of secular humanists is out to destroy the faiths of our children. And yet we must acknowledge that public schools do teach students to think about virtually all aspects of life in secular rather than religious ways, *as if* God were irrelevant and those secular ways of making sense of the world were sufficient. (More on this matter in Chapter 2.)

So, why did religion disappear from the curriculum? Quite simply, public education reflects the dominant ideas and ideals of our culture, and as American culture and intellectual life have become more secular, so has public education. We can see this in at least three ways.

1. *If the controversial nature of religion isn't an adequate explanation for the absence of religion from the curriculum, it is part of the*

explanation nonetheless. The Framers of our Constitution believed that, in the pluralistic culture of the new United States, government must be built on common ground; the divisiveness of religion was one reason they chose to disestablish religion. Similarly, it was the task of the early public, or *common,* schools of the 19th century to unite an increasingly individualistic and pluralistic culture; schools should teach what we hold in common, not what divides us. Because religion was divisive, schools began to marginalize it—not in one fell swoop, certainly, but gradually. "Americanism," by contrast, would unite us, and in an immigrant nation educators assigned it many of the tasks given to religion in earlier times and in more homogeneous cultures.

2. *Our civilization—and our educational institutions—grew more secular as the goals of life shifted to material wealth and happiness in this world rather than salvation in a world to come.* By the end of the 19th century the purposes of schooling (and of higher education) had become in large part economic: to pass on that practical knowledge that would enable individuals and the country to thrive economically.

3. *The extraordinary success of modern science in making sense of the world led to a devaluation of traditional religion.* Physicists and biologists saw no need to appeal to God in explaining the workings of nature, nor did psychologists or economists find the evidence of Scripture relevant in explaining human nature or the economy.

As a result, by the end of the 19th century, 50 years before the Supreme Court first addressed the place of religion in public schools, religion had largely disappeared from textbooks and the curriculum. True, a ceremonial husk of religion—school prayers, devotionals, and Bible reading—survived in some places (and occasionally until the present day). Still, religion has long been gone from the heart of education, from the understanding of life and the world conveyed in textbooks and the curriculum (Nord, 1995, chap. 2).

Of course, the almost complete secularization of education does not accurately reflect our culture. As we have noted, most Americans are (in varying degrees) religious; religion retains a good deal of vitality. What we must conclude, therefore, is that education mirrors only what have come to be the *dominant* ideas and ideals of modern culture and especially of intellectuals. We *disagree* about the significance and truth of religious claims.

What then should be the role of religious ideas and ideals in the public school curriculum when our culture is deeply divided about religion? How do we live with our deepest differences?

Taking Religion Seriously

We will argue there are two fundamental reasons—or families of reasons—for including religion in the curriculum, for taking it seriously. First, there are *civic* reasons. The American experiment in liberty is built on the conviction that it is possible to find common ground in spite of our deep religious differences. It is rooted in the civic agreement we share as citizens, in our principled commitment to respect one another. Properly understood, this means that we not exclude religious voices from the public square or from public education, but that we take one another seriously. For much of our history, Protestantism enjoyed a favored status in the ceremony, rhetoric, and often in the curriculum and textbooks of public schools. That was unjust; it meant that education didn't take others of different (or no) religious convictions seriously. In the 20th century the curriculum has often excluded religion. In *public* schools this is unjust; it means that we don't take religious people seriously. All sides need to recognize that we cannot resolve the current battles either by promoting a particular religion or by excluding all religion from the curriculum.

This civic framework is embodied in the religious liberty clauses of the First Amendment to the Constitution. For more than 50 years, ever since it first applied the First Amendment to the states, the Supreme Court has held that government, and therefore public schools, must be *neutral* in matters of religion—neutral among religions, *and* neutral between religion and nonreligion. It is not proper for public schools to take sides on religiously contested questions. We will argue that if schools are to be truly neutral they must be truly *fair*—and this means including in the curriculum religious as well as secular ways of making sense of the world when we disagree. Government can no more inhibit religion than promote it.

Second, there are *educational* reasons for taking religion seriously. A good *liberal* education should expose students to the major ways humanity has developed for making sense of the world—and some of those ways of understanding the world are religious. An exclusively secular education is an illiberal education. Indeed, we cannot systematically exclude the religious voices in our cultural conversation without conveying the implication that religion is irrelevant, that religious views have no claim on the truth. By conveying a limited (secular) range of views that students must, in effect, accept on authority for want of any understanding of the alternatives, we place them at a deep disadvantage in thinking critically about where the truth might lie.

These are not arguments for promoting religion or for indoctrinating students. They are arguments for including religion in the curricular discussion, for taking it seriously.

The New Consensus

Given the heated nature of our culture wars, it may come as something of a surprise to many that over the last decade a fairly broad consensus about the role of religion in public schools has developed at the national level among the leadership of many religious and educational organizations. This New Consensus has been articulated in a number of documents that we will discuss in Chapters 1 and 2. For now we simply outline the three major principles that form the foundation of the consensus. First, as the Supreme Court has made clear, the study of religion in public schools is constitutional. Second, the study of religion is tremendously important if students are to be educated about our history and culture. Third, public schools must teach about religion objectively or neutrally; their purpose must be to educate students about a variety of religious traditions, not to indoctrinate them into any particular tradition.

This New Consensus doesn't solve all the problems. Not everyone is part of it. Many people—indeed, many educators—haven't heard of it. We believe that the great majority of Americans would accept the basic principles underlying the consensus on reflection if they understood them, but, alas, all too many don't. And, of course, we are not so naive as to believe that *everyone* would accept the principles defining the New Consensus.

Moreover, the basic principles are open to varying interpretations. Just how important is religion? Important enough to bump other subjects from textbooks or the curriculum? Important enough to warrant classes in religious studies with certified teachers? And what does it mean to teach about religion "neutrally" or "objectively"— especially when we disagree deeply about the truth and meaning of religious claims? Obviously, more needs to be said.

In what follows, we approach the role of religion in the curriculum from the perspective of the New Consensus. It is our intention to build on the principles that ground the consensus and draw out their (sometimes surprising) implications for the curriculum, giving them substance, specificity, and relevance. Of course, not all advocates of the New Consensus will agree with our interpretation or application of the principles.

* * *

In Part One of our book we outline the basic civic, constitutional, and educational frameworks that we believe should govern the role of religion in the curriculum. In Part Two we discuss the role of religion in elementary education, moral education, and secondary school courses in history, civics, economics, literature and the arts, and the sciences. We also devote a chapter to religion courses; indeed, we hope that all teachers who deal with the Bible or world religions, whatever their subject, will read that chapter.

To provide some understanding of the conventional wisdom regarding religion in schools, we briefly review the new national education standards for what they say about religion (if anything), and we draw on our own study of textbooks to see how religion figures into them. (We recognize, of course, that most schools don't follow the standards and that good teachers don't just teach the texts.) We say something about what we take to be the major issues in each discipline, paying particular attention to what is religiously controversial. Finally, we draw out the educational implications: given our frameworks, given the major issues, given the different points of view, when and how should the curriculum or particular courses incorporate the study of religion?

Suggested Readings
and Resources

Our statement of the problem, and our account of the secularization of public education, are developed at considerably greater length in the Introduction and first two chapters of Warren A. Nord's *Religion and American Education: Rethinking a National Dilemma* (1995). The best general history of religion and public schooling is Robert Michaelsen's *Piety in the Public School* (1970).

In *The Myth of the Common Schools* (1987) Charles Glenn provides a good historical study of the role of religion in the common school movement of the 19th century, and in *Guardians of Tradition: American Schoolbooks of the Nineteenth Century* (1964) Ruth Miller Elson shows in detail how religion gradually disappeared from textbooks over the course of that crucial century. Although religion is not their primary subject, David Tyack and Elizabeth Hanson provide valuable perspective in their account of the professionalization of American education in *Managers of Virtue: Public School Leadership in America* (1982).

Three recent books on American higher education warrant mention, for to some considerable extent it is the academy that defines what is intellectually respectable and sets the curricular agenda for public schooling; each details the secularization of higher education in the United States. See George Marsden, *The Soul of the American University* (1994); Douglas Sloan, *Faith and Knowledge* (1994); and Julie A. Reuben, *The Making of the Modern University* (1996). For James Davison Hunter's influential interpretation of our culture wars, see his *Culture Wars: The Struggle to Define America* (1991).

PART

I

The Frameworks

1

The Civic and Constitutional Frameworks

"Congress shall make no law respecting the establishment
of religion, or prohibiting the free exercise thereof. . . ."

—Religious Liberty clauses of
the First Amendment to the U.S. Constitution

TAKING RELIGION SERIOUSLY IN THE CURRICULUM REQUIRES taking *religious liberty* seriously throughout the school culture. Without a shared commitment to principles of religious liberty, conflicts over religion and values can tear apart a community and create a climate of distrust in the schools. In many school districts, the mere mention of religion, much less substantive discussion, may trigger conflict. In other places, individual teachers may do a good job of including religion, but they often do so without clear district policies or administrative and community understanding of the proper role for religion in the public schools. In neither setting can religion or religious liberty be taken seriously.

The solution is for schools and communities to openly and honestly address religious liberty in public education. They might begin by asking: What are the civic ground rules for understanding the proper constitutional and educational role for religion in the public school? The starting point for this discussion should be the guiding principles behind the first 16 words of the First Amendment—the words that open this chapter. Properly understood and applied, these principles constitute a civic framework within which public schools can protect the rights of every parent and student while treating religion with fairness in the curriculum.

There is, of course, some risk in taking a proactive approach to religion-in-schools issues that have divided Americans since the founding of public schools. The greater risk, however, is to ignore the distrust and discontent that have led many parents to conclude, fairly or unfairly, that public schools are hostile to their faith and values. Ironically, as we shall see, religious issues in schools have actually become a good place to start building common ground. The growing consensus across the political and religious spectrum about the role of religion in the schools provides an unprecedented opportunity for educators to bring their communities together in support of a new approach to old conflicts.

Clearing away the confusion about how to apply First Amendment religious liberty principles in the schools isn't easy. Extremes tend to dominate the debate. On one end of the spectrum are those who advocate what might be called the "sacred public school" where one religion (theirs) is preferred in school practices and policies. Characteristic of the early history of public schools, this approach still survives in some parts of the United States. In more recent decades, some on the other end of the spectrum have pushed for a "naked public school" where religion is kept out in the name of a strict separation of church and state. The influence that this view has had on educators accounts for much of the silence about religion in the curriculum and the confusion about the religious liberty rights of students. Both of these models of public schools are unjust and, we would argue, unconstitutional.

We propose a third model that is consistent with First Amendment principles and broadly supported by many education and religious groups: the "civil public school," where people of all faiths and no faith are treated with fairness and respect. The starting point for our proposal is the shared vision of religious liberty that undergirds such a school. We will then consider how schools and classrooms may fully realize that vision.

The Civil Public School

A few years ago, the Association for Supervision and Curriculum Development, the National Association of Evangelicals, and the First

Amendment Center decided that the time had come for a new dialogue between public school educators and some of their severest critics, especially among conservative Christians. Much was at stake on all sides. Everyone at the table was painfully aware that culture-war battles in public schools tear apart the fabric of our society and greatly threaten efforts to reform schools.

The first meeting, in April 1994, opened with a list of disputes ranging from religious holidays and prayer to school reform and sex education. Hearing the litany of conflicts, a participant remarked that if we don't find ways to address our differences concerning religion and values in schools, then public education doesn't have much of a future. Ernest Boyer, representing the Carnegie Foundation for the Advancement of Teaching, suddenly hit the table, saying, "I wouldn't put it that way." The group looked surprised, well aware of Boyer's strong advocacy of public education. "No," he said emphatically, "if we don't do better in addressing these conflicts, it's not just public schools, but *our nation* that doesn't have much of a future."

We kept Boyer's warning before us as we struggled to craft an agreement that would help local schools and communities move from battleground to common ground. One year later, in the spring of 1995, 21 educational and religious groups issued a document entitled *Religious Liberty, Public Education, and the Future of American Democracy: A Statement of Principles.* For the first time in American history, organizations representing a broad spectrum of religious and political views—from right to left—articulated a shared vision of religious liberty in the public schools. The core of the agreement is captured in Principle IV, which states:

> Public schools may not inculcate nor inhibit religion. They must be places where religion and religious conviction are treated with fairness and respect. Public schools uphold the First Amendment when they protect the religious liberty rights of students of all faiths or none. Schools demonstrate fairness when they ensure that the curriculum includes study *about* religion, where appropriate, as an important part of a complete education.[1]

This articulation of First Amendment principles is as remarkable for who says it as for what it says. The National Education As-

---

[1]Free copies of the full *Statement of Principles* are available from the First Amendment Center, 1207 18th Ave. S., Nashville, TN 37212; telephone: (615) 321-9588.

sociation, the National School Boards Association, and the American Association of School Administrators joined with the Christian Legal Society, the American Center for Law and Justice, and Citizens for Excellence in Education. The Anti-Defamation League and the Union of American Hebrew Congregations are on the list, and so is the Council on Islamic Education and the Christian Educators Association International. Perhaps most remarkably, the Christian Coalition *and* People for the American Way are sponsors.

The *Statement of Principles* signals that there is a great deal of consensus regarding the relationship of religion to government and to public schools under the Establishment Clause of the First Amendment ("Congress shall make no law respecting an establishment of religion . . ."). We suggest that at the heart of this consensus is the idea that the public schools should be *neutral* in matters of religion.

For 50 years now, ever since its landmark ruling in *Everson v. Board of Education* (1947), the Supreme Court has taken *neutrality* as its touchstone in adjudicating Establishment Clause cases.[2] As government institutions, public schools must be religiously neutral in two senses: they must be neutral *among religions* (they can't privilege one religion over another); *and* they must be neutral *between religion and nonreligion* (they can't privilege religion generally over nonreligion).

What is not often appreciated is the fact that neutrality is a two-edged sword. Just as public schools can't promote religion, neither can they inhibit or denigrate religion. The courts have also been clear about *this*—but, of course, here is where the conceptual waters become muddy. What counts as inhibiting or denigrating religion?

We will argue that it is anything but neutral to ignore religion. Neutrality cannot mean hostility or even silence. It is, of course, true that public schools cannot be in the business of religious indoctrination; faith formation is properly the province of the family and religious institutions. But at the same time, schools have an obligation to make sure that religion is taken seriously. Neutrality, as we shall argue, requires *fairness* to religion.

Quite apart from the Court's interpretation of the Establishment Clause, we believe that justice requires that the curriculum of public schools be neutral in a pluralistic democracy. When the public dis-

---

[2]Everson v. Board of Education, 330 U.S. 1 (1947).

agrees deeply, public schools should not promote, much less institutionalize, one view and remain silent about others. Unlike private schools, *public schools* must take *the public* seriously. For example, because we disagree deeply about which political party has the better policies, it would violate our sense of justice for public schools to take sides, teaching only the policies and values of one party, leaving the other out of the discussion. We also disagree deeply, often on religious grounds, about how to make sense of our lives and the world; hence, public schools should not promote, much less institutionalize, any particular way of making sense of the world *be it religious or secular.* If public schools are to be built on common civic ground, they must be neutral when we disagree; they must take everyone seriously.

Before discussing more fully the implications of neutrality and the Establishment Clause for public schools, we should note that strong agreement also coalesces around the meaning of the Free Exercise Clause ("Congress shall make no law . . . prohibiting the free exercise [of religion] . . . ") in a public school setting. *Religion in the Public Schools: A Joint Statement of Current Law,* also published in 1995, expresses the consensus of 35 religious and civil liberties groups on the religious liberty rights of public school students. That same year, President Bill Clinton drew on the *Joint Statement* when he issued a directive through the U.S. Department of Education to all public school superintendents, outlining the constitutional and educational role of religion in the public schools. The National PTA and the First Amendment Center built on both documents to produce *A Parent's Guide to Religion in the Public Schools,* more than 250,000 copies of which have been distributed by schools and communities thus far.[3] Let's take a closer look at how these agreements provide a civic framework for a truly civil public school.

Religious Liberty Rights of Students

Many Americans continue to hold the mistaken view that the Supreme Court decisions in the 1960s concerning prayer and Bible

---

[3]*Religion in the Public Schools: A Joint Statement of Current Law* is available by writing to Religion in the Public Schools, 15 East 84th St., Suite 501, New York, NY 10028. The directive sent out from the U.S. Department of Education may be obtained by calling 1-800-USA-LEARN. Free copies of *A Parent's Guide to Religion in the Public Schools* are available from the First Amendment Center, Freedom Forum, 1101 Wilson Blvd., Arlington, VA 22209.

reading prohibited students from expressing their faith in a public school. Thanks in large measure to the president's directive, the message is finally getting through that the Court never struck down "prayer in schools"; it barred *state-sponsored* religious practices. In fact, students have extensive religious liberty rights while in school. School boards and school administrators should now have a clear picture of what it means to "protect the religious liberty rights of students of all faiths or none."

Under the First Amendment as interpreted by the courts, students do have the right to pray in a public school alone or in groups, as long as the activity does not disrupt the school or infringe on the rights of others. These activities must be truly voluntary and student initiated. For example, students may gather around the flagpole for prayer before school begins, as long as the event is not sponsored by the school and other students are not pressured to attend. Students also have the right to share their faith with others and to read their Scriptures. They do not have to leave their religion at the schoolhouse door. Only if behavior coerces or harasses others, or is disruptive of the educational process, should it be prohibited.

When it is relevant to the discussion and meets the academic requirements, students have the right to express personal religious views in class or as part of a written assignment or art activity. They may not, of course, force their classmates to participate in a religious exercise.

Most legal experts agree that students have the right to distribute religious literature in public schools subject to reasonable restrictions imposed by school officials regarding time, place, and manner. This means that the school may specify when and where the distribution may occur. But the restrictions should be reasonable, and the school must apply them evenly to *all* nonschool student literature.

In secondary schools, the 1984 Equal Access Act ensures that students may form religious clubs if the school allows other extracurricular clubs. The act is intended to protect *student-initiated* and *student-led* meetings. Outsiders may not "direct, conduct, control, or regularly attend" student clubs, and faculty sponsors may be present at religious meetings in a nonparticipatory capacity only. Schools must give student religious clubs the same access to school facilities and media as they give other extracurricular clubs.

Despite the broad agreement on all of these rights, some areas of disagreement remain—especially concerning student prayers at graduation or other school events. At present, there is no clear legal answer to this conflict because lower courts are divided about the constitutionality of student-initiated, student-led prayers at graduation exercises. Until the Supreme Court resolves the matter, school districts in various parts of the country will follow different rules.

The good news, however, is how much consensus exists on students' religious liberty rights in a public school. As President Clinton said in his speech announcing the guidelines, public schools need not be "religion-free zones."

Parental Rights and Responsibilities

A civil public school is also one that recognizes, in the words of the *Statement of Principles,* that parents have "the primary responsibility for the upbringing of their children, including education." At the very least, this should mean that parents are involved in shaping policies about religion and religious liberty in the schools.

Of special interest to parents, especially religious parents, are school policies concerning accommodation of student religious needs and requirements. Most school officials will try to accommodate parental requests to excuse a child from classroom discussions or activities for religious reasons if the request focuses on a specific discussion, assignment, or activity. At times, however, schools are unsure about when and how much to accommodate, particularly with the expanding religious diversity in their districts.

For several years, the Religious Freedom Restoration Act (RFRA), passed by Congress in 1993, made it more difficult for schools to ignore religious requests for excusal. Under the act, if parents could show that particular lessons or school policies substantially burdened a student's free exercise of religion, then the school would have to prove a "compelling state interest" in requiring attendance or enforcing the policy. When the Supreme Court struck down RFRA as unconstitutional in 1997, some of the pressure on school officials to accommodate religious requests may have been lessened.

Take, for example, a 1994 case involving a Sikh family in California. The family wanted to send their son to a public high school wearing a small ceremonial dagger in spite of the school's "no weapons" policy. During the court battle that followed, all sides agreed that school officials had compelling reasons for keeping all weapons out of the school. (Public schools have a number of "compelling interests," including health and safety of all students.) But using RFRA, the court agreed with the parents that the school's interest in safety could be preserved if the dagger—which all adult male Sikhs are required to wear—were riveted into its sheath (making it impossible to use as a weapon) and worn underneath the student's clothes.[4] Without RFRA, the Sikh family might well have lost that case.

It may be that without RFRA parents will find it more difficult to get exemptions for their children from general school policies. But we would argue that school officials should still take religious requests for accommodation seriously for at least two reasons. First, upholding the religious liberty of parents and students is the right thing to do. Many teachers and administrators understand this when they routinely grant requests for a student to be excused from participation based on religious convictions. A common example is the parental request for a child to opt out of a particular lesson or classroom activity. To be sure, the school has an important interest in teaching Sally to read. But giving Sally an alternate assignment for one book or a few stories is a good way to accomplish the school's educational goal while still protecting Sally's religious liberty.

Second, in most cases, parents may also appeal to another constitutional right, such as the right of parents to control the upbringing of their children or, on behalf of their children, the right of free speech. Though some recent lower court decisions seem to ignore or minimize parental rights, the Supreme Court has long recognized such rights.[5]

Free exercise of religion joined with either free speech or parental rights makes a powerful combination. The Supreme Court itself has indicated that the "compelling state interest" test may be used when free exercise claims are linked to at least one other constitutional right.[6] On legal grounds, therefore, public school officials are still well advised to make every effort to accommodate the needs and requirements of religious parents and students.

This does not mean that school officials can or should accommodate all opt-out requests, especially when such requests are ex-

---

[4] See Cheema v. Thompson, 67 F3d 883 (9th Cir 1995).

[5] See Meyer v. Nebraska, 262 U.S. 390 (1923) and Pierce v. Society of Sisters, 268 US 510 (1925).

[6] See Employment Division v. Smith (1990). 485 U.S. 660 (1990).

tensive. For example, schools could not accommodate parents who want their child to be excused from the world history class every time religion is mentioned, because religion frequently comes up (or ought to) in the study of world civilizations. Courts have recognized that public schools do not have to accommodate every request to opt out of portions of the curriculum.[7] Of course, it isn't always clear just where educators should draw the line. But when parents limit their request to particular lessons or activities, schools should try to provide an alternative for the student.

A number of schools have added another dimension to their excusal policies—one that is popular with many parents: opt in. This involves requiring parental notification and permission for students to be involved in potentially controversial lessons or activities. If, for example, a high school teacher decides to show an R-rated movie such as *Schindler's List* as part of the study of the Holocaust, parents would have to sign a permission slip for their child to see the film. Some school districts also use opt-in policies for participation in extracurricular student clubs. In this way parents know what is happening in the school and have the opportunity to keep their children out of activities they may find objectionable.

The effort to accommodate religious claims in public schools can be time-consuming and sometimes frustrating for educators, especially as religious diversity in the United States continues to expand. But it is well worth the trouble. By making every effort to accommodate, school officials not only fulfill their obligations under the First Amendment, but they also build trust between the school and parents.

Study of Religion

A civil public school that upholds religious liberty rights of parents and students would also ensure that the curriculum treats religion fairly and fully. We argue that if public schools "may not inculcate nor inhibit" religion, if they are to remain neutral concerning religion, then the curriculum *must* include religious as well as secular ways of understanding the world. Excluding religion, or barely mentioning it, is hardly neutral or fair. For many parents, the failure to take reli-

---

[7]See Mozert v. Hawkins County Board of Education, 827 F2d 1058 (6th Cir 1986).

gion seriously in the curriculum is strong evidence that public education takes sides against religion.

Under Supreme Court rulings, public schools clearly have permission to require that students learn about religion (leaving it to educators to decide where and how this should be done). The Court has not said when or if ignoring religion might violate government neutrality concerning religion. But the principles of neutrality articulated by the Court lend support to our contention that a neutral and fair curriculum must include study of religion.

In a series of decisions in the 1960s striking down state-sponsored religious exercises in public schools, the Court reaffirmed that "no establishment" prohibits the government not only from preferring one religion over another but also from preferring religion over nonreligion.[8] Writing for the majority in *Abington v. Schempp*, Justice Tom Clark argued that required religious exercises in public schools are a "breach of neutrality" barred by the First Amendment. He was careful, however, to make clear that government neutrality cannot result in hostility to religion. That is, government cannot prefer nonreligion over religion either. As Justice Clark wrote, the government may not establish a "religion of secularism" by opposing or showing hostility to religion. Neither should neutrality be taken to mean that the curriculum must exclude religion. On the contrary, the study of religion is important. In the frequently quoted words of the Court's *Schempp* decision,

> [I]t might well be said that one's education is not complete without a study of comparative religion or the history of religion and its relationship to the advancement of civilization. It certainly may be said that the Bible is worthy of study for its literary and historic qualities. Nothing we have said here indicates that such study of the Bible or of religion, when presented objectively as part of a secular education, may not be effected consistently with the First Amendment.

Clearly, including the academic study of religion does not violate the Establishment Clause. But is the school *required* to teach about religion in order to maintain neutrality? Justice Arthur J. Goldberg's

---

[8] See Engel v. Vitale, 370 U.S. 421 (1962) and School District of Abington v. Schempp, 374 U.S. 203 (1963).

concurring opinion in *Schempp* comes close to suggesting that the answer may be yes:

> It is said, and I agree, that the attitude of government toward religion must be one of neutrality. But untutored devotion to the concept of neutrality can lead to invocation or approval of results which partake not simply of that noninterference and noninvolvement with the religious which the Constitution commands, but of a brooding and pervasive devotion to the secular and a passive, or even active, hostility to the religious. Such results are not only not compelled by the Constitution, but, it seems to me, are prohibited by it.
>
> Neither government nor this Court can or should ignore the significance of the fact that a vast portion of our people believe in and worship God and that many of our legal, political, and personal values derive historically from religious teachings. Government must inevitably take cognizance of the existence of religion, and, indeed, under certain circumstances the First Amendment may require that it do so. And it seems clear to me from the opinions in the present and past cases that the Court would recognize the propriety of providing military chaplains and of the teaching *about* religion, as distinguished from the teaching *of* religion, in the public schools.

A public school curriculum that teaches secular ways of seeing the world while barely mentioning religious perspectives strikes us as a good example of the "passive hostility" Justice Goldberg says is prohibited by the First Amendment. The curriculum may well be one of those places where the government is required to "take cognizance of the existence of religion."

If the Court has not explicitly required that religion be included in the curriculum, we would argue that it ought to do so. Under the Court's own test for neutrality in *Schempp*, as well as in subsequent decisions, public schools may do nothing that has a primary effect of either advancing or *inhibiting* religion. We are convinced that the current curriculum does inhibit religion by marginalizing religion in our intellectual and cultural life, (implicitly) conveying the sense that religion is irrelevant in the search for truth in the various domains of the curriculum (as we will argue in Chapter 2). On both civic and educational grounds, a fair and neutral curriculum would include considerable study of religion.

The Role of the Teacher

Fairness and neutrality in the curriculum are possible only when teachers have a clear understanding of their role under the First Amendment. Teachers in public schools are employees of the government (or, better, they are there to act on behalf of all citizens). In that capacity, they are subject to the Establishment Clause and thus required to be neutral concerning religion while carrying out their duties as teacher.

The neutrality required of teachers by the First Amendment is intended to prevent the government from imposing religious or anti-religious views on students. True, in settings beyond the school, courts have let stand some traditional acknowledgments of religion in government settings (the Supreme Court itself opens with prayer). But when a captive audience of "impressionable young minds" is involved, the courts are stricter about practices that suggest state endorsement of religion.[9]

This constitutional requirement of neutrality limits in some respects the academic freedom of the public school teacher. Teachers have the freedom, indeed the obligation, to expose students to the marketplace of ideas. They may not, however, either inculcate or denigrate religion. When teaching *about* religion, the teacher, like the curriculum, does not take sides concerning religion. In the next chapters, we explore this matter in detail.

Does this mean a teacher may never mention personal religious views? What should happen when, for example, students ask the teacher to reveal his or her religion? We think that teachers are free to answer the question but should consider the age of the students before doing so. Middle and high school students may be able to distinguish between a personal view and the official position of the school; very young children may not. In any case, the teacher may answer with a brief statement of personal belief and not turn the question into an opportunity to proselytize for or against religion.

Teachers, like students, bring their faith through the schoolhouse door each morning. In our view, the Establishment Clause doesn't prohibit teachers from reading a religious book during non-instructional time, saying a quiet grace before meals, or wearing religious jewelry. If a group of teachers wishes to meet for prayer or

---

[9]See Roberts v. Madigan, 921 F2d 1047 (10th Cir 1991).

Scriptural study during the school day, we see no constitutional reason why they should not be allowed to do so as long as the activity is outside the presence of students and doesn't interfere with the rights of other teachers.

Constitutional problems arise when the teacher decides to use the classroom to either promote or denigrate religion. Parents in a North Carolina school district recently complained that their daughter's social studies teacher took every opportunity to make negative and sarcastic remarks about evangelical Christianity. On the other end of the spectrum, a Virginia teacher had to appear before the school board to answer complaints that she was using the curriculum, especially in December, to encourage students to accept Christ. In both instances, the behavior of the teacher was unconstitutional and unprofessional.

Although teachers may sometimes be confused about where to draw the line, most understand their obligation to model the First Amendment in the public school. A civil public school is a place where teachers are clear about how to apply religious liberty principles and are prepared to address religious issues in the classroom.

Finding Common Ground

We are convinced that creating a civil public school is the most effective way to move schools beyond the culture wars—to move from battleground to common ground. We have seen it happen in communities throughout the country.

Unfortunately, this model is still a tough sell in many school districts. Either they are currently violating the First Amendment by promoting religion and don't want to take the political risk of calling for change, or they try to ignore religion and see no reason to deal with it. Both attitudes fall into the "let sleeping dogs lie" theory of school administration. Too often it takes a crisis (usually a lawsuit) to move a district to act.

The failure of schools to be proactive concerning religious liberty and religion is not surprising. Administrators and school board members need only look at colleagues in other places who have been caught in the cross fire of charge and countercharge about such issues as prayer, equal access, the "December dilemma," or textbook selection. They see lawsuits, recall elections, dismissed superintendents, and divided communities. Why risk stirring up controversy?

Because the greater risk is not to. This is true for two important reasons.

First, applying religious liberty principles fully and fairly in public schools is not only the right thing to do, it is, as Ernest Boyer warned, urgently necessary if we are going to live with our deepest differences in the 21st century. As the religious diversity of the United States continues to expand, it will be increasingly important that public schools be places where religious liberty works and where we learn as much as possible about one another.

Second, the survival of public education may be at stake. The exodus from public schools is fueled in large measure by dissatisfaction with how schools address issues concerning religion and values. If schools act now, they can reverse the distrust and alienation that many citizens feel toward their schools. The New Consensus on religious liberty in schools and religion in the curriculum is an unprecedented opportunity to find common ground and to rebuild trust where it has been lost.

Yes, but how?

Civic Ground Rules

A good first step would be for the school board to appoint a community task force charged with finding common ground on the role of religion and values in the schools. When this was done not long ago in Ramona, California, a conservative Christian minister, a Jewish community leader, parents with diverse perspectives, teachers, and administrators worked together to produce a comprehensive policy on religion in the schools. Now adopted by the school board, the policy enjoys broad support in the community. Students and parents understand their religious liberty rights, teachers have a clear definition of teaching about religion (and support for doing so), and administrators have guidelines for dealing with issues concerning school calendars, religious symbols, and parental requests for excusal.[10]

The first task of any "common ground" effort should be to identify shared civic principles that can serve as ground rules for negotiating differences and working for consensus. One helpful place to

---

[10]Ramona's policy and other sample policies on religion in the schools may be found in *Finding Common Ground*, edited by Charles Haynes and Oliver Thomas, which is available from the First Amendment Center, 1207 18th Ave. S., Nashville, TN 37212; telephone 615-321-9588.

start can be the national agreements discussed earlier, especially *Religious Liberty, Public Education, and the Future of American Democracy: A Statement of Principles.* When an agreement is supported by a broad spectrum of religious and educational organizations, it provides a local school district with a new foundation (and a safe harbor) for confronting potentially controversial issues.

The civic ground rules that underlie the *Statement of Principles* and that are being used in Ramona, as well as in many other communities where agreements have been reached, are derived from three guiding principles of religious liberty:

• *Rights.* Religious liberty, or freedom of conscience, is an inalienable right for all. Public education must make every effort to protect the conscience of every parent and student.

• *Responsibilities.* As American citizens, we have a civic responsibility to guard that right for every person, including those with whom we deeply disagree.

• *Respect.* Not only *what* we debate, but *how* we debate is critical in a democracy. All parties involved in public schools should agree to debate one another with civility and respect, and should strive to be accurate and fair.[11]

In a growing number of communities from Snowline, California, to Wicomico County, Maryland, these civic ground rules provide a framework for constructive dialogue and a basis for agreement across deep differences.

Including the Stakeholders

Reaching agreement on civic principles means little unless the key stakeholders in public education are fully represented in the process and the wider community is informed of the results. The task force or committee should include parents and community leaders with a broad range of viewpoints, including those who have been most critical of the schools. It is crucial to identify among the critics those individuals who are interested in dialogue and open to working for

---

[11] The "three Rs" of religious liberty—rights, responsibilities, and respect—are more fully defined in the Williamsburg Charter, an agreement on religious liberty signed by nearly 200 national leaders in 1988. The full text of the charter appears in *Finding Common Ground* (Haynes and Thomas, 1994, 1996).

agreement on policy and practice. National organizations that represent the various constituent groups, especially those that have sponsored the *Statement of Principles,* are good resources for finding the right people to serve on a local task force.

In school districts scarred by culture-war battles, inviting in the critics may seem foolhardy. True, a small number of people on all sides of these issues oppose efforts to build bridges. But in our experience most people, when given the opportunity, will come to the table open to working for common ground. The benefits of this process far outweigh the risks. After all, building trust, modeling constitutional principles, and involving the community in their schools should be at the heart of our vision for public education.

Implementing the Vision

Finding common ground on religious liberty issues can raise high expectations in the community about school climate and performance. Without follow-through and careful implementation, all of the goodwill and trust gained during the process may be lost.

Schools in Wicomico County, Maryland, for example, made sure that they kept the community fully informed and involved as they developed their new policy. Through town meetings and use of the media, citizens knew what was going on and were able to participate in the discussion. When the school board adopted the policy, the superintendent made sure that it was disseminated to school personnel and parents. The district required all administrators to take part in an intensive seminar that prepared them to apply the policy's religious liberty principles in their decision making. It sent a number of teachers to a national institute for special training and provided workshops for many others on how to handle religion in the curriculum. The district developed new curricular resources and purchased others to help teachers teach about religions more accurately and fully.

Of course, all of these efforts to establish a civil public school aim at supporting and enhancing what happens in the classroom. Let's look briefly at one example, of many we could cite, of a classroom where the teacher takes religious liberty and religion seriously.

Martha Ball's Classroom

On any given day, a visitor to Martha Ball's 8th grade social studies class is likely to hear a lively discussion about religion. A teacher in

Salt Lake City, Martha is convinced that Utah history, indeed any history, cannot be properly taught without considerable study of religion. Like growing numbers of teachers across the nation, she is unafraid to take religion seriously.

What you will *not* hear in Martha's classroom are angry arguments about religion with name-calling and personal attacks. And you will *not* hear Martha Ball using her position as teacher to indoctrinate students—for or against any religion. As it happens, Martha is of the majority faith in Utah. Her students, however, view her as a fair-minded educator able to teach about various faiths and worldviews with balance and respect. There are at least two reasons why Martha is successful at integrating significant discussion of religion: first, she understands and applies the civic framework in her classroom; second, she has taken advantage of a number of educational opportunities that have prepared her to teach about a variety of religions with fairness and objectivity.

Religious Liberty for All

Martha begins each school year by asking her students to consider how the civic principles of religious liberty enable Americans to live with their deepest differences. She ties the discussion to the three key concepts of rights, responsibilities, and respect discussed earlier.

Students learn that the First Amendment is built on the conviction that religious liberty, or freedom of conscience, is an inalienable right of every person. At the same time they learn that this extraordinary commitment to religious liberty must be tied to a civic responsibility to guard that right for every citizen. They discuss how the rapidly expanding religious and ethnic diversity in the United States, including Salt Lake City, makes it more important each day that they recognize their civic duty to protect the rights of others—even those with whom they strongly disagree.

Civil and Respectful Debate

By taking responsibility for the rights of others, students understand that they are not being asked to compromise their own deep convictions—nor are they being asked to accept or condone the beliefs and practices of their classmates. They are committing themselves, as citizens, to discuss their differences with civility and respect.

Martha does not impose these ideas in her classroom. She presents them as civic principles that, when upheld, enable Americans to work together for the common good. She then asks her students to translate these principles into ground rules for their life together in the classroom. After writing and talking about what kind of class they want—how they want to be treated and how they should treat others—the students arrive at a shared understanding of "rights, responsibilities, and respect."

Through this process Martha sets the stage for civil debate and constructive dialogue. Students can address serious and controversial topics more readily because they are prepared to exchange views without personal attacks or ridicule. During a discussion of Utah history, for example, a student (who happened to be a Mormon) said, "Well, I know my church is the one true church." A Roman Catholic classmate spoke up: "But I know that *my* church is the true church." When the Mormon student started to get angry, Mrs. Ball asked him to recall the agreement reached by the class on the meaning of religious liberty. She reminded the students of how Roger Williams, a man of deep religious convictions, created a society where each citizen was free to choose in matters of faith. "What would Roger Williams say?" she asked the angry student. "What are the civic ground rules for this class?" He replied, "I guess I have to say that if I have the right to say that my church is true, then he has the right to say his is true." Martha's students learn that they have the right to express their religious beliefs, but they also understand the right of others to hold very different views. They can then go on to disagree with one another without going for the jugular.

Martha has discovered that when students commit themselves to civic ground rules she is able to teach more about religion, and the students enter into the conversation with greater interest and liveliness. Throughout the year, her students remind one another and Martha herself of the ground rules they have agreed to uphold. Her classroom becomes a microcosm of the American experiment in religious liberty at its best.

Conclusions

Agreeing to a civic framework is not a panacea for culture wars. The school district in Snowline, California, for example, adopted a set of policies and practices that reflect the "rights, responsibilities, and respect" guidelines in the *Statement of Principles.* But civic agreement has not inoculated the district from conflict and controversy. They continue to have disputes about a wide range of issues, from self-esteem programs to prayer. What has changed, however, is how controversies are addressed: the community finds solutions without bitter fights and lawsuits. A commitment to fairness and a concern for rights of conscience shape how the people of Snowline work for common ground.[12]

In a democracy there will always be winners and losers in public policy disputes involving public education. But if all sides have been treated fairly in the process, then those who may lose on a particular issue will remain supportive of the schools—especially if they win other debates. The issue of religion in the schools allows for plenty of opportunities for "winners" on all sides. As we have suggested, there are ways to say "yes" to a role for religion, even as the schools must say "no" to state-sponsored religious practices. The key is to begin with a shared vision of religious liberty that provides the civic framework for the debate.

For school districts interested in carrying out both the letter and the spirit of the First Amendment, it is not enough to acknowledge that there is an appropriate constitutional and educational role for religion in public schools. Even to pass policies that protect religious liberty rights and encourage teaching about religion is insufficient. A truly civil public school is built and sustained only when policies and practices are put in place with the broad involvement and support of the community. Administrators and teachers must be prepared to carry out these policies. Parents and students must be informed about the implications for the curriculum and the culture of the school. Only then is the school taking religious liberty and religion seriously.

The growing consensus on religious liberty and religion in the public schools provides a historic opportunity for finding common ground. Within the civic framework provided by the religious liberty clauses of the First Amendment we are able to debate our differences, to understand one another, and to forge policies and practices that protect the liberty of conscience of every parent and student. If we take this opportunity, a common vision for the common good may be possible in public schools—and in our nation—as we enter the 21st century.

---

[12]Jan Vondra, Assistant Superintendent for Curriculum/Education Services in Snowline Joint Unified School District, gives a fuller account of Snowline's experience in "Resolving Conflicts Over Values," (April 1996), *Educational Leadership* 53, 7: 76–79.

Suggested Readings
and Resources

Background documents and consensus guidelines for understanding the civic framework outlined in this chapter may be found in *Finding Common Ground: A First Amendment Guide to Religion and Public Education* (1994, 1996), edited by Charles C. Haynes and Oliver Thomas. For historical perspective on religious liberty and the First Amendment as they relate to education, see Chapter 3 of Warren A. Nord, *Religion and American Education* (1995). An excellent study of the origins and significance of the Religious Liberty clauses of the First Amendment is William Miller's *The First Liberty: Religion and the American Republic* (1987).

One of the best accounts of culture-war conflicts in public schools is *Battleground: One Mother's Crusade, the Religious Right, and the Struggle for Control of Our Classrooms* (1993) by Stephen Bates. For a full and provocative analysis of the culture wars, see James Davison Hunter's *Culture Wars: The Struggle to Define America* (1991) and *Before the Shooting Begins: Searching for Democracy in America's Culture War* (1994). In *A House Divided: Six Belief Systems Struggling for America's Soul* (1996), Mark Gerzon offers both a thoughtful analysis of the worldviews that divide America and very insightful approaches for finding common ground across our differences.

Extensive excerpts and annotations of the key Supreme Court cases involving religion in the schools may be found in *Religious Liberty in the Supreme Court: The Cases That Define the Debate Over Church and State* (1993), edited by Terry Eastland. A more complete anthology of these cases is *Toward Benevolent Neutrality: Church, State, and the Supreme Court* (1992), edited by Robert Miller and Ronald Flowers.

The Williamsburg Charter has greatly influenced our conception of a civil public school. *Articles of Faith, Articles of Peace: The Religious Liberty Clauses and the American Public Philosophy,* edited by James Davison Hunter and Os Guinness (1990), contains an excellent series of essays that provide a context for understanding the significance of the Williamsburg Charter.

For the latest developments in First Amendment law and new listings of resources for administrators and teachers, visit the First Amendment Center's web site (www.freedomforum.org).

2

The Educational Framework

ONE CAN'T BE AN *EDUCATED* HUMAN BEING WITHOUT UNDER-standing a good deal about religion. Just as there are civic and constitutional reasons for including religion in the curriculum, so there are educational reasons. And, just as those civic and constitutional reasons provide a framework for dealing with religion, so there is an educational framework that shapes how educators should deal with religion in the curriculum and in the classroom. Happily, these frameworks complement one another, for each is grounded in respect and the obligation to be *fair.* Fairness is, as we shall see, a virtue of considerable importance in the practice of *liberal* education, an education that enables students to think in an informed and critical way about the world.

We begin this chapter by describing the New Consensus about religion and the curriculum that has developed over the last decade. Although the influence of religion in history and its relevance to history courses are well accepted, the relevance of religion to other parts of the curriculum is much more controversial—and will require a good deal of our attention. We will explain why the study of religion is much more important than is usually recognized, discuss where in the curriculum it should be located, and provide guidelines for how to teach about religion in the classroom.

Much of our discussion in this chapter focuses on the role of religion in the liberal education that should characterize the upper grades. In Chapter 3 we will explore the more limited role of religion in elementary education.

The New Consensus

Our educational framework is grounded in the New Consensus that has developed over the course of the last decade. In 1988 a group of major religious and educational organizations—including the American Jewish Congress, the Islamic Society of North America, the National Association of Evangelicals, the National Council of Churches, the American Association of School Administrators, the National School Boards Association, AFT, NEA, and ASCD—endorsed a statement of principles entitled "Religion in the Public School Curriculum: Questions and Answers," which describes the importance of religion in the curriculum in this way:

> Because religion plays significant roles in history and society, study about religion is essential to understanding both the nation and the world. Omission of facts about religion can give students the false impression that the religious life of humankind is insignificant or unimportant. Failure to understand even the basic symbols, practices, and concepts of the various religions makes much of history, literature, art, and contemporary life unintelligible.
>
> Study about religion is also important if students are to value religious liberty, the first freedom guaranteed in the Bill of Rights. Moreover, knowledge of the roles of religion in the past and present promotes crosscultural understanding essential to democracy and world peace. (1988/ 1994, chap. 6, pp. 2–3)

In its report *Religion in the Curriculum*, the Association for Supervision and Curriculum Development concluded: "Clearly, decisive action is needed to end the current curricular silence on religion" (1988, p. 35). It recommended that textbook selection committees at all levels require the treatment of religion "in all curricular materials." The task is to "provide adequate treatment of diverse religions" and "their impact in history, literature, art, music, and morality" (ASCD Panel, 1988, pp. 35, 27). Teacher educators must ensure that teachers acquire the "substantive knowledge required to teach about religion in society," and all educators "should explore ways to foster public support for the teaching of rigorous, intellectually demanding accounts of religion in society" (ASCD, 1988, p. 40).

According to the National Council for the Social Studies, "knowledge about religions is not only a characteristic of an educated person, but is also absolutely necessary for understanding and living in a world of diversity." Hence, the study of religion "should be an essential part of the social studies curriculum." Such study should encourage "a comprehensive and balanced examination of the entire spectrum of ideas and attitudes pertaining to religion as a component of human culture" and should stress the influence of religion on history and on contemporary issues, "including its relation to economic, political, and social institutions as well as its relation to the arts, language, and literature" (1990, p. 310).

What do we conclude from these (and other) statements of the New Consensus?

• *First,* because of the powerful influence of religion on our history and culture it is essential—and not optional—to include religion in the curriculum.
• *Second,* the influence of religion is not limited to history; students must understand the relevance of religion to contemporary life.
• *Third,* religion is relevant to virtually all subjects of the curriculum.
• *Finally,* it is important for students to understand a variety of religions, not just their own.

Education, Religion, and the Search for Meaning

The fact that we often use the adjective *academic* (as in "that's academic") as a synonym for what is technical, trivial, and irrelevant, is telling. Too often educators (and students) lose sight of the forest for all the trees. Obviously a *good* education should provide students with *perspective,* with some sense of what is truly important. Education should initiate students—at least older students in the upper grades—into a conversation about what makes life meaningful.

Of course we disagree about what makes life meaningful, so let us put it this way. There appear to be *questions* that any reasonably thoughtful person must ask. What is the meaning of love—and what is the difference between sexuality and love? What does justice require of me—and of my country? When am I obligated to sacrifice my own good for that of someone else? What are the deepest sources of joy in life? How did the world begin? What sense can we make of suffering and of death? Is there progress in human affairs—and if so why? Is there a God? And how do I know any of this?

Many educators are tempted to leave some (if not all) of these questions to parents and religious communities. But, of course, *every* educated human being should have some grasp of the answers that people have given to these questions; these questions are not for religious folk only.

In any case, education can't avoid these questions. Much of the literature that students read in English courses revolves around them; in economics courses students are taught about human nature and values; in science courses students learn about how scientists understand the origins of the universe and of life. Of course most of the answers students encounter will be secular.

But there are both secular *and* religious ways of asking, reflecting on, and answering these unavoidable "existential" questions. An *educated* person should have some understanding of the major ways of thinking about them, and the resultant answers. Whether or not we think the various answers that religious traditions have given to these existential questions are reasonable, we must acknowledge the profundity of the attempts, their powerful influence on people's thinking and lives, and the universality of the concerns they address. It is truly extraordinary to think that we can claim to educate students while ignoring religious approaches to the deepest questions of human existence.

Religion and History

Of course, we don't ignore religion completely. We agree that students must learn about religion in their study of history.

And for good reason. Until the last several hundred years in the West, the dominant answers to these inescapable existential questions were religious. Indeed, for most of history the sacred and the secular were pervasively entwined, and religion pervaded all of life: from birth to death the sustaining rituals of life were religious; religion shaped and informed people's understanding of politics, war, economics, justice, literature, art, philosophy, science, psychology, history, morality, and their hopes for a life to come. If students are to understand *history* they must understand *religion*. This is not controversial.

Of course, the study of history is important, in part, because it locates us in "communities of memory" (to use Robert Bellah's [1985, pp. 153–155] fine phrase) that give definition to our identities. We are not simply individuals, ahistorical social atoms; we are born into cultures defined by languages and institutions, ideas and ideals, and we know who we are only when we have some sense of our inheritance. Whether or not we are religious, the religious past of our culture has played a powerful role in shaping us, and to be ignorant of this past is a little like being an amnesiac—choosing one's future without any sense of who one has been. History roots us in the past; it provides *cultural ballast.*

The study of history also provides us with critical distance from the present; it *liberates* students from parochial "present-mindedness." Indeed, by revealing the religious roots of our ideals and institutions, history gives students some sense of just how secular our civilization has become.

There is another reason why the study of religion's role in history is tremendously important. If history is replete with examples of ways in which religion has ennobled humanity and enabled people to flourish, it is also all too filled with examples of religious warfare and persecution. This makes the story of religious liberty, particularly as it is embodied in our constitutional tradition, important for students to understand.

The importance of studying history and one's place in it can't be overestimated—and we can't understand history without understanding religion.

Religion and Liberal Education

Of course, religion retains a good deal of vitality in our culture. Indeed, because many intellectuals continue to give religious answers to the profound existential questions of life, there is a vast *contemporary* religious literature that explores the implications of religion for virtually every subject in the curriculum: politics and economics, nature and psychology, literature and the arts, sexuality and morality. Our question now is this: What obligation do educators have to take seriously *live* religious ways of making sense of all of those areas of the curriculum that conventionally exclude religion from the discussion?

Worldviews

The astronomer Arthur Eddington once told a parable about a fisherman who used a net with a three-inch mesh. After a lifetime of fishing he concluded there were no fish shorter than three inches. Eddington's moral is that just as one's fishing net determines what one catches, so it is with conceptual nets: what we find in the ocean of reality depends on the conceptual net we bring to our investigation.

For example, the modern scientific conceptual net—or scientific method—allows scientists to catch only replicable events; the results of any experiment that cannot be replicated are not allowed to stand. This means that miracles, which are by definition singular events, can't be caught; scientists cannot ask God to replicate the miracle for the sake of a controlled experiment. Or, to take another example, scientific method requires that evidence for knowledge claims be grounded in sense experience—the kinds of experience that instruments can measure. But this rules out religious experience as a source of knowledge about the world.

Theologians, by contrast, have constructed different kinds of conceptual nets for catching dimensions of reality that, they claim, escape scientific nets. People within all religious traditions believe moral and religious experiences provide knowledge of a transcendent dimension of reality—of God. The Western religions—Judaism, Christianity, and Islam—have made sense of the world not in terms of universal causal laws, but narratives: events become intelligible not because they are lawlike, but because they fit in the plot of a story (as miracles might). Theologians take Scripture to be a source of knowledge (though liberals and conservatives read it in quite different ways).

In fact, how reasonable or "objective" a claim is—indeed, whether it makes sense at all—depends on the conceptual net we bring to the discussion. There is more to a *worldview* than the conceptual nets (or methodology) used by scientists or theologians or philosophers; still, we might say that worldviews are what is at issue.

For most of history, the governing worldviews of civilization have been religious; but over the course of the last several centuries in the West, modern science has come to provide the dominant worldview of our civilization and, as a result, shape our educational system. In the process, what counts as reasonable (and what counts as a matter of faith) has changed. True, if we *assume* the adequacy of the modern scientific worldview, religion is likely to appear as a matter of faith or even superstition; but why *should* we assume it?[1]

Subjects and Disciplines

The usual rhetoric notwithstanding, public schools don't teach *subjects*. Subjects are open to various interpretations—to the use of different conceptual nets for making sense of them. Instead, students are taught *disciplines*; they are taught to use particular conceptual nets to make sense of their subjects. They learn to interpret history as secular historians do; they learn to understand nature as secular scientists do; they learn to understand economics as secular social scientists do. In fact, they learn to make sense of every subject in the curriculum in terms of disciplines defined by secular (usually scientific) conceptual nets.

When students do, on occasion, study religion (in a history course, for example), they are taught to interpret its historical meaning in secular categories; they will not learn to interpret history in religious categories. This goes without saying. Indeed, nowhere in the curriculum is any effort made to justify the use of secular rather than religious categories and conceptual nets. Their adequacy is *assumed* and they are used *uncritically*—in spite of the fact that their adequacy is deeply controversial.

This is the core of truth in the claim that schools teach students the (functional) *religion of secular humanism* (Nord, 1995, chap. 5). The problem isn't so much the specific facts or beliefs or theories that

---

[1] The cultural authority of modern science is being challenged by more and more *secular* intellectuals who argue that we are entering a *postmodern* period in history. (The *modern* period is often dated from the Scientific Revolution and the Enlightenment, when science began to replace religion as the arbiter of rationality and truth.) Postmodernism means different things to different scholars, but we might define it in the most general terms as the conviction that there are no *objective foundations* for knowledge-claims. It is impossible to jettison the particularities of our cultural contexts; our understandings of the world are invariably shaped by our gender, ethnicity, class, language, unconscious minds, and ideological commitments.

Postmodernism is suspicious of all "metanarratives" or overarching accounts of reality—including that of modern science, which postmodernists see as just one among many narratives about how the world works, no truer or more reasonable (in any objective sense) than others. More about postmodernism as we proceed; our point for now is that in the postmodern world it is particularly naive to *assume* that science is the arbiter of rationality and truth. Or so many *secular* intellectuals now argue.

are or aren't taught, it is that public education nurtures a secular mentality. It assumes a secular, largely scientific worldview, and teaches students to make sense of their lives and the world in terms of that worldview. By providing students with secular conceptual nets only, by ignoring religion (except in a safely historical context), the curriculum conveys the idea that secular nets are adequate for catching all of reality and that religion is irrelevant to the search for the truth. As a result, religion is intellectually and culturally marginalized. No doubt most educators don't intend to do this, yet this is the result. (In Part II we will put flesh on the skeleton of this argument as we work through the various areas of the curriculum.)

Education and Indoctrination

As we saw in Chapter 1, there are civic and constitutional reasons of fairness for requiring that religion be included in the curriculum. It should be clear now that fairness is also required for *educational* reasons.

Philosophers often draw a distinction between education on the one hand, and socialization, training, and indoctrination on the other. Soldiers are trained to march and are socialized to follow the orders of their officers. Children are toilet-trained (rather than educated in toiletry), and, with some luck, they are socialized to obey their parents. In each of these cases, learning is more a matter of drill, discipline, and habit than of critical thinking. In matters of morality, politics, and religion we often use the word *indoctrination* rather than *training* or *socialization.* We indoctrinate children (or adults) when we teach (or socialize) them to accept doctrines, or a point of view, *uncritically.* By contrast, we educate children when we provide them with a measure of critical distance on their subjects, enabling them to think in informed and reflective ways about alternatives.

Public schools inevitably and properly train and socialize children: learning the basic skills of reading, writing, and arithmetic, for example, is largely a matter of training and drill; learning to be honest and on time is largely a matter of socialization.

With older children, however, the goal should be largely educational. We don't want to socialize or indoctrinate them into accepting positions on contested issues—issues about which we disagree. People in the United States, for example, are deeply divided between the Republican and Democratic parties. A *public* school has no business indoctrinating students into accepting the policies of either political party. Students can only think and act reasonably when they know something about the alternatives; indeed, we usually believe that the truth is most likely to be found when we hear both sides of the story, not one side only.

As students mature and proceed through the grades, the extent to which they are trained and socialized should diminish, while their education, properly conceived, should take root and grow. Education is the initiation of students into a discussion in which they are taught to understand, to take seriously, and to think critically about the contending voices in our world. This is often called *liberal* education— though "liberal education" is redundant, just as "liberal training" would be an oxymoron. A "liberal education," as we use the term, is not the kind of education advocated by the left wing of the Democratic Party; it is, rather, an education that requires students to learn something about the major ways humankind has developed for understanding their lives and the world.

It is not enough to teach the truth as one party in the disagreement understands it; if we teach only that view, students will not have the critical resources to make educated judgments about it. It is one thing to believe (what one takes to be) the truth; it is another thing to be *educated* to make reasonable judgments about it. Students will not be liberally educated, they will not be able to make reflective and critical judgments about anything that is religiously contested, unless they are taught about religious as well as secular ways of making sense of whatever is at issue. When we systematically and uncritically teach students secular ways of thinking about *all* "subjects" in the curriculum, we are in real danger of indoctrinating them (Nord, 1995, chap. 5).

Of course, one could argue in response that educators have an obligation to guide the thinking of students and that modern secular scholarship provides the most reasonable way of proceeding. But we *disagree* about what is reasonable when it comes to sexuality and politics and economics and the origins of the world—and much of the disagreement is related to religion.

In fact, what appears to be a secular consensus among scholars is artificial and misleading, for theologians aren't allowed to vote; they aren't allowed into the main quad of the academy (much less into public schools) but are exiled to divinity schools and seminaries and think tanks and religious bureaucracies.

Our argument is that when we disagree, at least when the disagreements cut deep, educators are obligated to give students some sense of what is at issue. If students are to be educated, if they are to think critically, then we must include religious voices in our curricular conversations.

To be clear we should say that this is an argument for fairness, not for neutrality; there is a difference. Just as a judge might be fair to the opposing parties in a lawsuit before passing judgment, so teachers might be fair to contending points of view before passing judgment. That is, while neutrality requires fairness, fairness doesn't require neutrality. Indeed, we believe that other things being equal educators have an obligation to guide the thinking of their students. But other things aren't equal when religion is at issue: *both* fairness *and* neutrality are required for the civic and constitutional reasons we gave in Chapter 1.

Nonetheless, it is important to keep in mind that it is often not at all *obvious* where the truth lies—and quite apart from these civic and constitutional constraints educators should show some humility in dealing with complicated and controversial questions. When fundamentally different worldviews shape the disagreements, it is not easy to say what the truth is.

Locating Religion in the Curriculum

If we are to take religion seriously, should we include it in existing courses, or do we need (new) courses in religious studies: religion in courses, or courses in religion? Our answer? Both.

In part because of the difficulty of creating new courses, advocates of the New Consensus usually argue for "natural inclusion" in existing courses: teachers should discuss religion wherever it "naturally" comes up. Of course, the study of religion has an established place in history courses and in English courses in which students read historical literature; but, arguably, they should also discuss religion in economics or biology or sex education courses when religious ideas, ideals, and influences in our culture shape the public discussion of justice or nature or sexuality—when it is "natural" to discuss them.

Natural inclusion presents two major problems. First, because teachers are trained to teach disciplines rather than subjects, religious ways of thinking don't come "naturally" to most economics, biology, or sex education teachers or textbook authors in their professional lives (no matter how religious they are in their personal lives). Indeed, they often explicitly reject such inclusion. The major science organizations have made it clear, for example, that science courses have no room for creationism. If discussions of creationism or religious interpretations of nature are to occur at all, they must take place elsewhere—most likely in history classes. Of course, history teachers aren't likely to view creation as part of their domain; it doesn't naturally come up there either.

The second problem with natural inclusion stems from the importance and complexity of religion. Given the amount of material that authors must cram into a history textbook, religion is apt to find little room even if its relevance is acknowledged. Making sense of religion requires some breadth of exposure, some sensitivity to competing worldviews, some grounding in theology. (Imagine if we tried to teach biology or economics by including them in history textbooks.) Of course, the variety of religious traditions and the complexity of religious language, symbolism, and theology make religion even more difficult for the typical (religiously illiterate) student to understand than those secular disciplines on which we lavish much more time and resources.

If we are to take religion seriously, if we are to acknowledge its importance and complexity, then we need to carve out space in the curriculum for courses in religion—or "religious studies" (which has become the term of choice in higher education). And just as we require science teachers to be certified in science, so religious studies should become a certifiable field for teachers of religion. Some schools do offer courses in religion—typically in the Bible or world religions, but these courses are inevitably electives and a very small minority of students ever take them. Our cultural priorities being what they are, this is not likely to change—though we might justifiably wonder why it is more important for a college-bound student to take 12 years of mathematics and no religion rather than 11 years of math and 1 year of religious studies.

We believe that high school students should be *required* to take at least one yearlong course in religious studies. Religion is too important and too complex to be handled adequately by natural inclusion; indeed, given the power of the secular disciplines in shaping the curriculum (and students' thinking about the world), we must grant religion at least a foothold in the curriculum to ensure a measure of critical perspective on secular education.

This, we believe, must be the ideal. But because we are not so naive as to think that our recommendation will gain wide acceptance, we suggest what may be a more realistic, two-pronged approach. First, we must emphasize natural inclusion. Teachers and textbooks must make clear that there are religious alternatives to secular ways of thinking. A *minimal fairness* would require that a first chapter in textbooks and an opening lecture or two in courses include some discussion of religious ways of thinking, perhaps in the context of a historical and philosophical overview of the subject at hand. Ideally, teachers and students would discuss those religious perspectives again at a later time, at critical points in the course. But second, to make possible a *robust fairness,* schools must begin to offer more *elective* courses in religious studies, especially as certified teachers become available and as students and their parents come to appreciate the importance of religion in the curriculum. A few communities might even consider requiring courses in religious studies.

How to Teach About Religion

The New Consensus is grounded in the Supreme Court's 1963 *Abington v. Schempp* decision in which, as we saw in Chapter 1, the Court affirmed the constitutionality of teaching about religion in public schools when done "objectively as part of a secular program of education."

According to "Religion and the Public School Curriculum: Questions and Answers" (the statement endorsed by 17 national religious and education organizations), the school's approach to religion should be "academic, not devotional." Schools "may sponsor study about religion, but may not sponsor the practice of religion." They "may educate about all religions, but may not promote or denigrate any religion" (1988, chap. 6, p. 2).

The guidelines of the National Council for the Social Studies require that the study of religion be "objective" and "academic in nature," and stress "student awareness and understanding, not acceptance and/or conformity." Such study should be "descriptive, non-confessional, and conducted in an environment free of advocacy." It should "involve a range of materials that provide a balanced and fair treatment of the subject" and be conducted with "sensitivity and empathy for differing religious points of view," investigating a "broad range" of "religious beliefs, practices, and values" (1990, p. 310).

ASCD puts it this way: "The central purposes of public schools are intellectual and civic . . . not religious. Religious education, or teaching *of* religion, is the job of parents and religious institutions, but teaching *about* religion is a legitimate purpose of public schools" (1988, p. 16). "The job of education is to educate, not to instill religious devotion" (p. 21).

The New Consensus, then, draws a sharp distinction between (unconstitutional) advocacy, indoctrination, proselytizing, and the *practice* of religion on the one hand, and, on the other, (constitutional) *teaching about* religion that is objective, nonjudgmental, nonsectarian, neutral, balanced, and fair.

It is worth pausing for a moment over the word *objective* because this is the word the Supreme Court used. Of course, what it means to be objective is not uncontroversial. Some scholars have concluded that there is no such thing as objectivity. Others equate objectivity with science. But both accounts of objectivity are controversial—not least among theologians.

It is fairly clear what the Court meant by "objectivity," however, for Justice Clark, in his majority opinion, and Justices Brennan and Goldberg in their concurring opinions, each made *neutrality* the touchstone of their decisions (as the Court has usually done in adjudicating Establishment Clause cases). We have argued, in turn, that neutrality requires both fairness and refraining from judgment. When we disagree on religious grounds, we can achieve neutrality only by including everyone in the discussion. On this reading, "objectivity" means being fair rather than being prejudiced—rather than *prejudging* conclusions by not taking everyone seriously.

Some educators believe that schools can maintain neutrality by not explicitly affirming or denying a point of view, in effect, by ignoring it. But this is naive. Consider an analogy. Traditional textbooks and curriculums that ignored the role of blacks or women in history and literature were neither neutral nor objective but, as we now recognize, deeply prejudiced. Similarly, to ignore religious voices is not neutral; rather, it marginalizes those voices, conveying implicitly their irrelevance to the search for the truth.

Diversity and Fairness

To be educated about religion is to understand something of religio*ns*, of religion in its diversity, just as to be educated about politics is to understand more than one's own political party. But, of course, not all religions can be included in the discussion; after all the school day consists of limited hours, and texts have only so many pages. We obviously cannot use the truth of a religion as our criterion for whether to include it, for we cannot assume judgments about truth if we are to be neutral. A more plausible, and less controversial, criterion is influence; indeed, in virtually all courses it is the influential ideas and ideals, theories and movements, that are considered. Almost inevitably the *major* religious traditions will make the greatest claim for inclusion because of their influence.

No doubt this is as it must be—though we would add the following caveats:

1. If teachers give the major religions the lion's share of time and space, they should include some discussion of "minor" or minority religions. Neutrality requires that educators not convey the sense that the major traditions are "normative" and that belonging to a minor (relatively uninfluential and seldom discussed) religion is either foolish or undeserving of respect.

2. In choosing among the less influential religions, it is wise and just to give attention to those that are practiced locally to give all children the sense that their traditions are taken seriously.

Must each major religion receive equal time in the curriculum? A great deal depends on context. In a course on American history it would be foolish to give equal time to Christianity and Confucianism because the *influence* of Christianity on America has been so much greater. A course on world religions that dealt exclusively or even primarily with Christianity and ignored Eastern religions would be deeply flawed.

If particular courses will inevitably take some religions more seriously than others because of relative influence, the curriculum must reflect some overall balance. We no longer believe that it is educationally sound to teach American or Western history only; and just as students must know something of world cultures, so they must know something of world religions if they are to be educated.

In some contexts efforts to provide a diversity of views and a balance between them have been deeply controversial. In the early 1980s, for example, several states passed "balanced treatment" laws requiring that "creation-science" be taught whenever evolution is taught. It *is* important for students to learn that there are diverse ways of thinking about the origins of life and humankind—religious as well as scientific. It is *also* important for students to learn that the vast majority of biologists and paleontologists reject creation-science as unscientific. We do not propose the quixotic position that science courses cease to be science courses. Religious accounts of nature—and a robust fairness—must be provided elsewhere in the curriculum and by teachers better educated about theology than most biology teachers are (though we shall also argue that biology texts and courses are obligated to be minimally fair).

In such cases we appeal to what we call the "Principle of Cultural Location and Weight." Teachers and texts are obligated to locate their positions on the map of alternatives, indicating what weight their views carry in their own disciplines and in the larger culture. Good teachers and texts should not convey to students the idea that there is only one way of thinking about a subject, when in fact there are many. Nor should they simply provide an array of alternatives without giving students some sense of which views are mainstream and which aren't, and for whom. Who believes what, for what reasons, and with what force?

It is important, then, that we avoid two quite different problems. First, educators must take diversity seriously. They should include all the major voices in the discussion. But, second, they need not accomplish this by means of a crude "balanced treatment" or "equal time" provision in particular courses; it is the overall curriculum that must be balanced and fair. In later chapters we will work through these issues in a number of contexts (including evolution and creationism) in much more detail.

The Many Dimensions of Religion

The great scholar of world religions Ninian Smart has distinguished seven *dimensions* of religion: doctrines (e.g., the Trinity, reincarnation); sacred narratives (e.g., the story of the Buddha, the story of the Exodus); ethics (e.g., the Torah, the Shari'a, the Sermon on the Mount); ritual (e.g., the Mass, daily Muslim prayer); religious experience (e.g., conversion experiences, mystical experiences); social institutions (e.g., monastic orders, the Temple in Jerusalem); and art and material culture (e.g., icons, temples) (1996).

These dimensions interpenetrate; cumulatively they define a worldview. While each dimension can be found in every religion, different traditions give different weight to them. Judaism, for example, has typically emphasized the social and ethical dimensions of religion; to be a Jew is to belong to a tradition, a community, and keep the Law. Jews have never defined themselves by creeds or doctrine; indeed, it is often held that one need not believe in God to be a good Jew. Christianity, by contrast, has historically been a creedal religion—requiring orthodox belief in "God the Father Almighty, maker of heaven and earth"—and conservative Protestants often hold that salvation hinges on belief. As a result, we often describe people as *practicing* Jews and *believing* Christians. Islam falls closer to Judaism than to Christianity in this regard. Yet again, Hinduism, Buddhism, and Taoism have often emphasized the *experiential* and *ritual* dimensions of religion. These distinctions are, of course, largely matters of degree—and, of course, there may be different emphases within different denominations or movements in a tradition.

Because so many teachers are Protestants, it is crucial that they recognize that other religious traditions are often unlike their own in placing much less emphasis on belief and doctrine—what the history texts often call the "basic teachings."

Understanding Religion from the Inside

If texts and teachers are to take religion seriously, if they are to be *fair* to members of a tradition, they must let the advocates of that religion speak for themselves, using the cultural and conceptual resources of their own traditions. The point is not to strain their world through our conceptual nets, but to hear what they say and see what they do in the context of their own beliefs, experiences, motives, and worldview—from *the inside,* as it were. Ninian Smart has called this *informed empathy*—using the symbols and narratives, the art and the rituals, the institutions and traditions of a religious culture to get inside the hearts and minds of people (1987, chap. 1).

(It is important to keep in mind that there is a huge difference between empathy and sympathy. Empathy is thinking or feeling *with* someone; sympathy is feeling *for* someone. Empathy is a matter of understanding and is, in a sense, morally neutral. Sympathy requires judgment; it is the feeling that someone merits our support. The point is not for students to sympathize with a religion, but understand it.)

Understanding a religion is not a matter of knowing a few *facts* about it, or being able to recite its core *beliefs*; it is more a matter of being able to make sense of the world in a particular religious way. It requires a different *gestalt* or consciousness, an appreciation of how the different dimensions of that religion shape a worldview.

Needless to say, it is not easy for students to think their way inside the hearts and minds of people in a culture or religion different from their own, and because most religious traditions make sense of the world in ways that are foreign to the conventional secular thinking of most students we can't expect a few paragraphs in a history text to accomplish the task.

Sensitivity to the different dimensions of religion is important in addressing the temptation to reduce religion to some set of beliefs. Consider an analogy. In educating students about music we are not content to have them read about the beliefs of composers and musicians, nor is it sufficient for them to scan sheets of musical notation or study acoustics. It is in *listening* to music—or better yet, in *performing* it—that students can grasp *from the inside* what music is all about. They make sense of music by experiencing it and, in the process, learning a new musical vocabulary, a set of categories that shape their developing appreciation for music. Similarly, scientists often claim that it is only in *doing science* that students can learn what science is.

For any number of reasons we can't require students to practice religion, but they can acquire some imaginative and vicarious sense of what it means to experience the world religiously from autobiographies and, even better, from literature, drama, film, and art. Indeed, because religious experience is often claimed to be *ineffable*, impossible to put into language, religions often function symbolically. Their natural language is poetry and symbol and metaphors that *point to* or imaginatively convey truths that cannot be said literally. Of course, the extent to which religious language is to be taken symbolically or literally is a major theological question. On almost any account, however, religion requires a different sensibility from science, and it is surely dangerous to assume that the skills of scientific thinking carry over to religion. The difficulty of conveying to students some understanding of religion is, as we've said, a powerful reason for requiring them to take a course in religion, studying it in some depth.

Understanding Religion from the Outside

Education isn't simply a matter of immersing students in several religious traditions so that they can grasp each, in turn, from the inside.

It is also important that teachers and texts approach religion *from the outside* in several senses.

A good liberal education will map the relationships of alternative ways of thinking about the subjects of the curriculum—and the world more generally. The point isn't to habituate students to living on a variety of unrelated islands of the mind, each defined by its own worldview, but rather to initiate them into a discussion about how different disciplines, different ways of making sense of the world, relate to one another. If understanding different religions from the inside is the necessary first step, the second step should be a *step back* from each of those religions to discuss how they relate to one another *and* to the secular ways of thinking about the world that pervade the curriculum. The point is to nurture some small measure of critical thinking.

It is, of course, interesting and important to consider what is *common* to religions—and what may distinguish all religious from secular ways of understanding the world. It is also important to understand the *deep differences* among religions; indeed, there may be little that religions have in common, shaped as they each are by their respective revelations, their different cultural and intellectual traditions.

It is also important to use the resources of modern secular scholarship to provide linguistic, historical, and cultural contexts for understanding religions. Sometimes this is a fairly straightforward matter of using nonreligious documents to help chart the development of a religious tradition, or understanding how language was used in ancient nonscriptural texts to throw light on what is meant in Scriptural texts. Of course, theologians and artists and the authors of Scriptural texts don't just work *within* enclosed religious traditions; they employ the conceptual resources of their cultures and respond to developments in the larger world. Religious texts and traditions are shaped, in part, by their cultural contexts so that understanding their contexts can often throw considerable light on religious texts and traditions.

Secular scholarship can also be used to *question* religious claims and undermine religion—and it cannot be the purpose of public education to immunize religion from criticism. A liberal education, as we have said, should initiate students into a discussion among advocates of *all* of the major points of view. But education must be structured so that this discussion is conducted openly and fairly, without coercion or prejudice, taking the contending points of view seriously.

Primary and Secondary Sources

John Stuart Mill once argued that it is not enough for students to hear the arguments of adversaries from their own teachers. Rather, according to Mill, students must hear the arguments

> from persons who actually believe them . . . in their most plausible and persuasive form. . . . Ninety-nine in a hundred of what are called educated men . . . have never thrown themselves into the mental position of those who think differently from them . . . and consequently they do not, in any proper sense of the word, know the doctrine which they themselves profane. (1859/1965, p. 287)

It is both simple justice and good education to let people speak for themselves.

This practice is especially true regarding religion, for the differences between religious and secular ways of talking about the world cut so deep that we are rightly wary, in our secular times, of the ability of textbook authors and teachers to say what is at issue religiously. Of course, the importance of art and literature in imaginatively and symbolically conveying religious ways of experiencing the world makes the use of primary sources essential.

Nonetheless, textbooks and secondary sources have their place as well. For younger students the coherence of a textbook may be as important as the encounter with contending points of view is for older students; it takes considerable intellectual maturity to work through the often confusing mix of voices found in anthologies of primary sources. And, as we've argued, secular scholarship and secondary sources have their place in the study of religion as well. As we see it, then, some kind of balance between primary and secondary sources is wise, but the use of primary sources—Scriptures, theology, art, autobiography, and literature—is essential.

Pluralism and Relativism

Many times, in dealing with controversial topics, we've heard teachers say, "There is no right answer." Sometimes, in their concern to be tolerant, teachers will say that all religions are fundamentally the same beneath their outward differences. Much of the multicultural movement emphasizes the (equal) respect due all traditions. And, as we have argued, for educational and constitutional reasons public schools, texts, and teachers must remain neutral on matters of religion.

Not surprisingly, many religious folks interpret all of this as relativism—the idea that no religion (or point of view generally) is any better or truer than any other. One of the most difficult tasks teachers have is to convey to students the difference between pluralism (and a tolerance or respect for people holding different views) on the one hand, and relativism on the other.

It is important to remember—and to remind students—that the disagreements among different religious and secular traditions are about *what the truth is*. If students come to believe that choosing a religious (or a political or scientific) position is like choosing what to eat from a buffet line, they will have misunderstood the nature of religion (and science) badly. From within each tradition, some foods are poisonous; others are healthy; and individuals certainly should not choose them on the basis of appearances or taste.

Of course, some religious traditions have historically been much more ecumenical than others. Hindus have often accorded divine status to Jesus and Muhammad and held that there are many paths to the truth (though not *all* paths lead there, by any means). Christianity, by contrast, has often been exclusivistic: none come to God but through Christ. There are religious liberals who believe that all religious traditions have some truth in them. There are secularists who believe that no religious tradition conveys the truth about anything of importance. And there are relativists and postmodernists who believe there is no such thing as truth.

Because of the civic ground rules of our democracy, and because public schools should be committed to a liberal education that takes seriously the various participants in our cultural conversation, we properly teach students *respect* for the rights of people in different religious and secular traditions. Indeed, teaching students to talk civilly about our differences is a tremendously important task of schools. But teachers must not take this to mean—and must not convey to students—that all religious traditions are equally true or equally false. That is another thing entirely.

As we noted in the last chapter, the constitutional requirement that schools and teachers be religiously neutral does not mean that teachers cannot express their own judgments in classes where students are mature enough to appreciate the difference between the unofficial "personal" view of the teacher and the official neutrality of the course. But this must be done with considerable care.

More important, students must learn how different religious and secular traditions criticize each other. Why do Muslims believe Islam to be superior to Christianity—and how do Christians argue otherwise? How do neo-Darwinians and various kinds of theologians criticize one another's positions? The point of a liberal education is not simply to expose students to an array of positions, but to initiate them into a continuing discussion about where the truth is to be found. But it cannot be the task of public school teachers to draw any official conclusions about such things.

Competence

Many members of minority traditions who might accept our educational framework in principle will also believe that in practice it is dangerous to include religion in the curriculum because teachers, no matter how well intentioned, will inevitably display their ignorance and prejudices. In a predominantly Christian culture, alternatives to Christianity won't receive knowledgeable or fair treatment, and teachers will end up advocating Christianity, even if subtly or indirectly.

This is a justifiable concern. The great majority of teachers are not prepared to teach about religion. Many know little about religious traditions other than their own—if they have one. We have articulated what we take to be *the ideal toward which we should be working*. That it is an ideal makes it no less important; if we want to improve, we aim at the ideal.

In any case, what is the alternative? We can't simply stop taking sides on religiously contested matters. After all, in teaching the secular disciplines teachers give (sometimes controversial) secular answers to religiously contested questions. And, of course, religion does surface here and there in textbooks now; it is unavoidable. Moreover, some teachers express their prejudices in class now, and some textbooks contain distorted and inadequate accounts of minority religions now. The solution cannot be to leave "well enough" alone, but to make teachers, textbook authors, and curriculum planners self-conscious and better informed about what they are doing.

Teacher Education

Working with teachers we have been struck, over and over again, by their desire to do what is right; and we have found that a very little consciousness-raising about the First Amendment and sensitivity to students from minority traditions can go a long way. Nonetheless, major reforms in teacher education are necessary.

• Teacher education institutions must teach all prospective teachers the civic and educational frameworks in their Foundations and Teaching Methods courses. Unfortunately, most teacher educators have little understanding of the frameworks; most schools of education simply do not take religion seriously.

• Every teacher education institution should offer an elective course for prospective teachers on religion and education (perhaps jointly planned and taught by faculty in the department of religious studies and the school of education) that deals in some depth with the issues discussed in this book.

• All teachers who deal with religiously contested matters should know something about the relationship of religion to their particular subjects and disciplines. Ideally, they should be required, as part of their certification, to take at least one course relating religion to their subject (Religion and Science, Religion and American History, Religion and Literature, etc.). Whether required or not, departments of religious studies should make such courses available as electives.

• While awaiting these reforms, universities and school systems should address these topics in a variety of summer seminars and inservice workshops.

• If there are to be courses in the Bible or world religions, there must be teachers competent to teach them. Religious studies must become a certifiable field, requiring at least an undergraduate minor. Schools *must not* phase in courses in religion until there are competent teachers.

• State departments of education should set certification requirements and review curriculums, setting standards for the inclusion of religion at appropriate places in the curriculum.

• Administrators must understand the civic and educational ground rules if teachers are to feel safe teaching about religion. Coursework for administrators must include study of the relationship of religion and education.

• Neither teachers nor administrators will feel safe unless school boards adopt religion policies that make it clear that religion is an appropriate and important part of the curriculum. These policies should emphasize that religion is included for educational reasons, not for proselytizing. The development of these policies should be exercises in defining common ground in which representatives of various local constituencies work together to establish ground rules within the constraints of the Constitution.

• To do the job well, teachers must have good textbooks and resource materials. A good deal of material already exists in some areas of the curriculum (history, literature, and social studies, for example), but there is very little material elsewhere (the sciences, economics, and religious studies itself). To address this need publishers must be convinced there is a market for such material; states need to create such markets.

Conclusions

It is important to recognize the harmony between our civic and educational frameworks. Just as we are obligated for civic reasons to treat people and subcultures with respect by taking their religious traditions seriously, and just as the Establishment Clause of the Constitution requires fairness to religious ways of thinking for the sake of a true neutrality between religion and nonreligion, so a properly liberal education requires that religious voices be included in the curricular conversation.

Second, we would point out that although there are religious arguments for taking religion seriously in schools, we haven't appealed to them. Our civic, constitutional, and educational frameworks, and the arguments for using them, are fully secular. It is not the task of public schools to proselytize or promote any particular religion—or religion generally. Their task is to educate students about various religions, fairly.

Finally, we note once again that what is at issue is a matter of considerable importance. To teach students only secular ways of thinking about the world risks indoctrination. The point of a liberal education is to initiate students in a critical discussion of the major ways of making sense of the world so that they are in some position to responsibly judge what is true and good all things considered. If students are to be liberally educated, they must learn a good deal about religion—and if this is to happen, significant reforms are necessary.

* * *

Having developed our civic and educational frameworks, we now go on in the following chapters to apply the frameworks to various areas of the curriculum. This chapter has emphasized liberal education and critical thinking—concerns primarily of the upper grades; the next chapter looks at elementary education and reviews what (more limited) role there might be for religion there.

Suggested Readings and Resources

The argument of this chapter is developed at considerably greater length in Chapters 5–7 of Warren A. Nord, *Religion and American Education: Rethinking a National Dilemma* (1995). In developing our framework, we have drawn on the work of Ninian Smart: see especially Chapter 1 in *Religion and the Western Mind* (1987). *Finding Common Ground: A First Amendment Guide to Religion and Public Education,* cited earlier, is an excellent anthology of documents and essays dealing with religion and public education.

Elmer John Theissen's *Teaching for Commitment: Liberal Education, Indoctrination, and Christian Nurture* (1993) is an insightful and sophisticated study of religion and indoctrination. *School Wars: Resolving Our Conflicts over Religion and Values* (1996) by Barbara Gaddy, T. William Hall, and Robert J. Marzano, comes close to the position we have taken but without appreciating how deep the problems cut. Nel Noddings's *Educating for Intelligent Belief or Unbelief* (1993) is a provocative exploration of some of these issues.

In *The Moral and Spiritual Crisis in Education* (1989), David Purpel explores his theme insightfully from the perspective of liberation theology and the Cultural Left. *Curriculum, Religion, and Public Education: Conversations for Enlarging the Public Square* (1998), edited by James T. Sears with James C. Carper, includes a wealth of essays addressing these issues from a variety of perspectives. Richard McMillan's *Religion in the Public Schools: An Introduction* (1984) provides helpful perspective.

Finally, two older anthologies are still worth reading: *Religion and Public Education* (1967), edited by Theodore R. Sizer, and *Public Education Religion Studies: An Overview* (1981), edited by Paul Will, Nicholas Piediscalzi, and Barbara DeMartino Swyhart.

P A R T

II

The Curriculum

3

Elementary Education

THE *PRESENCE*, NOT THE ABSENCE, OF RELIGION OFTEN TRIG-gers controversy on the elementary school level. Frequently the fight centers on the perennial "December dilemma"—the crèche in the school lobby, the Christmas play, the visits by Santa in the classroom, and other holiday activities.

As lamentable as they are, Christmas conflicts could provide schools with a valuable opportunity to rethink how they treat religion in the curriculum throughout the year. That rarely happens. Faced with a crisis, most schools take the path of least resistance. Christmas becomes "winter holidays." Teachers continue holiday activities in December but carefully avoid mentioning Jesus. Such tortured efforts to keep Christmas without Christ lead to some very odd overreactions by teachers. One Nashville teacher told us with pride in her voice that she had managed to celebrate Christmas in her classroom for 23 years—and she hadn't mentioned Jesus once! This would be funny if it weren't so painfully revealing about the confusion surrounding religion in many elementary school classrooms.

Fortunately some school districts now recognize that it is wrong to either promote *or* ignore religion in the elementary schools. They have found another approach—one that is both just and constitutional. In Williamsville, New York, for example, the district turned a conflict about holidays into an opportunity to involve the community in developing a policy on the place of religion in the curriculum. As a result, the elementary school teachers have learned how to take religion seriously without violating the First Amendment. Walk into a Williamsville elementary school just before Christmas and you will probably find students learning about what Christians actually *believe* about Christmas. At other times during the year, you will hear teachers and students discussing other religious traditions in ways that are accurate and fair.

In elementary schools these discussions of religion focus on the generally agreed upon meanings of the holidays, customs, basic beliefs, and histories of the major religions. Only as children become more mature should teachers ask them to think more critically about differences among religions and within religions—and, of course, the tensions between religious and secular ways of understanding the world.

But as Williamsville discovered, even the most basic teaching about religion in elementary schools is hard work. When young, impressionable children are involved, it is easy to understand why parents—and courts for that matter—have a heightened concern about religious issues. Nevertheless, the results in Williamsville and elsewhere have been worth the effort. Community support for the schools is stronger, parents have more trust in teachers to handle religious issues, and students are getting a better education. In this chapter we will argue that all school districts should do what Williamsville is doing. We begin with a discussion of why religion belongs in the elementary grades and then suggest how school districts might include study of religion without stirring a fight.

The Case for Religion in the Elementary Curriculum

When a crisis hits, communities like Williamsville discover that objections to the inclusion of religion are loudest if elementary schools are involved. This is particularly true in the primary grades, although many parents and educators are nervous about the ability of even upper elementary students to handle discussions of religion. Leave religion to the family and faith communities, goes the familiar argument, and wait until students are older to discuss the role of religion in history and society.

Of course, we agree that formation of faith is the job of families and religious communities. But, as we have already discussed at length, learning about religion is not the same as religious indoctrination. Far from being a way to usurp the role of parents or clergy, study of religion in the elementary grades is part of the core of the schools' mission to provide a good education and to prepare students to live in a democratic society. Properly considered, the study of family, community, various cultures, the nation, and other key themes and topics important in the early grades all require some discussion of religion.

At the same time, as we noted in Chapter 2, the fear of religious indoctrination is not without foundation. There are teachers today, as there have been in the past, who may use their position to promote their own faith or to be hostile to religion. That is why we urge that teacher education include more exposure to the First Amendment as well as to the study of religion.

But the fact that it isn't easy to achieve a fair and balanced elementary curriculum is no reason not to try. Silence about religion can also be a form of indoctrination—however unintentional. The notion that individuals can understand all of human life and history without reference to religion is itself a view of life that is antithetical and hostile to religious claims.

The New Consensus and Standards

As we discussed in Chapter 2, the New Consensus concerning religion in the curriculum should help to dispel fears among educators about dealing with religion in the early grades. Religious and educational groups from across the religious and political spectrum have agreed that there are many opportunities on the elementary level for study about religion.

This view is also reflected, at least in principle, in the *Curriculum Standards for the Social Studies* issued by the National Council for the Social Studies (NCSS). The standards mention religion in 2 of the 10 thematic strands that "form the framework of the social studies standards" (NCSS, 1994, pp. 21, 25).

These kinds of statements give permission for more mention of religion, but whether they will encourage serious treatment of religion in the elementary curriculum remains to be seen. The NCSS standards, for example, fail to do more than make a passing reference to religion. When the standards spell out what is meant by teaching "Culture" in the early grades, they do not explicitly mention religion. They emphasize "culture and cultural diversity." They tell us that students should explore the ways "groups, societies, and cultures address similar human needs and concerns," and "describe ways in which language, stories, folktales, music, and artistic creations serve as expressions of culture and influence behavior of people living in a particular culture" (NCSS, 1994, p. xiii). Much in the study of cultures, of course, could very well involve teaching about religious practices and beliefs. But *none* of the sample classroom activities for teaching this theme, or any other theme, in the early grades deal with religion (NCSS, 1994, pp. 49–75). This is odd, given the centrality of religion in most cultures. Perhaps the authors of the standards assume that religion will come up naturally. In our experience, however, if religion is ignored in the framework or the textbook, it will be ignored in most classrooms.

On balance, however, the NCSS standards are a potential step forward for the study of religion in elementary schools because they encourage the study of different cultures, the development of chronological thinking, and the inclusion of primary sources and historical narratives in the early grades. The same might be said of the *National Standards for History.* Although the K–4 history standards include only a couple of brief mentions of religion, there are many opportunities to include religion in the study of various cultures and historical narratives. The history standards explicitly encourage inclusion of religious ideas and events in the upper elementary grades (National Center for History in the Schools, 1996).

The California Example

According to the traditional model of elementary education—a model widely adopted until very recently—young children are not ready for history, much less religious events and people in history. In this view, the child's focus should be on immediate surroundings and the present-day world of family, school, neighborhood, and community. As it is usually practiced, this approach leaves little room for religion beyond mentioning a few symbols and places of worship.

Fortunately, in the last decade educators and developmental psychologists have successfully challenged these assumptions about children's learning (Gagnon, 1989, pp. 175–177). Like the standards just discussed, some state frameworks, notably the *History-Social Science Framework for California Public Schools,* now encourage considerable discussion of history in the early grades. Again, this opens the door for study of religion. In California, beginning in kindergarten, students "reach out to times past," and in grades 1, 2, and 3 they learn about various cultures and read stories about historical figures. Students tackle California history in grade 4, begin American history in grade 5, and study ancient civilizations in grade 6. On all levels, the framework offers many opportunities, some stated and some implied, for study of religion (California Department of Education History-Social Science Curriculum Framework and Criteria Committee, 1987, 1997).

This is no accident. The drafters of the California framework intend a history-enriched primary curriculum and history-centered upper elementary curriculum to encourage more study of religion. We have found that in practice the framework has led to more discussion of religion in California classrooms, particularly in 6th grade.[1] Sixth grade students are studying Hebrew religion (including passages from Hebrew Scripture), the origins and spread of Buddhism, Confucian teachings and influence in China, and the teachings of Jesus and the rise of the Christian church. Charlotte Crabtree, a leader in the California effort and a member of the influential Bradley Commission on History in the Schools, summarizes the case for religion this way:

> Elementary school studies of U.S. and world history, necessarily centered on the lives of people in order to motivate and sustain children's interest, also provide fruitful opportunities to explore with children the important role of ideas, religion, and the arts in shaping individual behavior and group culture, and in instituting or restricting change. No adequate understanding of human history is possible, we believe, without examining people's most dearly held religious and secular beliefs and the influences of those beliefs upon their ethical and moral commitments and choices, and

---

[1] Some textbook publishers have responded to the California call for more study of religion, most notably Houghton-Mifflin. Although uneven in its treatment of religion in California and U.S. history, the 6th grade world civilizations text includes significantly more about religion than previous textbooks. The California 3Rs Project, discussed in Chapter 4, is a statewide effort to provide teachers with educational opportunities and classroom resources for teaching about religions.

upon their actions in political, economic, and social life. (Gagnon, 1989, pp. 184–185)

We agree. Study of human society and history, including religious society and history, should begin in the earliest grades. Elementary education provides the foundation—the basic knowledge and skills—for the more complex and challenging discussions that come later. Leaving religion out not only gives a distorted and false view of the world and human nature, it deprives students of the tools they will need for further study in middle and high school.

The Core Knowledge Approach

Another influential assault on the view that young children are not developmentally ready for study of religion comes from E.D. Hirsch Jr., founder of the Core Knowledge movement. Hirsch is convinced that students need to be introduced to at least the basic ideas and stories of the world's religions at a young age as preparation for critical understanding later on. Beginning in 1st grade, religion should be treated as an integral part of the great world civilizations and a shaping force in world and U.S. history. These first discussions of religion focus on the core beliefs and symbols as well as on important figures and events.

Hirsch's ideas about what children need to know concerning religion are reflected in the Core Knowledge Sequence, now used in at least several hundred schools throughout the United States. Study of the history of world religions begins in 1st grade with introductions to Judaism, Christianity, and Islam and a discussion of the religion of ancient Egypt. Second graders learn something about Hinduism, Buddhism, Confucianism, and Greek myths. In 3rd grade, students are introduced to Roman religion, the spread of Christianity, Byzantium, Constantine, Viking religion, Native American religious beliefs, and the religious motives for coming to America during the colonial period. Fourth graders tackle the Christian Church in the Middle Ages, the spread of Islam, Islamic civilization, the Crusades, and religious art. By 5th grade students are discussing the Reformation; the Counter-Reformation; the Eastern Orthodox Church in Russia; Shinto and Buddhism in feudal Japan; the Aztec, Maya, and Inca religions; and the Mormons in the story of westward expansion in the United States. Finally, in 6th grade, students examine monotheism, covenant, and other central ideas of Judaism and Christianity; and, in American history, religious issues in the story of immigration and social reform (Holdren and Hirsch, 1996).

Clearly, the Core Knowledge approach takes religion seriously in the early grades. The major faiths of the world are well represented, though Core Knowledge places more emphasis on biblical literacy because of the pervasive influence of the Bible in American culture. Are most elementary teachers prepared for this challenge? Probably not, no more than they are prepared to teach other parts of the Core Knowledge Sequence. But the fact that curricular materials and some educational opportunities are available to support the sequence should help to address this challenge. The Core Knowledge Foundation has assembled an outstanding list of resources for introducing religion to young children, as well as sample lessons developed by teachers.[2]

Even with offers of support and assurances of legality, teaching about religion still frightens some school officials. We spoke with administrators at two Core Knowledge schools in Tennessee and Kentucky who reported that they are not using the religion components of the sequence, though one said that the school plans to do so in the future. By contrast, the Nashville schools, which adopted Core Knowledge in fall 1997, are including all of the content concerning religion.

Religious Diversity and Freedom

Placing religion at the core of what students need to know is necessary for civic as well as academic reasons. High school student Chana Schoenberger discovered how important "core knowledge" about religion can be while attending a summer program at the University of Wisconsin at Superior. Eight faith groups were represented among the 20 students who participated with her in the program: Jewish, Roman Catholic, Methodist, Hindu, Muslim, Mormon, Jehovah's Witness, and Lutheran. She was amazed at how little they knew about one another—and what they did "know" about other

---

[2] We are indebted to Mary Beth Klee of Crossroads Academy in Hanover, New Hampshire, for alerting us to the various ways in which the Core Knowledge movement addresses religion in the curriculum. Klee gives workshops to teachers on teaching about world religions in the elementary school using the Core Knowledge approach.

faiths was distorted and wrong. The ignorance of her peers bothered her, but what hurt was when the teacher casually remarked (in reference to using government money for his study wisely) that he "wouldn't want them to get Jewed." When Chana returned to school that fall, she decided to get involved in a program to inform other students about the various religions in the school. "People who are suspicious when they find out I'm Jewish," she wrote later, "usually don't know much about Judaism" (Haynes and Thomas, 1994, 1996, chap. 7, pp. 11–12).

As Chana and her friends discovered, America is a very diverse place. In fact, the United States is the most religiously diverse country on earth, and, if polls are to be trusted, the most religious of all Western nations. According to one recent survey, 79 percent of Americans say religion is an important part of their life. On a weekly basis, 71 percent of Americans claim they pray, 40 percent attend religious services, and 43 percent read the Bible (Angus Reid Group, 1996).

In much of the rest of the world, such deep and diverse religious commitment is rarely accompanied by political civility. We need only think of Bosnia, India, Sri Lanka, and many other nations across the globe. Thanks in large measure to the religious liberty provisions of the First Amendment, the United States is the exception to this tragic pattern. But Americans seem to forget that the American experiment of living with deep religious differences is still new and fragile. Our culture wars should be a sufficient reminder that religious arguments matter. If allowed to deepen unchecked, they can poison our public life—including our schools—with hatred and division.

The task of sustaining this unprecedented experiment in religious diversity and freedom begins in kindergarten. Students should learn in the earliest grades that we are different in how we understand the world, and that our civic agreements protect our right to be different. Simultaneously, of course, they must learn how citizens deal with religious and other differences in the classroom, neighborhood, and wider community. Even the youngest children can begin to practice what the *Williamsburg Charter* terms the "Golden Rule for civic life": Our rights are best protected when we guard the rights of others, even those with whom we disagree (Haynes and Thomas, 1994, 1996, Appendix A, p. 11). These two aims—some basic knowledge of the religious beliefs and practices of others and a commitment to our civic framework of religious liberty—should be essential components of the elementary school curriculum.

The Major Issues

No matter how persuasive the argument or how good the curriculum, including study of religion in the elementary grades will not be easy. Even as this chapter was being written, a call for help came from a Nashville elementary school that had recently introduced the Core Knowledge curriculum. An angry parent objected to the use of the Bible by her child's 6th grade teacher when teaching about the ancient Hebrews. The teacher was using the Bible appropriately and following the curriculum guidelines of the school, but the parent couldn't understand why the Bible is allowed in a public school.

Parents are understandably nervous about how teachers will present religion to their children. Will they promote one religion over others? Are they prepared to teach about various faiths fairly and accurately? When the Nashville schools first adopted Core Knowledge, the district did much too little to prepare teachers to teach about the many religious ideas, symbols, individuals, and history required by the curriculum. Some teachers worked hard to prepare themselves. Others weren't sure how to handle religion. Faced with explaining the idea of covenant in the Hebrew Scriptures, one well-intentioned, but slightly confused teacher finally blurted out to her 6th graders that God "made a deal" with Abraham.

Fear of controversy (or poor teaching) should not deter public schools from dealing with religion in the curriculum. It can be done, but it takes work. Parents have the right to expect that teachers will receive appropriate staff development and curriculum resources. In places where this is done, the vast majority of elementary teachers report strong parental support for religious literacy, including biblical literacy. Most of them begin each year by informing parents about what they will be doing in the study of religion and why. In their experience (and ours) parents overwhelmingly favor including religion once they understand the constitutional and educational rationales for doing so.

Religion and Religious Holidays

With all of the challenges, taking religion seriously is not as costly or controversial as ignoring religion or including it in ways that are unconstitutional. The "December dilemma" mentioned at the beginning of this chapter is the best illustration of what we mean. Put a crèche in the school lobby (with a menorah and a Christmas tree), as one school district did in December, and you are threatened with a lawsuit for promoting religion. Remove the crèche (but leave the Menorah and tree), and many Christians protest that their faith is now excluded, and some Jews ask if this means that school officials don't consider the Menorah a religious symbol. When the superintendent tries to take it all away, even more people get angry.

As we mentioned at the outset, Williamsville and other school districts have found a better way: teach *about* religion, including religious holidays. Because (unfortunately) many school districts link much of the elementary curriculum to holidays, and because (again, unfortunately) holidays may be one of the only times in many schools when religion gets mentioned, it is important to say something about what academic treatment of religious holidays entails.

The same coalition of religious and education groups that sponsored "Religion in the Public School Curriculum" (discussed in Chapter 2) also produced "Religious Holidays in the Public Schools: Questions and Answers."[3] Finally, after many years of bitter arguments, a broad consensus has been reached on religious holidays in public schools:

> The study of religious holidays may be included in elementary and secondary curricula as opportunities for teaching about religions. Such study serves the academic goals of educating students about history and cultures as well as about the traditions of particular religions in a pluralistic society. (Haynes and Thomas, 1994, 1996, chap. 10, p. 2)

This is a constitutional approach that addresses deeply held convictions of people on both sides—those who don't want public schools to promote religion and those who don't want public schools to become religion-free zones. For example, in our experience most conservative Christians would much prefer that schools teach something about the religious meaning of Christmas rather than promote the shopping mall version of the holiday. And people who oppose religious celebrations in public schools will usually support the academic study of Christmas.

What does this agreement look like in the classroom? The crèche, the menorah, the crescent and star, and other religious sym-

---

[3] Sponsors of this statement include such diverse groups as the American Jewish Congress, the Christian Legal Society, and the Islamic Society of North America.

bols are used as teaching aids. Traditional carols and music from other traditions are sung and played as part of the study of music. In short, as long as there is an educational goal, religious art, music, literature, and symbols have a place in the elementary classroom. The important distinction for teachers to keep in mind is the difference between teaching about religious holidays, which is permissible, and celebrating religious holidays, which is not.

The key skill an elementary teacher needs when teaching about religious traditions is the ability to teach through attribution (e.g., "Many Christians believe that . . ."). In this way teachers avoid injecting their personal views into the discussion while allowing the religious tradition to speak for itself.

No matter how careful they are, however, if teachers limit their study of holidays to Christian—or even Christian and Jewish—celebrations, they create a perception of unfairness. They must make an effort to teach a variety of traditions at various times of the year. As we discussed in Chapter 2, a fair and neutral curriculum will include a diversity of views. Those holidays that are central events in the major traditions should be considered, along with those that may have special significance for people in the local community.

School assembly programs in December are a special challenge, given that Christmas concerts and Nativity pageants have a long and cherished history in many schools. The sponsors of "Religious Holidays in the Public Schools" advise schools to "devise holiday programs that serve an educational purpose for all students—programs that make no students feel excluded or identified with a religion not their own" (Haynes and Thomas, 1994, 1996, chap. 10, p. 3). This means that the December holiday program should include religious music—to leave out traditional Christmas carols would be absurd and unfair—but such concerts should include a variety of music, secular and religious.[4] The coalition also agrees that Nativity pageants or plays portraying the Hanukkah miracle are inappropriate in public schools. Reenactment of these sacred events puts the school in the

---

[4] When "Religious Holidays in the Public Schools" was first released, a state superintendent wrote to ask if the coalition meant to suggest that a performance of Handel's *Messiah* would have to be mixed with some secular music in a school program. He has a point. Surely a school chorus may sing a great work of music that happens to be religious in content without "balancing" it with other music. But we still advise that schools be especially careful in December because of the historic battles in public schools at that time of year. Handel's *Messiah* might not cause a stir in May, but it is sure to spark controversy in December.

position of sponsoring a devotional experience that more appropriately belongs in a church or synagogue.

It is particularly unfortunate when schools attempt to justify Christmas celebrations (as opposed to programs with an educational purpose) by mixing in a celebration of Hanukkah. Two constitutional wrongs do not equal a constitutional right. It is also wrongheaded to focus on Hanukkah as the chief opportunity to teach something about Judaism. Hanukkah is a minor Jewish holiday (and it is *not* the Jewish Christmas). Passover, Rosh Hashanah, or Yom Kippur are all much better choices for substantive teaching about the Jewish faith.

But what about the cultural Christmas with its trees and wreaths, or the cultural Easter with its eggs and bunnies? In our view, the first obligation of a school district is to find a way to treat religious holidays academically. Then, once a commitment is made to appropriate study of religion, the district is in a better position to tackle trees and bunnies. When dealing with these cultural symbols, the question may not be a legal one (after all, the majority of the Supreme Court justices have indicated that they see the Christmas tree as a secular symbol), but rather "what is the right and sensitive thing to do in our community?" Whatever the courts say, many parents and students see cultural Christmas and Easter decorations and activities as promotion of religion, while others, particularly conservative Christians, are offended if such symbols are all that students learn about the Christian faith.

The solution is for schools and communities to sit down together and come to some agreement about how their schools will treat both religious and cultural holiday symbols. When districts do this, they find much support for academic treatment of religious holidays, and, building on that agreement, they find ways to tone down the cultural trappings. It may not be illegal, but it is surely insensitive to have weeks of Santa and Frosty throughout the school. Teachers and administrators shouldn't assume that everyone expects Santa on Christmas morning or a visit from the Easter Bunny on Easter Sunday. Art projects and other class activities should give students a choice that respects the kinds of celebrations, religious or otherwise, that their families practice. Rather than pulling out the school tinsel or other decorations, let student-initiated art decorate the halls at various times of year, including December. In these and similar ways, elementary schools can finally get beyond the debate about where to put the crèche or menorah and begin to teach students what these and other symbols actually mean in the traditions they represent.

Role-Playing

If Nativity pageants are inappropriate in an assembly program, what about reenacting other religious ceremonies in the classroom as a hands-on way to teach about religions? Some elementary school teachers, for example, role-play the Seder meal as part of the study of Judaism. Isn't this a valuable activity for getting students to empathize with the religious traditions they are studying?

Although some texts and curriculum guides suggest such activities, we advise against them. No matter how carefully planned or well intentioned, role-playing religious ceremonies risks undermining the integrity of the faith involved. This may be more of a problem for some traditions than for others. Reenacting the Catholic Mass, for instance, would surely raise more objections than reenacting the Seder meal. But in all cases, the possibility that a moment or ritual considered sacred might be trivialized or mocked, even unwittingly, is too great to risk. The other problem, of course, is the very real possibility that the activity will violate the conscience of students who participate. Even if they volunteer, students may not be aware of the religious implications of what they are doing.

Yes, we encourage helping students to get inside the religions they study, what we described in Chapter 2 as "informed empathy." But instead of reenactments, we suggest using audiovisual resources and primary source documents (and objects) to give students some feel for how individuals practice the rituals of the faith.

Literature

One of the most natural and appropriate ways to include teaching about religion in the elementary grades is through children's literature. Carefully chosen stories from and about the various religions help students to get some sense of what these traditions are all about—to see them from the inside.

Although there has been some improvement in recent years, reading texts for elementary grades are still poor in their treatment of religion (as Paul Vitz documented in his famous study more than a decade ago). Writers of basal readers, as well as many teachers, have been afraid to include stories with religious themes, ideas, and images. Sometimes a story from Hindu or Buddhist legends might sneak in, but rarely one from Judaism or Christianity (Vitz, 1986).

Fortunately, however, things are beginning to change as state guidelines such as those of California acknowledge the importance of including study about religion in the curriculum. Today there are a growing number of books for children about the world's major faiths—literature books and history books—suitable for use in public schools. The widely praised *Molly's Pilgrim* by Barbara Cohen is a good example of a book for primary grade children that includes religious belief and practice as a natural part of the story. For upper elementary students, Mary Pope Osborne's *One World, Many Religions: The Ways We Worship* is a scholarly, but lively, introduction to the major faiths.

The key is to select material that is both accurate about the religion under discussion and intended for a broad audience. If using sacred texts, teachers should be careful to put the story in the context of learning *about* the religion. Again, attribution is important: the children need to understand that they are learning about what the people of a particular religious tradition believe and practice. Devotional books intended for faith formation or religious education should not be used in a public school classroom.

Guest Speakers

An additional resource might be a guest speaker. In Nashville recently an orthodox Jewish Rabbi gave 6th graders in an elementary school a firsthand account of what it means to be a Jew. The students were fascinated, asking about everything from the little things they noticed ("Why don't you shake hands with women?") to big ideas they were studying ("What does it mean to keep kosher?").

Although presentations like this can bring religion alive for students, we do have a few concerns. First, the teacher must put the visit in context, noting, in this case, that the speaker represents one of several major perspectives about Jewish law and life within Judaism. Second, the teacher must make sure that the guest has the background necessary for an academic discussion of the faith. Third, the teacher must be sure that the guest understands what is expected of him or her. Guest speakers on religion must be informed about the First Amendment guidelines for teaching about religion and know exactly what they are being asked to speak about.

Students should not be asked what their faith is, much less to speak as a representative of that faith. They are free, of course, to speak about their faith as long as their comments are germane to the discussion. But the teacher should not rely on students to "fill in the gaps" about their religion.

Conclusions

An elementary school curriculum that ignores religion gives students the false message that religion doesn't matter to people—that we live in a religion-free world. This is neither fair nor accurate. Silence about religion also denies students the promise of a good education. If they are to understand the world they live in, they must be exposed at an early age to the religious dimensions of society, history, literature, art, and music. Without this foundation, they will be unprepared for the more complex and critical study of the upper grades. Finally, students must begin in the primary grades to learn about the rights and responsibilities of religious liberty, the fundamental principles that sustain our nation across deep and abiding differences.

Despite what we believe to be a strong case for including religion in the elementary curriculum, we have tried to emphasize just how difficult it is to take religion seriously when young and impressionable children are involved. Nowhere in public schools do teachers need to be more cognizant of the power of their example than in the early grades. That is why the First Amendment framework we outlined in Chapter 1 must be clearly and firmly in place in the elementary school. And that is also why staff development programs and academically sound resources focused on teaching about religions must be made available to all elementary teachers.

We began our discussion by invoking the example of Williamsville, New York. We could add Ramona, California; South Orangetown, New York; and many other places that are now working to take religion more seriously in their schools. No, it isn't easy. But the renewed trust between parents and teachers, the broad community support for doing the right thing, and the enrichment of the curriculum are some of the very important reasons why the effort is worthwhile—and vital to the future of public education.

....

Suggested Readings
and Resources

Elementary teachers need a concise description of the various religious groups that they encounter in their classroom and teaching. We suggest *America's Religions: An Educator's Guide to Beliefs and Practices* (1997) by Benjamin J. Hubbard, John T. Hatfield, and James A. Santucci, available from Teacher Ideas Press (telephone: 800-237-6124). A discussion of each tradition is followed by a helpful section on possible classroom concerns.

Teachers also need a calendar noting major religious holidays with brief descriptions of their significance. One can be obtained from The National Conference (telephone: 212-206-0006).

Resources for teaching children about religion in history, art, music, and literature are listed in *Books to Build On: A Grade-by-Grade Resource Guide for Parents and Teachers* (1996), edited by John Holdren and E.D. Hirsch Jr. Public school teachers need to preview carefully all of the recommended books that deal with religion to make sure that they are accurate and that they are not intended for devotional use. For more information about Core Knowledge, contact the Core Knowledge foundation (telephone: 800-238-3233).

Using suggestions of classroom teachers, the First Amendment Center has compiled a list of children's literature with religious ideas and themes appropriate for use in a public school (telephone: 703-284-2826). The center also provides *Living With Our Deepest Differences: Religious Liberty in a Pluralistic Society,* a set of lessons for upper elementary students about the meaning and significance of religious liberty in American history.

We strongly urge that parents be informed about how religion will be treated in the classroom. One approach is to make available to parents *A Parent's Guide to Religion and the Public Schools,* a brief pamphlet published by the National PTA and the First Amendment Center (available free from the center, The Freedom Forum, 1101 Wilson Blvd., Arlington, VA 22209).

4

History

FEW EDUCATORS DISPUTE THE IMPORTANCE OF STUDY ABOUT religion in history. The New Consensus is strongest on this point. Consensus, however, does not necessarily mean commitment to change. Despite some improvement in textbooks and state frameworks, we see few signs that schools are taking religion seriously in history or elsewhere in the social studies. When religion appears, the treatment is usually superficial, sometimes inaccurate, and almost always inadequate.

The agreement to teach about religion in history is often more political than educational. When legislatures or boards of education in North Carolina or West Virginia call for more study of religion, little or nothing happens in the way of staff development to ensure that this actually occurs. Sometimes controversial topics not wanted in other parts of the curriculum—creationism, for example—are officially placed in the social studies. But, again, rarely do such actions translate into actual programs and resources that prepare teachers to teach the controversy.

How should schools treat religion in history and other social studies courses? In Chapter 3, we indicated how schools might treat study of religion in the social studies component of the elementary classroom. Here we focus on the middle and high school grades. Although we recognize that social studies on all levels is a field of study that includes many disciplines, in this and the following chapter we will discuss three areas—history, civics, and economics—widely studied in U.S. public schools.

Textbooks and Standards

In the mid-1980s, a series of textbook studies called attention to the poor treatment of religion in textbooks for world and United States history. These studies, combined with concerns raised by textbook trials in Alabama and Tennessee, helped create the New Consensus discussed in Chapter 2. All sides agreed: students must learn a good deal about religion if they are to understand history.

More than a decade has passed, but textbooks have yet to take religion seriously. Why is this important? Because the vast majority of decisions about what to teach in the history classroom are based on the textbook. We are aware (and grateful) that a significant number of excellent classroom teachers go beyond the text and use supplemental resources. But constraints of time, pressure to cover a tremendous amount of material, and lack of access to quality supplemental materials push most teachers to rely heavily on the textbook. Even when teachers want to deal with religion, they often feel ill-prepared to do so and unsure about how it should be done. Confronted with these obstacles, if the textbook avoids religion, so will most teachers.

The news is not all bad. According to the American Textbook Council, there has been some improvement in the treatment of religion in the new generation of history texts (Sewall, 1995, pp. 15–16). Many of the changes involve brief mentions of religion, though some constitute substantive discussion of religious ideas and events, particularly in world history. Some of the credit for the changes that have occurred must be given to the *History-Social Science Framework for California Public Schools* (California Department of Education History-Social Science Curriculum Framework and Criteria Committee, 1987, 1997). Not only does California call for more teaching about religion on all grade levels, state officials have let textbook publishers know that inclusion of religion will be an important criterion for adoption.

Despite this progress, textbooks are still woefully inadequate in their treatment of religion. World history texts do provide brief accounts of the basic teachings and practices of the major religions as they appear in history, but, in our view, the texts do not give enough

space to the topics to enable students to make sense of these traditions. In the texts we examined, religion virtually disappears after
1750. The authors say nothing about the various religious ways of
interpreting history and give no attention to the major theological
developments in the last two centuries.[1]

United States history texts are no better. They mention religion
occasionally, especially in relation to political and social developments. Beyond brief discussions of Native Americans and Puritans,
however, they say little or nothing about the beliefs and practices of
any other religious traditions. In accounts of American history after
the Civil War, religion disappears almost entirely. If we exclude their
treatment of the Holocaust, each of four texts we examined devotes
more space to railroads than to religion for the entire post-Civil War
history of the United States. Again, the texts discuss no religious interpretations of history, and with the exception of short accounts of
what was at issue in the Scopes trial, the texts include no discussion
of theology after the Civil War.[2]

The *National Standards for History,* published in 1996 (National
Center for History in the Schools), are intended to raise the level of historical thinking and understanding in all grades and courses. In view
of the controversy surrounding national standards in general and the
history standards in particular, it remains to be seen how influential
they will be in reshaping the teaching of history and improving the content of textbooks. Whatever the outcome of that debate, it is important
to take note of how the standards treat religion because they reflect the
current thinking of many educators within the discipline of history.

In some ways the standards are generous to religion. Almost 17
percent of the elaborated standards in world history include some
reference to religion. Under these standards, students would learn
about the basic beliefs and practices of the major religions as well as
how these faiths influenced the development of civilization in succes-
sive historical periods. The U.S. history standards include religion less
frequently—in just under 7 percent of the elaborated standards (and
many of these are only brief mentions of religion). Nevertheless, if these

---

[1] The four texts we reviewed are *World History: Peoples and Nations* (HBJ 1993);
World History: Patterns of Living (Prentice-Hall 1993); *History and Life* (Scott Fores-
man 1993); and *History of the World* (Houghton Mifflin 1993).

[2] The four texts we reviewed are *The United States and Its People* (Addison-Wesley
1993); *History of a Free Nation* (Glencoe 1992); *History of the United States*
(Houghton Mifflin 1991); and *The Americans: A History* (McDougal Little 1992).

standards guided curriculum leaders and textbook writers, study of religion in world and U.S. history would be expanded considerably.

In other more significant ways the standards fail to take religion seriously. Given the quantity of material to be covered, the time available to learn about the major religions is too limited for students to grasp what it means to understand the world or history religiously. Furthermore, like textbooks, the standards seriously understate the role of religion after 1750 in world history and after the Civil War in U.S. history. They make no mention of significant theological developments in the modern era, including the Second Vatican Council, one of the most important theological events of the last several hundred years. Of the 11 examples of "long-term changes and recurring patterns in world history," none deals with religious history. Finally, the standards assume that history should be interpreted only in secular categories. They do not ask students to consider how historical events and developments are interpreted by faith traditions such as Judaism, Christianity, and Islam, each of which see a religious meaning and purpose in history, or by Eastern traditions that view the cycles of time in very different ways.

Religious Interpretations of History

Standards and textbooks notwithstanding, there is more than one way to conceptualize history. True, history has become a secular discipline and most contemporary historians use secular categories to construct their narratives. But surely a liberally educated person ought to know that there are claims for religious meaning in history that a secular approach cannot convey. For millennia, people in many faith traditions have understood history as the arena of divine action. Indeed, some contemporary historians, as well as millions of adherents to Judaism, Christianity, and Islam, continue to interpret history in religious categories. Without exposure to religious conceptions of history, students will understand little about how history has been interpreted for much of the development of Western civilization; they will learn that all of history should be interpreted only in secular ways.

The Bible as History

The educational implications of ignoring religious views of history are considerable. We may illustrate our point by looking briefly at the

Bible, a religious account of history of central importance to millions of people throughout the world.

We can, of course, learn a great deal about history from the Bible, but what we take to be historical in the Bible will depend on how we interpret it, and the criteria we use to assess the validity of historical claims—both of which are matters of much controversy.

Consider, for example, the following passage from a high school world history textbook:

> Because the Egyptians feared the Hebrews, they made them slaves. The Hebrew leader Moses led the Hebrews from Egypt to Palestine. Under the rule of their early kings—Saul, David, and Solomon—the Hebrew nation prospered. . . . King Solomon died about 900 B.C. Then Palestine split into two kingdoms. The kingdom of Israel was formed in the north. The Kingdom of Judah was formed in the south. The Kingdom of Israel lasted for 250 years. Then it was destroyed by the Assyrians. (Leinwand, 1986, p. 24)

Consider now the biblical account:

> When Pharaoh let the people go, God did not guide them by the road towards the Philistines. . . . God made them go round by way of the wilderness towards the Red Sea. . . . And all the time the Lord went before them, by day a pillar of cloud to guide them on their journey, by night a pillar of fire. (Exodus 13:17–18, 21, *The New English Bible*)

Moreover, according to the Scriptural account, it was God who made Israel a great nation, and it was God who raised up the Assyrians and Babylonians to punish Israel for its sins.

The Bible provides what is often called *sacred history*. It makes sense of history in terms of God's purposes and actions. The biblical authors saw the hand of God behind the exodus—and all the miracles, experiences, and events they wove into their historical narratives. For those who accept the Bible as Scripture, God is at work in history, and there is a religious meaning in the patterns of history.

Many religious conservatives believe that the Bible can be read *literally* as history—and, no doubt many of the historical claims made in the Bible are accepted by secular scholars. But using the methods of secular historical scholarship scholars are unable to discern miracles, divine causality, or religious meaning in history. At best, secular history must remain silent about the actions of God in history. Religious liberals offer a third alternative in claiming that many parts of the Bible must be read as *myth*—meaning not that they are false, but that they can't be taken to be *literally* true. There may not have been a *literal* pillar of fire, for example, but the purposes of God were fulfilled in the liberation of the Hebrews from oppression and in the religious life of Israel.

Sometimes, to make study of the Bible more "acceptable" in public schools, educators are willing to jettison the miracles and accounts of God's interventions in history. But this too is problematic, for it radically distorts the meaning of the Bible. And yet to include the miracles and religious interpretations of events inevitably opens the discussion to controversy and conflicting accounts of how to interpret them.

Sorting out what is *historical* is complicated and controversial, and teachers who teach the Bible as history need to be sensitive to the differences between conventional secular history, and the varieties of sacred history. They should be prepared to include a number of different perspectives—religious and secular—on the historicity of the Bible.

Much of the recent conflict about teaching the Bible as history in public schools is rooted in the inability of some advocates of this approach to differentiate between secular and sacred history. Our position is that if students are to be *educated* about the Bible, and if it is to be studied *neutrally*, they must learn something about the contending ways of assessing the Bible as history. They cannot be uncritically taught to accept the Bible as literally true, as history. Nor should they be uncritically taught to accept as historical only what secular historians find true in the Bible.

We believe that in addition to including discussion of the Bible in history and literature courses, elective Bible courses can be a good idea if carefully conceived and properly taught. But, again, given the complexity of the debate about the historicity of the Bible, teachers who deal with the Bible as history need a great deal of sophistication. We suspect that a literary approach may be more manageable, though here too teachers need to be sensitive to the Bible as a sacred text, as Scripture (as we will argue in Chapter 6). Because the Bible is so important, and because its interpretation is so controversial, we will address how to teach about the Bible at considerably greater length in Chapter 8.

The Puritan View of History

Learning about the Bible as sacred history is also crucial in the study of American history. An obvious example is the Puritan conception of history as articulated by John Winthrop in his lay sermon "A Model of Christian Charity," delivered to his fellow Puritans aboard the *Arabella* just as they reached Massachusetts Bay in 1630:

> Thus stands the cause between God and us. We are entered into covenant with Him for this work; we have taken out a commission, the Lord hath given us leave to draw out our own articles. . . . For we must consider that we shall be as a city upon a hill, the eyes of all people are upon us. (Winthrop, 1630/1956, p. 83–84)

Clearly this is a religious interpretation of history, a biblical view that sees all of history in terms of God's actions and purposes. But should teachers take the time to get inside the biblical worldview as understood by the Puritans? If a liberal education is the aim, then the answer must be yes.

Everyone agrees that learning *something* about Puritans is important. Indeed, Puritans generally get more space in U.S. history textbooks than any other religious group. Unfortunately, most of these accounts of Puritans are superficial, largely negative, and, in many cases, simply wrong. They emphasize the intolerance and persecution perpetuated by Puritans (though they do not examine the roots of the conflicts). We would agree that the narrative should include the flaws of Puritanism (or of any religious movement), but educators must make the picture more complete and coherent by also presenting how the Puritans themselves viewed their mission. Few texts attempt to explain theological issues important to Puritans, and none deal fully with the Puritans' conception of history. By most accounts, therefore, Puritans are important for how they influenced (mostly negatively) early colonial history, but what they actually believed and how they viewed the world are largely irrelevant. The text could put the same space to much better use.

The solution is not simply to add more information about how Puritans and other religious groups shaped social and political developments in American history. Religion is not just important for its influence on events; religion seeks to answer fundamental questions about human existence and history. If we want students to struggle with these questions and to think critically about history, then it is important that they study how various faith traditions *conceive* history.

In the case of the Puritans, Winthrop's lay sermon is a good place to begin. In his address, Winthrop locates the great migration of Puritans at the center of the world's history. Reminding his hearers of why they had traveled so far at such great sacrifice, he describes their mission in New England as nothing less than an agreement with God to fulfill the divine plan for humanity. Their covenant would require them to establish a "holy commonwealth" and Christ's true church in anticipation of the Second Coming. Modeling themselves on ancient Israel, the founders of the Massachusetts Bay Colony saw themselves as called by God to change the course of history.

Without exposure to this conception of history, much in the rest of the American story is difficult to comprehend. How else would students make sense of the similarity and differences between ideas of covenant in the 17th century and ideas of constitution in the 18th? How would they comprehend the many U.S. foreign policy debates that reflect ongoing arguments about America's special mission as "a city upon a hill?" What will California students understand about the foundations of their public schools, libraries, and state universities— all of which were founded by missionaries from New England attempting to realize the Puritan ideal? These are but a few of many examples of the Puritan sources, for better and for worse, of much in the American nation and spirit.

At the end of the 20th century, something very close to the Puritan reading of sacred history continues to shape debates about the meaning of the United States. Millions of Americans view the movement of history and the American destiny through the lens of convictions that echo the Puritan covenant. Many conservative Christians continue to resonate deeply to a vision of the United States that is "divinely blessed" with a special mission in the world. In this view, we were founded as a "Christian nation," and our future prosperity and freedom depend upon acknowledging the divine source of our blessings and our liberties. The clash between this conception of the United States and other views, religious and secular, has fueled the debate about school prayer and other culture-war issues for nearly 40 years. To understand these competing positions, students must know that there are alternative ways to think about this nation and its destiny. Some of these alternatives are religious.

U.S. and world history courses are replete with opportunities to alert students to religious conceptions of historical events. In the painful history of the Middle East—to cite one obvious example in world history—Jews, Muslims, and Christians have long had competing convictions about God's purposes in that region of the world. For much of American history, religious interpretations of events have shaped our self-understanding as a nation. During the Civil War, for instance, many on both sides saw the conflict as a religious war, involving divine judgment on our nation. Whatever the illustration, our point is the same: If students are to be liberally educated about the meaning of history, they must learn that traditional religious and modern secular ways of understanding history are fundamentally different.

Religion in History

Beyond attention to religious ways of interpreting history, what should the teaching of history include about religion? The answer is not merely to mention religion more often—a common tactic in the textbook world. Coverage, though significant, is not sufficient. *How* religion is discussed is as important as the number of pages devoted to it.

Getting Inside Religion

To begin with, it is not enough for textbooks and teachers to briefly summarize major beliefs and practices. Students need to explore the religious experiences and convictions at the heart of the major world religions. In the study of Islam, to take one significant example, students need to know something about key theological conceptions such as the meaning of the word *Islam,* the strong emphasis on the absolute transcendence and oneness of Allah, and the way in which the Qur'an is understood as immediate revelation. The teacher should also say something about the religious core of Muslim life, especially as exemplified during the early community under the prophet Muhammad and the "rightly guided" caliphs—a period that becomes paradigmatic for Muslims in subsequent eras. Teachers can best accomplish this if they employ strategies and resources that allow Muslims to speak for themselves. Exposing students to Scriptures and primary source documents and literature, as well as using film and qualified guest speakers, provides students with the opportunity to encounter religion as directly as possible.

The aim should be to help students see the Islamic worldview from the inside. They should have the conceptual tools with which to grasp core concepts such as the religious meaning of the *umma*—the Muslim community—beyond the many national, ethnic, and political differences in Islamic societies. They should be able to discuss such crucial topics as the spread of Islam, then and now, as a religious phenomenon of profound importance in world history and in our own time—a topic that most texts explain solely in political or sociological terms. Of course, they must learn about the political and sociological impact of Islam through the centuries, and, yes, they must learn about the cultural differences within Islam. But understanding Islam, or any faith group studied in world history, requires first understanding the theological claims and religious experiences that have shaped how believers make sense of the world. This is what we described earlier as *informed empathy*.

Multiculturalism

Our suggestion that the study of history include efforts to "get inside" religious perspectives parallels the call for a more multicultural curriculum. Many advocates of multicultural education advance arguments similar to ours about the need for an empathetic understanding of the many cultures and ethnic groups that have shaped both world and U.S. history. And, much like our position, their stance pleads for a curriculum that is both fair and reflective of a truly liberal education.

In light of these parallel arguments, it is striking that most proposals for multicultural education virtually ignore religion.[3] Enriching the world history curriculum with the voices of ethnic and cultural groups neglected in the past is essential. But for a great many people (Hindus are a good example), the depth of tribal, ethnic, or cultural identity has been historically and inseparably tied to religious conviction and practice. To teach about world cultures and to minimize or gloss over religion would result in a superficial and mistaken multicultural education.

---

[3] See, for example, the *Curriculum Guidelines for Multicultural Education* (1991) published by the National Council for the Social Studies, Washington, D.C.

Much the same can be said in U.S. history. Teaching about African Americans, Native Americans, Latino cultures, and others without significant discussion of religion would be an impoverished and distorted discussion. There is another consideration as well. For millions of Americans throughout our history, the most profound definition of their identity is in terms of religion—not ethnicity or nationality. Just as it is essential that women, African Americans, and others be included in the curriculum, it is vital that the religious voices now absent in the study of U.S. history be heard. American religious history is more than the history of Puritans, Protestants, or even Christians. And as we noted in Chapter 2, whether or not we are religious, we are shaped by the religious past of our many cultures.

Although we agree with an approach to multicultural education that seeks to diversify the curriculum, we should note at least two ways in which our proposals for including religion differ from some of the more ideological and controversial versions of multiculturalism. First, we have already made the case for a civic framework, grounded in First Amendment principles, as the ground rule for addressing our differences in a public school classroom (and in our life together as Americans). Some multiculturalists disparage these and other principles and values of the American republic and Western civilization as "Eurocentric" and oppressive. Although we agree that teachers should discuss both virtues *and* vices of the West and the United States, we would argue that public schools have an obligation to teach and uphold the democratic first principles of the U.S. Constitution with its Bill of Rights. Yes, many of these principles are derived from European sources and from the biblical traditions. (And these roots should be taught.) And, yes, they have yet to be fully and fairly applied in American society. But however imperfect the realization of the ideal, our constitutional arrangement embodies the shared principles and ideals that define us as a nation—and undergird what we do in the public schools. We must distinguish between the principles and their application. In many ways the story of American history is the story of the ongoing struggle to expand the application of these principles more fairly and justly to all citizens.

Second, we are concerned about versions of multiculturalism that fail to take religious differences seriously. Religions and cultures differ in ways that are deep and abiding; their values and convictions often collide with one another. Students need to learn that although people share many core human values, religions make very different claims about what is ultimately true. This is not to suggest that there is no absolute truth; only that we differ about the nature of truth. Students should not get the impression that all claims are equally valid (or equally false)—many of these claims are mutually exclusive. Nor should we push them to accept cultures or religions that are antithetical to their own convictions. But we should expect them to respect the *rights* of all, even those with whom they disagree. Beyond that, they need to learn how to engage differences thoughtfully and to think critically about what they are learning concerning themselves and others.

Some of the cultural and religious claims or practices studied may not only be in conflict with one another, but also with the civic principles and agreements of our society. This too should be discussed so that students are prepared to address questions that have been long debated in our history: What are the limits of religious liberty? Where do we, as a nation, draw the line when religious or cultural practices come into conflict with societal norms or American law? For a nation as religiously diverse and free as the United States, these are central questions that every generation must reconsider.

Dissent and debate are crucial for the survival of liberty. The First Amendment framework itself protects our right to be different and encourages us to engage one another in honest and open debate. Students should learn early on that the public square of America is often a messy and contentious place. What is fortunate and admirable about the American project is that our civic agreement as embodied in the Constitution provides the guiding principles that enable us to negotiate our conflicts with civility and respect. Schools are where citizens learn how this arrangement ought to work. We should simultaneously learn that we are deeply different *and* that we have the civic principles that enable us to live with even our deepest differences.

Coverage

If students are to have the opportunity both to empathize—to see religious traditions from the inside—and to think critically about differences, then history textbooks will need to devote more space, and teachers more time, to religion. The immediate response of many educators and textbook publishers is that there is not enough room in the curriculum to give more coverage to religion. If that is the case, then we would argue that different choices may need to be made.

To cite a particularly egregious example, when one text gives Jesus less than half the space devoted to Eleanor of Aquitaine or, in another, to Joseph Stalin, then someone is making poor educational decisions about what is important for students to learn. In the space Jesus *is* given, most texts say something about love and forgiveness, but little or nothing about the fact that Christians see Jesus as God incarnate. There is little discussion of the nature of sin and salvation, the coming of the Kingdom, the significance of the Resurrection story, or other key Christian teachings and experiences contained in the New Testament. Without some understanding of these concepts, many subsequent developments in Western civilization make little sense.

Beyond reordering priorities, educators need to rethink the approach to key themes and topics. Students cannot adequately understand the American Revolution, for example, without studying the First Great Awakening, part of what John Adams characterized as the change in "religious sentiments" that was the "real American revolution." [4] The story of immigration is incomplete and distorted without study of the centrality of religion in the immigrant subcultures formed in America between 1880 and 1910. Study of the founding and development of the African-American churches provides the best foundation for understanding much about American history, including Reconstruction and the civil rights movement. As these examples suggest, taking religion seriously is not always a matter of "adding on" to what the curriculum already covers. It may mean teaching required key topics and themes in a different way.

We are acutely aware that finding more room in the curriculum for *anything*, however worthy and relevant, is an enormous challenge. Including more about religion, as we noted earlier, is particularly challenging in view of the importance and complexity of religious studies. Of course, the problem isn't just that textbooks don't *mention* religion enough; it is that they don't say enough to *make sense* of religions—and they make no effort to convey any sense of what it means to interpret history religiously. As we have argued, it may very well be that only by requiring students to take a course in religious studies can we address these concerns adequately. Nevertheless, history courses can at least strive for what we have called minimal fairness by giving much more attention to the key religious ideas and developments that have shaped the great world civilizations.

---

[4] John Adams writing to Hezekiah Niles in 1818.

Theological Developments

Most textbooks leave the reader with the false impression that religion is something that used to matter a long time ago but no longer makes much difference in the lives of modern people. This is untrue, of course. Religion remains a powerful force in the lives of most people in the United States and across the globe.

Students can make better sense of the last two centuries of world history if they have some understanding of such theological developments as the rise of literary and historical biblical criticism, debates within Roman Catholicism since the Second Vatican Council, the fundamentalist response in various traditions to religious liberalism and modernity, and the impact of science and psychology on religious thinking. Theology matters in the modern world.

This is true in recent U.S. history as well. A few examples: The rise of Christian fundamentalism in the late 19th century continues to have a profound impact on American life and politics. Reform, Conservative, Orthodox, and Reconstructionist Jews in the United States have reasserted their Jewish identity in bold new ways. Theological debates about the role of women in various traditions have been an important dimension of the larger debate about the role of women in American society. The list is long: theological ideas and differences continue to shape many of our most controversial public policy debates—including those over abortion, justice, war and peace, and, of course, education, as we shall see in upcoming chapters.

A number of American theologians have had an impact on our history. The Catholic theologian John Courtney Murray played a major role in redefining religious freedom in America and in the deliberations of the Second Vatican Council. One of the towering public intellectuals of our century, Reinhold Niebuhr deeply influenced debates over social justice and foreign policy, in part by arguing for a "Christian Realism" that took sinfulness more seriously than was commonly done. Martin Luther King Jr. was a theologian—a point typically ignored in the textbooks. His theology of social justice was drawn, in large measure, from the Bible and his understanding of the Social Gospel.

True, religion has lost its preeminence in the modern era, particularly in the West. But for many people in the United States and throughout the world, profound theological issues are at the core of their encounter with modernity. (Even the fact that the world has become increasingly secular cannot itself be comprehended without study of various religious responses to secularization.) In the rest of this book, we move beyond history and make the case for the relevance of religion and study about religion to other dimensions of our life in contemporary society.

Innovative Resources for the Study of Religion in History

The vast majority of the hundreds of history teachers with whom we have worked want to include more study of religion in their courses. But how are they to get the necessary resources and support? For the teacher, the challenge of achieving even minimal fairness in the treatment of religion when teaching world and U.S. history is daunting to say the least. Few teachers have much background in religious studies. Few state frameworks encourage in-depth study of religion. And the new generation of textbooks is only marginally better than the old. Until these larger changes occur, what can teachers do to take religion seriously in history? Fortunately, some innovative resources and strategies are available now.

The 3 Rs Projects

The First Amendment Center at Vanderbilt University supports initiatives in several regions of the country designed to address religious liberty issues in public schools. Based on the principles of "rights, responsibilities, and respect" discussed in Chapter 1, these programs help communities find common ground on a wide range of conflicts and concerns involving religion and public education. In addition to policy development, one of the primary goals of the projects is to prepare teachers to teach about religion in ways that are constitutionally permissible and educationally sound.

The most extensive of these programs is the California 3 Rs Project, begun in 1991. Co-sponsored by the California County Superintendents Educational Services Association, the project has an extensive network of resource leaders and scholars throughout the state providing support for classroom teachers. Teachers trained by the project give workshops for their colleagues on the constitutional and educational guidelines for teaching about religion. Religious studies scholars from local colleges and universities are linked with school districts to provide ongoing expertise and periodic seminars on the religious traditions that teachers are discussing in the curriculum.

Utah has a similar statewide project that anticipates building a network of resource leaders in all of Utah's school districts by the year 2001. In Georgia, the state Humanities Council runs an ongoing 3 Rs program that works with teachers in each region of the state. Texas, Oklahoma, and Pennsylvania have 3 Rs Projects in various stages of development.

Oxford University Press

At long last, a series of scholarly works on religion written for young readers is being produced. Edited by Yale University professors Jon Butler and Harry Stout and published by Oxford University Press, *Religion in American Life* will be a 17-volume series authored by some of the nation's leading scholars in the field of religious studies. The first four volumes are scheduled to appear in the fall of 1998.

The series will be an invaluable resource for teachers of junior and senior high school students. Teachers of U.S. history will find all of the volumes most useful, but teachers of world history, government, and literature will also be able to use many of the volumes in a variety of ways. Three chronological volumes give the religious history of the United States from the colonial period to the present. Nine volumes cover significant religious groups in America, including Protestants, Catholics, Jews, Muslims, Native Americans, and followers of Eastern faiths. Four volumes address specific topics—women, church-state issues, African American religion, and immigration—that are of special importance in understanding the role of religion in American life.

With the addition of these books to school and classroom libraries, students and teachers will have access to scholarly works that fill the gaps left by inadequate textbook treatment of religion. In fact, the chronological volumes would themselves be an excellent textbook for an elective course on religion in America or religion in U.S. history. A teacher's guide, prepared by the First Amendment Center, will suggest ways to use the volumes for supplemental reading and research projects in history and other courses.

On Common Ground CD-ROM

Another groundbreaking resource for students and teachers is a CD-ROM entitled *On Common Ground: World Religions in America*, pub-

lished in 1997 by Columbia University Press. This multimedia resource uses text, primary sources, photographs, music, film, and the
spoken word to bring alive the extraordinary religious diversity in the
United States. Prepared by Harvard Divinity School professor Diana
Eck, the CD-ROM draws on the Pluralism Project, a Harvard-based
study that has documented America's religious landscape.

Using the CD-ROM, students can find out about the practices
and beliefs of America's many faith traditions and explore the religious diversity of 18 cities and regions. Fifteen different religions are
represented, from the long-established Native American, Christian,
and Jewish traditions to more recent arrivals such as Hinduism and
Buddhism.

What is especially impressive about this resource is how it uses
documents, photographs, film, and music to evoke information directly from the practitioners of each faith, allowing students to have
some experience of the religion from the inside. It is also noteworthy
in its discussion of differences within various traditions (e.g., Orthodox and Reform Judaism). It even includes issues debated within various traditions—women and Islam, for example. In short, this is an
essential resource for every secondary social studies and literature
classroom.

The Ackland Art Museum Project

An educational model that has tremendous potential for introducing
students to the world's major religions is the Five Faiths Project being
developed by Ray Williams, Curator of Education at the Ackland Art
Museum, University of North Carolina at Chapel Hill.

The project grew out of the Ackland's successful curriculum-
based gallery lessons. For a number of years now, teachers have
brought students—ranging from primary grades to college level—to
the museum to learn more about the world's religions through art.
The Ackland's collection now includes artworks from Hinduism,
Buddhism, Judaism, Christianity, and Islam. In their encounter with
paintings, sculpture, and ritual objects, students engage these traditions in immediate and powerful ways.

The Five Faiths Project is planning to expand in a number of
exciting directions. An interactive gallery computer station will enable
students to learn more about a religious work of art in its cultural
context. This is important. Religious objects in the Ackland's collection—a Russian icon, a statue of the Hindu deity Ganesha, and

others—were created for sacred settings and practices quite unlike their present museum home. Through the interactive computer program, students will see and hear the ritual occasions, locations, and stories that give these objects their full meaning.

The Ackland has also made a commitment to provide North Carolina teachers with preservice and continuing education focused on the study of religion. Teachers will learn from outstanding scholars in religious studies, visit local places of worship, and meet religious leaders. Not only will they learn about the major religious traditions, but they also will discover how to enrich their courses with the study of religion and religious art.

For schools in other areas of the nation without access to the Ackland, the museum plans to produce a CD-ROM with accompanying curriculum guides. These materials will help teachers bring the study of religion to life through music, personal stories from practitioners of each faith, photographs, and videoclips placing the art in its original context. All of this will be available through the Ackland's home page on the World Wide Web.

The Ackland's Five Faiths Project will be a model that we hope local museums throughout the nation will replicate. Hundreds of community and university art museums have collections of religious art that have the potential to be an invaluable resource for teachers and students. If adopted by other museums, the Ackland model has the potential to fill a crucial gap in the curriculum, and perhaps to revolutionize the relationship between museums and schools.

Suggested Readings and Resources

The First Amendment Center supports the 3 Rs Projects discussed in this chapter and will provide information about those programs and other opportunities for teacher education in religious studies. The center also disseminates *Living with Our Deepest Differences: Religious Liberty in a Pluralistic Society,* a series of lessons for inclusion in courses at the elementary, junior high, and senior high levels. For more information about these and other resources, contact the First Amendment Center by calling 703-284-2826 or visit the web site: www.freedomforum.org

For more information about the series *Religion in American Life,* contact Oxford University Press, 198 Madison Ave., New York, NY 10016-4313. The CD-ROM *On Common Ground: World Religions in America* is available through Columbia University Press (telephone 800-944-8648). The World Religions Project may be contacted by writing to Ray Williams, Curator of Education at the Ackland Art Museum, University of North Carolina at Chapel Hill, Chapel Hill, NC 27599.

In 1990 an ASCD panel prepared a curriculum guide to significant developments in U.S. history in which religion was a key factor. It is published in *Religion in American History: What to Teach and How* by Charles Haynes (1990). The same volume includes a variety of primary source documents and strategies for using them to teach about religion in U.S. history. For an in-depth discussion of creative strategies for using primary sources in the classroom, see David Kobrin's excellent book *Beyond the Textbook: Teaching History Using Documents and Primary Sources* (1996).

The National Humanities Center provides TeacherServe, an online curriculum enrichment service for high school history and literature teachers. One of their instructional guides, *Divining America: Religion and the National Culture,* covers a range of topics important for teaching American history, from Puritanism to the civil rights movement. Created by scholars and master teachers, this material will help teachers include substantive study of religion in American history courses. The interactive nature of the site gives teachers the opportunity to ask questions and make suggestions about the content of the site (http://www.nhc. rtp.nc.us:8080/tserve/tserve.htm).

A number of other organizations offer resources appropriate for teaching about religion in public schools. The Religion and Public Education Resource Center offers a variety of curriculum guides, sample lessons, and other materials. The center is directed by Dr. Bruce Grelle, Department of Religious Studies, California State University–Chico, Chico, CA 95929-0740. The Council on Islamic Education (P.O. Box 20186, Fountain Valley, CA 92728-0186) draws on a network of university scholars to provide public school educators with resource materials and workshops for teaching about Islam. Education About South Asia—Vidya (P.O. Box 7788, Berkeley, CA 94707-0788) has resources for teaching about the religions of the Indian subcontinent. The World Religions Curriculum Development Center offers print and audiovisual curriculum materials on world religions (6425 West 33rd St., St. Louis Park, MN 55426).

An excellent short discussion of the many faith groups found in U.S. schools appears in *America's Religions: An Educator's Guide to Beliefs and Practices* by Benjamin J. Hubbard, John T. Hatfield, and James A. Santucci (1997). Included are concise descriptions of the basic beliefs and practices of some 22 religious groups. Especially helpful for teachers are the sections in each chapter on classroom concerns and common misunderstandings and stereotypes. The guide is available from Teacher Ideas Press (P.O. Box 6633, Englewood, CO 80155-6633).

Two of the best histories of religion in America are Sydney Ahlstrom's *A Religious History of the American People* (1972), a classic work of extraordinary scholarship, and Martin Marty's *Pilgrims in Their Own Land*

(1984), a somewhat shorter, very readable general history of religion in America. For studies that focus on Catholicism and Judaism, see Jay Dolan, *The American Catholic Experience* (1987) and Arthur Hertzberg, *The Jews in America* (1989). Catherine Albenese's *America: Religions and Religion* (1981) is particularly good on religious pluralism. *Retelling U.S. Religious History*, edited by Thomas Tweed (1997), includes a good collection of essays that explore how the traditional narrative of American religious history needs to be expanded and rewritten to include neglected traditions.

For a superb collection of essays on religious ways of interpreting the meaning of history and the nature of historical study, see *God, History, and Historians* (1977), edited by C.T. McIntire. *Religious Advocacy and American History* (1997), edited by Bruce Kuklich and D.G. Hart, is a good collection of essays that explores the relationship of religious and secular assessments of American history.

For a lengthy guide to readings and resources for teaching about the world's religions, see Chapter 9 of *Finding Common Ground*, edited by Charles Haynes and Oliver Thomas. See also the "Suggested Readings and Resources" for teaching Bible and World Religions in Chapter 8 of this volume.

5

Civics and Economics

ALTHOUGH CIVICS AND ECONOMICS ARE BOTH "SUBJECTS" IN social studies, they are typically conceived and taught in significantly different ways. The *historical* story of America and our constitutional tradition are at the heart of the study of civics; economics, by contrast, is taught ahistorically. Civics is a *subject*, open to consideration from a variety of disciplinary perspectives; economics is conceived as a discipline—a "hard" social science—rather than as a subject open to different interpretations. Civic education is *moral* education; it initiates students into the roles and responsibilities of citizenship. Economics texts and teachers eschew moral language and categories.

As the national standards make clear, the implications for religion are significant. The civics standards are replete with references to religion; indeed, of all the national standards they are the most sensitive to religion. The economics standards, by contrast, ignore religion completely; of all the standards they are the most hostile to religion.

Civics

However much we disagree about the *separation of church and state* now—and we disagree a good deal—for most of history people agreed that the domains of religion and government overlapped in many ways. Students need to understand both the historical relevance of religion to government and the contemporary controversies over their relationship.

Standards and Textbooks

The relationship of religion to government, politics, and law is a recurring theme of the *National Standards for Civics and Government.* Indeed, if we look at the standards for high school civics courses we find some 30 references to religion. The references are often historical, but unlike the history standards, which relegate religion largely to the premodern world, the civics standards also emphasize the importance of understanding the role of religion in the *contemporary* United States.

We cannot do justice here to the many ways in which religion is woven into the standards but will suggest something of this richness by listing recurring themes. Students should understand

1. How, historically, various religious visions (grounded in the Judeo-Christian tradition, the Protestant Reformation, and Puritanism) have shaped government and American society;

2. Conceptions of the relationship of God to law (particularly natural law and natural rights theories);

3. The importance of religious liberty and the meaning of "separation of church and state" in our constitutional tradition;

4. Religious pluralism and the role of various religious groups in American politics;

5. The role of religion in creating conflict in the United States and other nations; and

6. How religion can challenge allegiances to the nation.

Perhaps our primary concern about the standards is that they (like the history standards) are so comprehensive that their emphasis on religion will be lost as teachers make difficult decisions about what to include in their limited time.

Religion has been all but lost in the four civics texts we reviewed.[1] Although each says something about religious liberty and the First Amendment, the accounts are typically brief (only one paragraph in one text). None says anything significant about traditional

---

[1] The four civics texts we reviewed are *Civics: Participating in Our Democracy* (Addison-Wesley 1992); *American Civics* (HRW 1992); *Civics: Responsibilities and Citizenship* (Glencoe 1994); and *Civics: Government and Citizenship* (Prentice-Hall, 1990).

religious conceptions of the state, or religious sources of law or natural rights. (While each text highlights the paragraph from the Declaration of Independence that includes the phrase "endowed by our Creator with certain inalienable rights," only one comments—in a single sentence—on the relevance of God to rights.) No text includes any discussion of higher law or religious arguments for civil disobedience (though each discusses Martin Luther King Jr., who did make such an argument). The texts ignore the role of religion in contemporary politics. Two texts do include short sections on school prayer and the role of religion in public education. In sum, although the texts include a little about religion here and there, the discussions are almost always perfunctory, and the texts fall far short of the standards.

The Major Issues

Our discussion of the major issues in civics education will overlap, but also go beyond, references to religion in the standards.

• *Religious liberty and the liberal state.* In his famous sermon onboard the *Arabella*, John Winthrop, governor of the new Massachusetts Bay Colony, said this: "Thus stands the cause between God and us: we are entered into Covenant with him." We shall be as one body, he continued, always having before our eyes our commission from God to "walk in His ways and to keep His Commandments and His Ordinance, and His laws" so that "the Lord our God may bless us" and shall "delight to dwell among us" (1630/1956, pp. 82–84). One hundred fifty-seven years later, when the Framers explained the authority of the Constitution of the new United States of America, they wrote: "We the people . . . do hereby ordain and establish this Constitution of the United States of America"—and failed to mention God at any point in their document.

Until the 18th century, most people in the West believed that the authority of government was grounded in religion; the "powers that be" are ordained by God. The laws of states were to reflect divine or *natural* law. States had established religions, and people assumed it was the state's proper task to enforce religious conformity. People were born into a "station with its duties." The spheres of government and religion overlapped if they didn't quite coincide. Indeed, historically there was little in the Jewish, Catholic, Orthodox, or Islamic traditions that argued for separating religion and government.

In the 17th and 18th centuries a new view of government began to develop. People came to understand government as the result of a "social contract" between free individuals, and its authority now derived from the consent of the governed. People were born free, possessing among other natural rights the right to religious liberty. The purpose of government was no longer religious, but (as the Declaration of Independence put it) the protection of life, liberty, and the pursuit of happiness. Gradually, the roles of church and state were separated.

How do we account for this change? A part of the explanation is that the religious wars and persecution that followed in the wake of the Reformation did a great deal to discredit religion. When religion proved too divisive, it became necessary to develop a new moral framework that didn't require religious consensus. Of course the new United States was made up of a welter of contending religious groups, and as each of them was somewhere in the minority, each in turn saw the benefits of religious liberty and secular government at the federal level. Social peace required it.

But there were theological and philosophical as well as pragmatic arguments for religious liberty and the idea of a *liberal* state. (Here we use "liberal" in its classical sense: the liberal state maximizes individual liberty.) The Protestant Reformers insisted that human institutions—the church and the state—should not come between individuals and God; we should be free to follow the dictates of our consciences. No doubt Protestant countries continued to have established churches for some time, but the idea of a "free conscience" gradually began to shape Protestant thinking about government— particularly in America, through Roger Williams, William Penn, and then, in the 18th century, a multitude of Evangelicals. Indeed, to some considerable extent, we owe the religious liberty clauses of the First Amendment to an alliance of Evangelicals (especially Baptists) and Enlightenment Deists, such as Thomas Jefferson, who emphasized religious liberty (or freedom of conscience) as a "natural" right grounded in a religion of reason.

It is important that students understand the traditional religious conception of government, the historical backdrop of religious persecution and warfare, and the developing consensus about religious liberty that led to the First Amendment. No doubt we disagree about the proper limits to religious liberty, but the ideal has long been part of our political consensus and is now endorsed by virtually all religious traditions in the United States.

• *The separation of church and state.* From the earliest days of our Republic, most Americans have agreed that religious liberty requires *disestablishment*—separating the institutions of religion and state. Indeed, the decision by the Framers to disestablish religion (on the federal level) is arguably the most momentous advance for religious liberty in history. But from the very beginning there has been much disagreement about how much "separation" the First Amendment's Establishment Clause requires.

As we have noted, for the past 50 years—ever since *Everson v. Board of Education* (1947)—the majority of Supreme Court Justices have interpreted the Establishment Clause to require a "wall of separation between church and state." Government must be neutral among religions and between religion and nonreligion; it cannot promote, endorse, or fund religion or religious institutions. This has been, and is, the liberal or "separationist" reading of the Establishment Clause.

Dissenting voices on the Court (including the current Chief Justice) take what is sometimes called an "accommodationist" view: the Establishment Clause prohibits the government from creating a national church or favoring one religion over another, but it does not prohibit general acknowledgment of religion by government (such as allowing nonsectarian prayers at school-sponsored events) or allowing religious groups to receive government funding on the same basis as secular groups (through vouchers for religious schools, for example).

For many religious conservatives, much is at stake in this long-running debate about the meaning of the Establishment Clause. They see the separationist position in its strictest applications as hostile to religion and religious expression. On the other end of the spectrum, many religious liberals and secularists view any government funding of religious groups and any government expression of religion, however indirect or nonsectarian, as a violation of conscience and a stepping stone to an unholy alliance of church and state.

Students need to be familiar with this ongoing controversy over the "separation of church and state" and the meaning of the Establishment Clause. Debate about the constitutional relationship of religion and government is at the heart of many recent and current conflicts over public policy, and the direction the Supreme Court takes on this question will do much to shape the kind of nation we will be in the 21st century.

• *Morality and politics.* Religious conservatives often argue that the courts have used the Establishment Clause to marginalize religion and secularize public life. The resulting "naked public square," to use Richard John Neuhaus's term (1984), is often criticized for undermining the sense of moral and religious community that sustains civic virtue and social relationships and provides a context of meaning for our politics.

People within the Western religious traditions have understood God to require justice of us, and not simply personal moral virtue; traditionally, the religious goal has been to transform society, to bring about the Kingdom of God. This has been a goal for religious liberals as well as for conservatives. Although we are now likely to associate religious politics with conservative Christianity, a generation ago religious liberals grounded their support of the civil rights and antiwar movements in their religion (while many conservatives believed that religion and politics must be kept separate). No doubt religion continues to provide the (ultimate) conceptions of morality and justice for much of our politics, both conservative and liberal—even if politicians don't quote chapter and verse to justify their positions (or even know the relevant citations). Of course, some know it quite well: within recent years, two Christian ministers (Jesse Jackson and Pat Robertson) have run for president, and religious organizations have played an increasingly prominent role in our politics.

Part of what makes our culture wars so difficult is that religious conservatives and liberals approach moral and political issues from such strikingly different worldviews. We noted in our Introduction James Davison Hunter's (1991) influential analysis of how our different ways of justifying our most fundamental values almost inevitably lead to conflict over issues such as abortion, sexuality, the family, education, and the meaning of America. Many conservatives ground their positions in biblical texts and historical revelation, whereas liberals believe in moral and religious progress that allows them to reform their traditions. To make sense of our politics, students need to understand the religious worldviews that shape our culture wars and the ongoing debate over the proper role of religion in politics.

• *Individualism.* Religious critics from both the Left and Right have been critical of modern (secular) individualism with its relentless emphasis on the self. From within all religious traditions persons are understood to be social beings rather than individualistic social atoms; we have natural obligations to help others, not just voluntary contractual relationships.

• *Pluralism.* The United States has become increasingly pluralistic religiously in ways that complicate (and sometimes enrich) our politics. Interestingly, although the multicultural movement has exerted great influence in education, it has essentially ignored the extent to which our deepest sense of identity is often rooted in religion. Again, many of the issues relate to "the meaning of America" and our sense of community. How do we live together with our deepest differences? To what extent should our laws help to sustain distinctive religious communities, traditions, and institutions, rather than level differences and nurture a common culture? For example, what can be said for and against vouchers that would enable people to educate their children in their own religious traditions rather than in public schools? Many religious conservatives are strong supporters of the parental rights movement because they believe the state and its various regulatory agencies have too much authority over their children. Should public policy rely on and provide greater financial support for "mediating structures" such as religious organizations in addressing poverty and welfare reform?

There is, of course, a foreign policy dimension to these issues. To what extent should the United States (and international organizations such as the IMF and World Bank) attempt to "impose" secular Western ideals and institutions on nations where more traditional, often religious, ideals and institutions offer alternative models for development?

• *Authority and allegiance.* Within virtually all religious traditions allegiance to God takes precedence over allegiance to the state, and patriotism is in constant danger of becoming a kind of idolatry—exalting something limited into something absolute. In his "Letter from Birmingham Jail," Martin Luther King Jr. argued that segregation laws were not binding (indeed, they were not "true" law) because they violated "natural law"—the law of God. For King and other leaders of the civil rights movement, allegiance to that higher law justified civil disobedience. Many opponents of abortion argue in similar ways for civil disobedience.

Through civics classes schools place a powerful emphasis on making students good citizens and good Americans; it is also tremendously important that students appreciate the widespread religious concern about nurturing an uncritical allegiance to the state. Students need to understand different views of the nature of the state's authority—and its limits. Should state law conform to "natural" (or divine) law—and what if it doesn't? When is civil disobedience (or even revolution) justifiable?

• *Key public policy issues.* Virtually all public policy issues can be debated on religious grounds, but several issues relating to the proper role of government are of profound importance within religious traditions. For many religious conservatives the great moral issue of our time is abortion—which they take to be murder. Students should understand why. For many religious liberals, the key issues are those of social justice and the role of government in "liberating the oppressed." For some members of minority religions, the problem of minority rights is omnipresent in a society in which most people are at least nominally Christian. Students must learn to look at the actions of government through the eyes of people in various religious communities if they are to understand our politics and make educated judgments about justice and government.

• *Religion and public education.* Finally, many of these issues come together, and become personally relevant for students, in considering the role of religion in public schools. Students should understand the major court rulings regarding prayer, Bible reading, and religious liberty. They should also acquire historical and religious perspectives on the governing ideals of public education as a civic institution: What values do public schools properly nurture in a multicultural and religiously pluralistic culture?

The Educational Implications

A good deal of what is taught in civics texts and courses is not controversial. We can agree on much of the relevant history; the Constitution and the court rulings that have determined its meaning are part of an "objective" historical record. But civics courses inevitably engage fundamental questions about which we disagree deeply: the meaning of America; the separation of church and state; the wisdom of court rulings; the moral grounds of public policy; and the relative authority of the state and religion. Often these disagreements are grounded in our different worldviews. To be liberally educated, students must hear the different voices in our cultural conversation and begin to think critically about them.

Schools should supplement civics textbooks with primary source readings chosen, in part, to reflect the differing points of view in our ongoing conversation about government and religion. Students should read John Winthrop, Roger Williams, and Thomas Jefferson on church and state. They should read Martin Luther King Jr. on civil rights and civil disobedience—and compare King's arguments with those who advocate civil disobedience as a response to abortion. Multicultural texts should explore what it is like for members of minority religious traditions to live in a predominantly Christian culture—and the implications for our civic values and institutions.

According to the national standards, the goal of civic education "is informed, responsible participation in political life by competent citizens committed to the fundamental values and principles of American constitutional democracy." This requires acquiring "a body of knowledge," "intellectual and participatory skills," and the development of "traits of character" that promote the "healthy functioning" of the body politic (Center for Civic Education 1994, p. 1). That is, civic education is a form of moral education. It requires that students be initiated into the office of citizen—defined by social practices, obligations, and rights.

Classrooms must exemplify and nurture those "traits of character" or civic virtues—the rights, responsibilities, and respect—that we discussed in Chapter 1. Students must take one another—with their differing ideas, values, and traditions—seriously. Although students are certainly not obligated to agree with one another, they should treat one another with respect. Of course, the civic virtues are developed not just in studying government, but in the practice of student government and in the "ambience" of schooling. Perhaps most important, teachers and texts are obligated to practice these virtues by taking seriously—by including in the discussion—the contending voices in our cultural disagreements over government.

Economics

Because there is considerable concern in our culture about the relationship between God and mammon, it is a little surprising that there appears to be no concern about the relationship between economics, as we usually teach it, and religion.

Standards and Textbooks

In an astonishing statement the editors of the *National Content Standards in Economics* write in their Preface that the standards were developed to convey a single conception of the world of economics—

the "majority paradigm" or "neoclassical model" of economic behavior, for to include "strongly held minority views of economic processes" would only risk "confusing and frustrating teachers and students who are then left with the responsibility of sorting the qualifications and alternatives without a sufficient foundation to do so" (National Council on Economics Education [NCEE] 1997, p. viii).

Using neoclassical theory, the standards eschew moral and religious language and convey a *value-free* conception of economics as a social science. People "usually pursue their self-interest" (NCEE, 1997, p. 8)—and there is no discussion of altruism or of occasions on which people shouldn't pursue their self-interest. Adam Smith's "invisible hand" is still at work: "The pursuit of self-interest in competitive markets generally leads to choices and behavior that also promote the national level of economic well-being" (NCEE, 1997, p. 18). Competition increases productivity and is praised; there is no discussion of any moral or social costs related to competition. Profits are an all-important incentive. Technology and economic growth are uncritically praised. Economic decisions should be matters of cost-benefit analysis. A benefit is "something that satisfies your wants" (NCEE 1997, p. 4), and there are no good or bad, right or wrong wants. All value judgments are essentially subjective. As long as the marginal benefit of an activity exceeds its marginal costs, "people are better off doing more of it" (NCEE, 1997, p. 4). Tradition has no inherent value, according to the standards. Economics is a science, as "people respond predictably to positive and negative incentives" (NCEE, 1997, p. 7). Not surprisingly, the standards are fairly critical of government—and remarkably uncritical of markets.

The standards do not discuss unions, class differences, the environmental costs of development, consumerism (or materialism), or poverty as a moral problem. They never use moral or religious language, nor do they ever require students to understand anything about morality or religion. Nowhere is there any discussion of justice, the sacred, or the dignity of human beings.

Although grounded in neoclassical theory, the four high school economics texts we reviewed are not quite so narrowly conceived as are the standards.[2] Each includes, for example, historical sections

---

[2] The four economics texts we reviewed are *Economics* (Addison-Wesley 1993); *Scholastic Economics* (Scholastic, Inc. 1991); *Applying Economics Principles* (Glencoe 1994); *Economics: Today and Tomorrow* (Glencoe 1991).

on labor unions and on Marxist and socialist alternatives to market economies. Although the texts claim that most behavior is self-interested, that the profit motive is fundamental, and that competition is essential to the successful functioning of the economy, they avoid universal statements and sometimes acknowledge that a more altruistic range of motives may come into play—though they provide no criteria for assessing the relevance or reasonableness of such motives and noneconomic goals, and they insist that values are "subjective" preferences. They often raise moral questions (albeit implicitly more than explicitly) but provide no resources for resolving them. For example, each text describes alternative tax systems (progressive and regressive), but they present no discussion of moral criteria or theories that might be used to assess their respective merits. Several of the texts include statistics on poverty that raise questions about justice, but they avoid any use of moral categories in assessing poverty. One of the texts includes 17 considerations relevant to choosing a career, but other than "union or non-union workplace," none is in any way moral or religious, and the idea that one's career might be a "calling" is not considered. None of the texts includes any discussion of consumerism, Third World poverty, or the impact of economics on the environment. In their combined 1,800 pages there are no more than a half-dozen sentences that refer to religion in any way; each is a passing reference of no substance.

The Major Issues

Not surprisingly, the major issues for economics often overlap those relating to government and civics courses.

• *History and secularization.* Until the 18th century, the marketplace, like government, was shaped to some considerable, if lessening, extent by religious ideals and traditions, and it is important to keep in mind that the freedom in "free enterprise" is freedom from religious as well as from governmental regulation. So, for example, within the new market economies of the West usury, which had once been a sin, was rehabilitated as interest in order to facilitate the accumulation of capital; supply and demand replaced the conception of a just price; guilds collapsed before the need for free and mobile labor; charity and begging, once virtues and signs of saintliness, became vices; self-interest and acquisitiveness, once vices, became

the governing virtues of the economic world; and intellectual authority came no longer from theologians and philosophers but from the
value-free calculus of that new (secular) specialty, economics.

This new way of thinking about economics went hand and glove
with the Industrial Revolution and a torrent of economic energy that
transformed society and, in the process, undermined traditional culture. As the economist Joseph Schumpeter put it, an essential characteristic of market economies is their *creative destructiveness* (1972,
p. 83), for they require ceaseless change, competition, technological
advances, mobile labor, and the creation of new wants. We should
remember that in the 19th century the advocates of market economies were called "liberals" or "radicals," and their staunchest opponents were often those conservatives who saw their world crumbling
before their eyes. Much of the current criticism of "Westernization" in
Muslim cultures stems from this recognition.

Whatever their destructive effect on traditional cultures, however, market economies have proven extraordinarily successful in
creating consumer goods and raising standards of living. One result,
not surprisingly, has been "consumerism" or "materialism"—an increasing cultural fixation on consumer goods that has redirected
many people's fundamental orientation in life. No longer do most people understand themselves as living in a "vale of suffering" with their
eyes fixed on the spiritual goods of the world to come; rather, they
have tasted the goods of the marketplace, found them good, and are,
as a result, ever more focused on the "pursuit of happiness" in the
world at hand. To some considerable extent the goals of the economic
system have usurped the role of religion in shaping our lives and our
culture.

We are largely oblivious to the connection, however. Indeed,
according to the sociologist Robert Wuthnow, the American middle
class has no notion of the claims that religion once made on the economic world:

> Asked if their religious beliefs had influenced their choice of
> a career, most of the people I have interviewed in recent
> years—Christians and non-Christians alike—said no. Asked
> if they thought of their work as a calling, most said no.
> Asked if they understood the concept of stewardship, most
> said no. Asked how religion did influence their work lives or
> thoughts about money, most said the two were completely
> separate. (1993, p. 200)

• *Economics as a discipline.* There is, of course, a vast theological literature on the relationship of religion and economics. (Perhaps no subject in moral theology has been so extensively discussed by Catholic and Protestant theologians over the last century.) This literature is almost completely ignored by economists, and *is* completely ignored in the national standards and in textbooks. Economics is taught not as a subject that might be studied using theological as well as secular methodologies, but a discipline. We teach students to think about economics *as secular social scientists understand it.*

• *Neoclassical theory.* As the standards make clear, the particular view that underlies much contemporary economic thinking is neoclassical economic theory, which grew out of the market revolution, the seminal work of Adam Smith, and the Enlightenment understanding of the world. Perhaps the most significant points of tension flow from the fact that economics is conceived as a science, and as such is "value free."

In classical and neoclassical economics people are understood to be essentially self-interested; hence the importance of the profit motive and competition in economics. No religion has ever taken this view of human nature, however. Religions have placed rather more emphasis on cooperation and community, and even those theologians who have most emphasized human depravity and original sin have held that it remains our duty to rise above self-interest and act as God would have us act. Interestingly, studies by economists show that students who study neoclassical theory become more self-interested as a result of their coursework (Frank, Gilovich, and Regan, 1993). Arguably, the prevalence of self-interest in human nature is, in part at least, a historical product of, among other things, our economic institutions.

Economists typically teach that we should use cost-benefit analyses to make decisions, though any religious perspective suggests both practical and theoretical problems with such an approach. As economists discuss them, the costs and benefits are those that accrue to people; yet most religious traditions tell us that we must consider the effects of our actions on all of God's creation— and on God. All religious traditions take obligations to future generations seriously, but cost-benefit analyses typically "discount" the future because the long-term effects of our actions aren't safely predictable. Cost-benefit analyses give extraordinary power to economists and other experts, and they discount tradition, conscience, and nonscientific ways of knowing. Almost inevitably, cost-benefit analyses weigh measurable (that is, material) costs and benefits and leave out of the equation what is sacred—those spiritual aspects of life that cannot be quantified. (How, for example, do we measure the value of the survival or extinction of a species in preparing an environmental impact statement?) Perhaps most fundamentally, cost-benefit analysis involves weighing relative harms and goods— whereas most religious ethics is grounded in duties and the claim that some things are right and wrong in themselves and are not subject to weighing.

According to neoclassical theory the purpose of the economy is to maximize "preference satisfaction." Economics is "value free" and cannot privilege some preferences over others. Needless to say, it is all but impossible to maintain some sense of the sacred when all preferences are merely subjective and we think about everything in cost-benefit terms. The Sabbath and religious holidays cannot be kept holy, for there is no such thing as sacred time. Much advertising plays on themes of sexuality, power, and greed in ways that corrupt human dignity and sacredness of life. In theory (and, as a result, almost inevitably in practice) the Bible and pornography are interchangeable consumer goods.

Like modern political theory, neoclassical theory has emphasized individualism over community. Indeed, market economies and neoclassical theory have made a virtue of competition. Of course, Adam Smith believed that the common good—the "wealth of nations"— would flow from the competition of self-interested individuals in a free economy. Within virtually every religious tradition, by contrast, society is understood communally: we are born into webs of obligation with other people, with God, and with all of creation.

• *Poverty, wealth, and consumerism.* The standards give no moral weight to the needs of the poor, yet virtually every religious tradition has placed special emphasis on compassion and the duty to help the poor and oppressed: God has a special concern for the widow and orphan, for the "least" among us. Almsgiving is one of the Five Pillars of Islam. Compassion is perhaps the fundamental Buddhist virtue. Whether the *state* should redistribute wealth is controversial on religious as well as secular grounds, but many contemporary theologians take God's concern for the poor to mean that our theories of economic justice must be broadly redistributive in some sense.

Although some religious traditions (Catholicism and Buddhism, for example) have found special virtue in monasticism and vows of poverty, most have not condemned wealth per se, but rather the undue attachment to wealth that keeps us from God. Although there are exceptions, virtually all religious traditions condemn contemporary consumer culture precisely for nurturing attachments to wealth and the material goods of this life. Of course, the economic system thrives by nurturing our acquisitiveness, creating stronger (and new) desires for consumer goods, requiring that we devote ever more time, energy, and education to economic pursuits. There have been and currently are religious movements that equate spiritual salvation with worldly wealth, but the religious mainstream is deeply wary of the effects of wealth and consumerism on our spiritual lives.

Of course, the pervasive poverty of the Third World—and the wealth of the First World—creates a moral problem of profound importance. Many theologians (not least Pope John Paul II) have spoken out forcefully regarding justice and the obligations of wealthy nations to the Third World.

- *The environment and economic growth.* The effects of economic growth on the environment have become catastrophic—we might even say "religious"—in their implications. Western theology has not been particularly sensitive to environmental issues until the last several decades, but discussions of stewardship and the sacredness of nature have become pervasive in contemporary theology. We shall have more to say about the environment and nature in Chapter 7; for now we simply note that economics must not ignore the implications of economic growth on nature, and the intersection of theological with economic and scientific categories for understanding and assessing economic growth.

- *Work.* From within all religious traditions, work must be understood in moral and spiritual as well as in economic terms. There are, of course, moral rights that should protect workers from exploitation, and working conditions must respect the dignity of people. Whether this requires, in particular cases, unions, affirmative action programs, or worker participation in decision making, may be debatable, but it is essential to ask these questions. Of course some work, even if freely undertaken, is by its very nature degrading (its contribution to the GNP notwithstanding). From within many religious traditions, work is regarding as a *calling*, as a way in which we fulfill our obligations to God by using our talents for the good of humanity. (We might note how the idea of a *profession* has all but lost its connection to public service as professionals have become little more than experts-for-hire.)

• *Capitalism.* While there is an Evangelical Left, religious conservatives are often advocates of capitalism—sometimes on Scriptural grounds, sometimes on more general moral and political grounds. Negatively, conservatives note the harsh treatment the Socialist and Marxist Left has accorded religion; positively, they argue that freedom in the marketplace complements freedom in the civic domain so that capitalism and democracy go hand in hand. Ever since the Social Gospel movement at the end of the 19th century, religious liberals, by contrast, have tended to be critical of capitalism, noting ways in which it has exploited people and appealing to Scripture for conceptions of justice and the "liberation of the oppressed" that require some form of democratic socialism or a mixed economy and welfare state. Over the hundred years between Pope Leo XIII's encyclical *Rerum Novarum* and John Paul II's *Centesimus Annus,* Catholicism has charted a "middle course" between the Left and Right in matters of economics. Much Islamic thought has been highly critical of capitalism, in part because of its internal conceptions of justice and society, and in part because of the powerful role capitalism plays in the Westernization of the Islamic world.

Some theologians would maintain that it is anachronistic to argue that the Bible, the Talmud, or the Qur'an endorses either capitalism or socialism—creations of the 18th and 19th centuries—though Scripture surely does make claims about morality and justice that are not compatible with all economic systems. For our purposes, however, what is important is less the conflict between Right and Left, than the tension between secular and religious ways of thinking about economics. Do the secular categories of modern economic theory exhaust or distort our understanding of the economic world?

Consider an analogy. Many religious liberals readily accept evolution as God's way of doing things. All too often, however, religious liberals have been naive in failing to distinguish between the idea of evolution (which may be interpreted in theological categories as the working out of God's purposes) and neo-Darwinian evolution (which denies the relevance of religious categories and is explicitly purposeless). Similarly, in defending capitalism, many religious conservatives naively accept neoclassical economic theory and an essentially secular understanding of economics. Just as there may be ways of reconciling evolution and religion, so there may be ways of reconciling capitalism and religion. Of course, a scientist always has the option to argue that science gives only a partial account of nature, and an economist always has the option to argue that neoclassical theory gives only a partial account of the economic world. The problem is that we teach both science and economics without giving students any sense of their possible limitations. Just as most scientists are professionally oblivious to religion, so are most economists.

The Educational Implications

To be liberally educated, students must learn something about religious as well as secular ways of thinking about economics; if they are to receive an education that is religiously neutral they cannot be taught uncritically to think about economics in exclusively secular ways that, in effect, marginalize the religious alternatives.

How should we teach economics? At the least, the opening chapter(s) of any economics text and the opening session(s) of any economics course should put the discipline of economics into broad historical and philosophical perspective. Students must learn that the ways of thinking about economics they will study are controversial, that there are religious alternatives, and something about the major alternatives. We've noted that most economics textbooks include chapters on Marxism and socialism; why not on religious accounts of human nature, justice, and economics as well? Teachers must know enough about religion to alert students when texts convey religiously controversial assumptions and claims, and they should use primary sources drawn from a variety of religious traditions to supplement texts in dealing with particularly important, religiously contested issues.

We find the claim made in the economics standards that only neoclassical economics should be taught (lest students and teachers become confused about the alternatives) to be appalling. Of course, students should learn about neoclassical theory, but they should learn something about the alternatives, both secular and religious. Indeed, moral and spiritual concerns so pervade our economic life that to teach economics apart from them is an educational travesty.

* * *

The state and the market are (along with modern science) the dominant institutions of modernity, and if students are to be educated they must be able to put the conventional assumptions of contemporary politics and economics into historical and cultural perspective. Indeed, it is particularly important that they appreciate the depth of the religious critique of these institutions.

In spite of our technology, economic growth, prosperity, liberty, and growing sensitivity to human rights, we find ourselves caught up in a catastrophic environmental crisis, mindless consumerism, massive poverty, senseless violence, and, in the richest of countries, something that looks very much like a crisis of spirit. The claim that progress inevitably marches to the beat of secular modernity is dubious.

From almost any religious perspective a significant part of the problem has been that modern civilization has marginalized religion. Arguably, the most important issues relating to both politics and economics are moral, even spiritual. The national civics standards do reasonably well in suggesting the importance of including religious voices in the conversation; the economics standards and texts are oblivious to religion and to the requirements of a liberal education.

Suggested Readings and Resources

Thomas Curry provides a superb account of religion in the colonies on the eve of the First Amendment in *The First Freedoms: Church and State in America to the Passage of the First Amendment* (1986). In *The Search for Christian America,* three respected evangelical historians, George Marsden, Mark Noll, and Nathan Hatch, argue that America was conceived as an essentially secular state. For a historical defense of the separation of church and state in America, see Isaac Kramnick and R. Laurence Moore, *The Godless Constitution: The Case Against Religious Correctness.*

The liberal or "separationist" position in the debate over the meaning of the Establishment Clause is forcefully argued by Leonard Levy in *The Establishment Clause: Religion and the First Amendment* (1986). Robert Cord provides the conservative or "accommodationist" alternative in *Separation of Church and State: Historical Fact and Current Fiction* (1982).

Ronald Flowers offers a helpful summary of recent Supreme Court rulings in *The Godless Court? Supreme Court Decisions on Church-State Relationships.* For collections of Supreme Court rulings on religion clause cases see the "Suggested Readings and Resources" that follow Chapter 1.

For a very good historical anthology of Jewish statements of the relationship of religion and government, see *Religion and State in the American Jewish Experience* (1997), edited by Jonathan D. Sarna and David G. Dalin; for a variety of contemporary Jewish assessments, see *American Jews and the Separationist Faith* (1993), edited by David G. Dalin. John Courtney Murray's *We Hold These Truths: Catholic Reflections on the American Proposition* (1960) is something of a classic. Murray's influence was felt at the Second Vatican Council: see its "Declaration on Religious Freedom" (in the *Documents of Vatican II*, 1966).

In *The Naked Public Square: Religion and Democracy in America* (1984) Richard John Neuhaus argues from a neoconservative perspective that the absence of religion in our public space has created a dangerous vacuum in our culture. Stephen Carter echoes Neuhaus's concerns from a more liberal vantage point in *The Culture of Disbelief: How American Law and Politics Trivialize Religious Devotion* (1993). We have noted several times the influential work of James Davison Hunter in mapping the role of religion in our culture wars; see his *Culture Wars: The Struggle to Define America* (1991). In *Habits of the Heart* (1985) Robert Bellah and his colleagues provide a wealth of historical and sociological perspectives on the role of religion in American cultural politics. *Religion in America* (1989), one of the "Opposing Viewpoints Series" published by Greenhaven Press, includes a variety of readings on the role of religion in American life suitable for classroom use. *The Ethics of War and Peace: Religious and Secular Perspectives* (1996), edited by Terry Nardin, includes essays that provide good summaries of approaches to war and peace in the major Western religious traditions. *Muslim Politics* (1996) by Dale Eickelman and James Piscatori is a finely nuanced study of politics on all levels. Bruce Lawrence's *Shattering the Myth: Islam Beyond Violence* challenges the predominant stereotypes of Islam in relation to violence and gender issues.

Our position in the section on economics is developed more fully in Warren A. Nord, *Religion and American Education* (pp. 30–35, 144–148, and 296–302). Two classic studies of the historical relationship between religion and economics still make good reading: Max Weber's *The Protestant Ethic and the Spirit of Capitalism* (1904–1905) and R.H. Tawny's *Religion and the Rise of Capitalism* (1922).

A good collection of excerpts from major works, both liberal and conservative, on religion and the economy can be found in *Christian Social Ethics* (1994), edited by John Atherton. *Religion, Economics and Social Thought* (1986), edited by Walter Block and Irving Hexham, is a rich collection of contemporary essays written from within the Christian, Jewish, and Islamic traditions. There are brief summaries of the implication for politics and economics of the major religious traditions in *Ethical Issues in Six Religious Traditions* (1996), edited by Peggy Morgan and Clive Lawton. E.F. Schumacher's essay "Buddhist Economics" in his *Small Is Beautiful: Economics as If People Matter* (1985) is a classic. Robert Wuthnow's *Rethinking Materialism* (1995) is a good collection of essays on the spiritual significance of American materialism.

The most important recent Christian assessments of economics and justice would include Pope John Paul's encyclical *Centismus Annus* (1991) and the National Conference of Catholic Bishops' *And Justice for All* (1986), both of which argue for welfare state capitalism. Michael Novak's *The Spirit of Democratic Capitalism* (1982) is the major defense of capitalism from a religious perspective; Gustavo Gutiérrez's *A Theology of Liberation* (1971) is the seminal statement of liberation theology. *A Cry for Justice: The Churches and Synagogues Speak,* edited by Robert McAfee Brown and Sydney Thomson Brown, is a good sourcebook of essays on the major religious statements on economics. Gary Dorrien's *Soul and Society* (1995) is a superb history of 20th century Protestant political and economic theology.

6

Literature and the Arts

FOR MORE THAN A MILLENNIUM IN THE WEST, THE GREATEST theme of the painter was the life and death of Christ, and the greatest task of the architect was to build a cathedral. The greatest work of literature in the thousand years before Shakespeare is Dante's account of hell, purgatory, and paradise. Some would say that the greatest work of art after Shakespeare is Milton's *Paradise Lost,* others, *Faust*—works that also give God His due, albeit via the devil. Indeed, for much of history, the glory of art has been the glorification of God. Even *modern* literature and art often speak to religious questions—in nontraditional ways; the relationship is deeper than we might expect.

We begin this chapter with a brief review of textbooks and the national standards for teaching literature and the arts before discussing what we take to be some of the major issues relating to religion and literature and the arts. We pay special attention to teaching the Bible as literature and look briefly at what might make the performance of religious art objectionable in public schools, before suggesting a number of educational implications.

Standards and Textbooks

Literature

The national *Standards for the English Language Arts* encompass a good deal more than literature. Students need to be literate regarding lab manuals, reference materials, journals, computer soft-ware, databases, CD-ROMs, laser disks, films, television, newspapers, speeches, editorials, advertisements, letters, bulletin board notices, and signs, to name just a few of the media discussed in the standards (International Reading Association [IRA] and the National Council of Teachers of English [NCTE] 1996, pp. 6, 15, 39–40). Indeed, of 12 standards, only 2 deal *explicitly* with literature. The first requires that students "read a wide range of print and nonprint texts to build an understanding of texts, of themselves, and of the cultures of the United States and the world" and that among these texts "are fiction and nonfiction, classic and contemporary works" (IRA and NCTE, 1996, p. 27). The second standard requires students to "read a wide range of literature from many periods in many genres to build an understanding of the many dimensions (e.g., philosophical, ethical, aesthetic) of human experience" (IRA and NCTE, 1996, p. 29). Other standards deal with textual interpretation, effective communication, linguistic structures, research, information technologies, linguistic diversity, English as a second language, and the use of language to pursue students' goals in life—though literary texts are occasionally discussed under the heading of these standards as well.

There is no discussion of religious texts, though there are three passing references to religion in the 69 pages of the standards. Texts chosen for study should "reflect the diversity of the United States' population in terms of gender, age, social class, religion, and ethnic-ity" (IRA and NCTE, 1996, p. 28). In discussing cultural diversity the standards suggest that students might explore "the history of oral cultures and their many philosophical and religious traditions" (IRA and NCTE, 1996, pp. 41–42). At another point, the standards note that African folk narratives and Greek myths "can be read as delight-ful, entertaining stories, as representations of mythic archetypes, or as cultural, religious, or philosophical histories of particular regions or people" (IRA and NCTE, 1996, p. 27). That is, the sole references to religion are made in passing, are located in distant times and places, or are included primarily to address questions of cultural diversity.

It is true that the second standard explicitly emphasizes the importance of literature in illuminating the ethical and philosophical dimensions of experience; this might be taken to include religious experience, and this is important. But the standards make nothing of it. There is no discussion of religious literature or of the Bible or Scriptures from other religious traditions.

High school literature anthologies are somewhat more sensitive to religious literature than are the standards. Textbooks that organize world literature, British literature, or American literature by historical periods typically include a good deal of religious literature; indeed, such literature is unavoidable. Many textbooks are organized by theme or genre, however, and use literature drawn primarily from the 19th and 20th centuries that is almost always secular. (Although recent literature is typically more secular than historical literature, it often appears that recent religious literature is slighted in these texts.) Excerpts from sacred Scriptures make token appearances in most world literature texts, as do excerpts from the King James Bible in anthologies of British literature. Almost always the excerpts are chosen for their literary rather than their religious significance—Psalms rather than Genesis or the Gospels, for example.

The Arts

The *National Standards for Arts Education* emphasize the importance of the arts given our "need for meaning" and our "pursuit of the abiding questions: Who am I? What must I do? Where am I going?" (Consortium of National Arts Education Associations [CNAEA] 1994, p. 5). The preface to the standards points out that because so much of a child's education is devoted to the "linear" logic of language and mathematics, the arts are particularly important in teaching a "different lesson" in that they "cultivate the direct experience of the senses; they trust the unmediated flash of insight as a legitimate source of knowledge. Their goal is to connect persons and experience directly, to build the bridge between verbal and nonverbal, between the strictly logical and the emotional—the better to gain an understanding of the whole" (CNAEA, 1994, p. 6). And, indeed, a recurring theme in the standards is the importance of relating the arts to other aspects of life. One of two references to religion in the standards is an example of this, showing "how the sacred and secular music of African Americans contributed to the civil rights movement" (CNAEA, 1994, p. 13). In fact, the preface to the standards makes the general point that because art is "a powerful force in the everyday life of people," it "is essential that those who construct arts curricula attend to issues of ethnicity, national custom, tradition, religion, and gender" (CNAEA, 1994, p. 14). The standards include no subsequent discussion of religion, however.

Like the language arts standards, the arts standards might be viewed as broadly permissive. For example, one standard requires that students understand the visual arts "in relation to history and cultures." For high school students this means that they be able to "differentiate among a variety of historical and cultural contexts in terms of characteristics and purposes of works of art" (CNAEAS, 1994, p. 71). Obviously this can't be done for many cultures and historical periods without bringing religion into the discussion. Still, the standards never single out religion as being of any special relevance or importance in performing or studying the arts.

The Major Issues

Historically, the domains of art, literature, and religion have overlapped in a number of ways. First, there is sacred literature or *Scripture*—poetry, proverbs, parables, and myths—that is taken to be *revelatory* and acquires *canonical* status within a tradition: the books of the Bible, the Talmud, the Qur'an, Buddhist sutras, the Vedas, the Mahabhrata, and the Tao te Ching, for example. Second, there are art and noncanonical literature that use the symbols and language, the images and conceptual resources, of a particular religious tradition (and that may illustrate, draw on, or allude to scripture)—Dante's *Divine Comedy*, Michelangelo's Pietà, or the great cathedrals and mosques and temples. Third, there is art and literature that grapples with religious questions, not from a position of orthodoxy within a tradition, but from the periphery, questioning a tradition, perhaps reformulating or "resymbolizing" it, perhaps rejecting it, but all the while presupposing some understanding of it—Melville's *Moby Dick*, Camus' *The Plague*, or Salman Rushdie's *Satanic Verses*, for example.

Consequently, we must be careful in talking about religion and art as if they are obviously distinct domains of life. Indeed, as we suggested in Chapter 2, religion is often expressed in art and literature; art is a *dimension* of religion.

• *Subjects and disciplines.* Because modern art and literature have become increasingly secular over the past several centuries, and because of the increasing specialization and professionalization of the academic disciplines, literary and art criticism have become increasingly secular and autonomous disciplines in the academy. For example, according to the "New Criticism" that dominated English departments for so much of this century, literature could be understood in purely literary or aesthetic categories, apart from any larger cultural or religious context. Crudely put, literature is one thing, religion is another. For a variety of reasons this view of literary criticism has broken down over the last several decades. Indeed, the task of much contemporary *culture studies* and *postmodern criticism* is to expose the cultural and ideological contexts and subtexts, purposes and prejudices of writers and artists. One result has been a growing emphasis on interdisciplinary work—including study of the relationship of religion, literature, and the arts. Still, postmodernists have typically been much more interested in race, gender, and class, than in religion.

No doubt a good deal of religious art and literature is included in historical survey courses, but what range of contexts and conceptual nets should teachers and texts use to make sense of it? Our argument is that if students are to be liberally educated they must have some sense of the religious as well as the more narrowly secular (literary and art critical) meaning and significance of art and literature. That is, Art History and English are best understood as subjects, whose works and texts are open to religious as well as secular interpretations. Teachers must approach art and literature with enough theological sophistication to illuminate their religious dimensions. We will work though an example of this shortly in considering the Bible as literature.

• *Art as revelation.* There are a variety of ways in which literature and art might be religious. The paintings and stained glass in medieval cathedrals told the Christian story in images for people who couldn't read, and much religious art is essentially a visual illustration of the *words* of Scripture. The Eastern Orthodox tradition of Christianity has a quite different understanding of art, however: an icon is not simply an illustration of Scripture, but is itself revelatory; the beauty of the icon reveals God's divinity. Indeed, there are forms of revelation that *cannot be put into words.* The aesthetic categories of harmony, beauty, and the sublime have often been taken to characterize our experience of God, and, as John Dixon has put it, "systematic thought can occur in languages other than the verbal" (1984/ 1995, p. 277). Styles of art can illuminate different conceptions of God and reality—conceptions that may create or correlate with "verbal" theologies but are not necessarily reducible to them. So, for example, Dixon traces the influential "Tuscan theologies" of Giotto and Duccio through our cultural history.

Or consider the religious dimensions of the romantic movement. Historically, people understood reality to be "multidimensional," embodying moral and spiritual as well as purely factual (or scientific) dimensions. The scientific revolution and the Enlightenment *flattened* reality, however. The tendency was to believe that everything that could not be accounted for scientifically (beauty, goodness, and God, for example) must be merely subjective and exist only in our minds. Reality was nothing more than matter-in-motion. Romanticism was a reaction against the Enlightenment, a reassertion that reality was richer than science claimed it to be. Aesthetic experience—nurtured through poetry and myth, painting and music—*reveals* a dimension of reality that slips through the holes in the conceptual net of modern science.

In his "Lines Composed Above Tintern Abbey," William Wordsworth wrote that he discerned in nature a

> . . . presence that disturbs me with the joy
> Of elevated thoughts; a sense sublime
> Of something far more deeply interfused,
> Whose dwelling is the light of setting suns,
> And the round ocean and the living air,
> And the blue sky, and in the mind of man;
> A motion and a spirit, that impels
> All thinking things, all objects of all thought,
> And rolls through all things. (1798/1950, p. 164)

Wordsworth's poem should not be read as an autobiographical commentary on the state of his mind, but as the expression in art of a revelatory experience of God in nature. No doubt Wordsworth expressed himself in language, but it was not language as a scientist would use it, but as a poet or artist uses it, to express and evoke what cannot be said "literally." Indeed, through the theology of Friedrich Schleiermacher—the most influential Protestant theologian since Calvin—the themes of romanticism came to shape much of modern liberal theology.

The literary critic T.R. Wright has suggested that literature and theology have a common enemy: the pervasive and pernicious literalism of our scientific age (1988, pp. 13–20). One of the great values of studying literature and literary criticism is that they make clear the many ways in which language (and religious literature) can convey meaning. Religious texts—the Bible not least—often employ poetry and parables, symbols and metaphors, to convey religious meaning.

It is also important to keep in mind that unlike the sciences, the Western religions—Judaism, Christianity, and Islam—have all understood reality as a narrative. Like a novel, history has a meaning, a plot line in which God's purposes are revealed and realized. Events acquire their intelligibility not because they fall under universal causal laws but because they make sense in terms of the narrative.

• *The diversity of religious approaches to art.* While we need to be sensitive to nonverbal forms of revelation, nonetheless, the Western religions have traditionally emphasized verbal revelation. God acts through language, and God's actions are revealed through language in scripture. And God *said:* let there be light. In the beginning was the *Logos*—the *Word.* The Qur'an has traditionally been understood to be the verbal revelation of God. The Eastern religions have placed a much greater emphasis on intuition and mystical experience that cannot be expressed in language, and, as a result, art and aesthetic categories play a considerably greater role in revealing the nature of ultimate reality. To some extent this distinction is a matter of degree and emphasis; there are mystics within the Western religions, for example.

Of course, we need to be careful when we characterize Scripture as the "Word" of God. As we have noted, many theologians have claimed that the truths of the Bible are expressed symbolically or allegorically, rather than literally. Catholics have traditionally been open to a variety of ways of reading Scripture; the Protestant reformers and contemporary religious conservatives have, by contrast, placed considerably more emphasis on a "literal" reading of the Bible, as God's verbal revelation. Some religious traditions take the Creation story in Genesis 1 to be literal historical/scientific fact; others do not. All of this is, of course, controversial.

There are other significant differences among the Western religions. The Islamic and Jewish traditions, for example, include a strong prohibition on artistic images of God (and often of people): thou shalt make no graven images. Christians have not, typically, held to such prohibitions; God was incarnated in human form as the man Jesus, and artistic images of God have been common in Christianity—though "iconoclastic" Christians, like the Protestants of the Reformation, have often taken to smashing images that, they believed, had become objects of worship themselves, separating people from God. Judaism and Islam do not believe in an incarnated God, but rather in a transcendent God who cannot be captured in images. Similarly, the Protestant Reformers emphasized the transcendence of God rather more than did medieval Catholics.

• *Creativity.* Romanticism emphasized spontaneity, genius, imagination, individuality—the creativity of the artist; and, increasingly over the last two centuries, it has become the task of the artist to do more than mimetically convey the (religious) truths of tradition. In fact, theologians have often drawn on the insights of literature and art, just as they have drawn on the insights of modern science, to reshape their traditions. Or, to pick another example, the existentialist movement in philosophy, literature, and the arts had a profound effect on theology, as writers and theologians—from Fyodor Dostoevsky to Paul Tillich—used new themes, symbols, and languages to recast their understanding of God and the human condition. Art and literature may be religious—or perhaps we should say *spiritual*—in the absence of traditional religious language and iconography—as, for example, in some of the paintings of Kandinsky and Rothko.

Here we find another tension between liberals and conservatives. Scholars often draw a distinction between "high" art, which is self-consciously creative and constantly reconceiving its relationship to the traditions that spawn it, and "traditional" art, which is rooted in, and sustains the images and symbols and narratives of, a tradition. For many religious conservatives much of modern art and literature is unscriptural and irreligious, even sacrilegious, whereas for many artists and liberal theologians, much modern art embodies attempts to discover deeper levels of meaning and to resymbolize God (or the spiritual) in ways that speak to us in our times. Advocates of high art often find traditional religious symbols, narratives, and motifs naive, sentimental, and irrelevant.

• *Secularization and the search for meaning.* We have emphasized the religious significance of the aesthetic qualities of art and literature, but aesthetics and form can be (over)emphasized at the expense of content. Virtually all "great" literature and art address and deepen our understanding of those existential questions about the meaning of life that are inescapable for any reflective person: Who am I? What is the nature of my humanity? How do I make sense of suffering and death? What is justice? What is my duty in life? For what can I hope? What is love? What is the human condition? Often these are called "religious" questions, in part because religions have traditionally provided widely accepted answers to them, in part because they are *ultimately important*. There are, of course, secular ways of thinking about these questions as well. Hence we might say that literature and art address the central "existential" questions of life in *both* secular and religious ways (though sometimes this distinction is hard to draw).

As we have noted, much, if not most, of the art of ancient, medieval, and early modern Western civilization was explicitly religious. By the end of the 19th century, however, most literature and art had not only ceased to be overtly religious, it had ceased to assume a religious worldview. Indeed, the world of much (though certainly not all) modern art and literature is a world without God, in which "the center no longer holds." William Barrett has suggested that the themes that obsess modern(ist) writers and artists are "the alienation and strangeness of man in his world; the contradictoriness, feebleness, and contingency of human existence; the central and overwhelming reality of time for man who has lost his anchorage in the eternal" (1962, p. 64). Andrew Delbanco has recently characterized our literary life as embodying a "culture of irony" in which belief is impossible, all talk of morals sounds moralistic, and heroes are debunked. In the ironist's eye, Delbanco claims, "every pretender to legitimate authority becomes a Wizard of Oz, and the point is to draw aside the curtain" (1995, p. 212). Of course, students sometimes fail to appreciate the spiritual void in much modern art and literature because they have no sense of what it is like to live in a God-centered world.

An educated person should appreciate the historical context of modern art and literature, the developing "dialectic" in our cultural conversation about God, and the human condition as it is worked out in art and literature. What is important is not simply the aesthetic dimensions of art and literature; it is the moral and political and religious insight into the human condition. Of course, not *all* modern literature and art embrace the abyss. Religious experience and tradition continue to shape some art and literature; this is important as well.

• *Popular literature and art.* T.S. Eliot once confessed to the "alarming" realization that it was not great literature but literature read "purely for pleasure" that had the most powerful and potentially insidious influence on us because we read it so casually and uncritically. Indeed, he suggested, it affects us "as entire human beings; it affects our moral and religious existence"—and for the worse (1932, p. 27). Many religious parents would agree, finding television, advertising, movies, and video games subversive of their moral and religious values.

Of course, much popular art is religious. Warner Sallman's portrait of Christ may be the most popular and reproduced image in all of history, there is a flourishing market in "Christian fiction," and angels are popular on television; even in the youth culture there is Christian rock and rap, and the extraordinarily popular *Star Wars* trilogy of films is deeply religious. Still, Eliot's point is important: popular art is immensely influential in *uncritically* shaping children's attitudes toward sexuality and violence and authority and a good deal else. Children need to learn to think in a critical and informed way about popular as well as "high" art and literature.

The Bible as Literature

In all of history no book has had so powerful an influence on literature and art—or on life generally—as the Bible (though, neither the arts education nor the English language arts standards mention it). In its 1963 decision on Bible reading, the Supreme Court ruled that although the Bible may not be read devotionally in public schools it *is* constitutional to study the Bible for its "literary and historic" qualities. As we have seen, anthologies in world and British literature often include excerpts from the Bible and other scriptures—and there are Bible *courses* scattered here and there.

Educators often draw a contrast between courses called The Bible *as* Literature and The Bible *in* Literature, the latter dealing with ways in which later writers have used Biblical allusions, language, stories, and symbols. Courses in The Bible *as* Literature typically approach the Bible as they would any literary text. The purpose of such courses is often to convey a rudimentary Biblical literacy, a grasp of the language and the major stories, symbols, and characters. Some more advanced courses may employ literary scholarship that deals with the nature of authorship, narratives, archetypes, and a host of literary-critical questions that draw on an understanding of ancient languages, non-Biblical cultures, and contemporary literary theory. There is a tension, however, to which teachers must be sensitive, between reading the Bible as literature and reading it *as Scripture*—that is, as a religious text sacred to a tradition, which is to be interpreted using the theological resources of that tradition.

Let's take as an example the Song of Songs. On the surface (read "literally") it appears to be a poem about carnal love. Modern scholars don't claim to know who wrote it (according to tradition it was written by Solomon), but there is some evidence that it developed out of earlier predecessors in non-Biblical cultures, was sung irreverently in taverns of the first Christian century, and was treated as a simple love song in early times. Yet it is a book of the Bible. Indeed, during the Middle Ages it was more frequently copied than any other book of the Bible. Two of the greatest medieval scholars wrote extensively on the Song of Songs: for Rashi (Rabbi Solomon ben Isaac of Troyes) it was a song about God's love for His people—the Jews; for St. Bernard of Clairvaux, it was about Christ's love for His church and the yearning of the soul for union with God in love. Both offered careful readings of it that drew on other Biblical texts and the resources of their respective religious traditions; indeed, for them the text can't be understood apart from the theological tradition for which it is Scripture.

The great historian of religion Wilfred Cantwell Smith has written that we read the *Bhagavad Gita,* if we are Hindus,

> in order to understand the world, and our life within it; and if we are historians, in order to understand how the world has been seen by Hindus, to understand what the *Gita* has been doing to people these two thousand years or so as under its influence they have gone about their daily business, and their cosmic business. (1993, p. 34)

The *Bhagavad Gita* and the Song of Songs are not simply, or even primarily, literary or historical texts; they are *Scripture;* that is, they are texts that people within a tradition take to provide an understanding of God and their relationship to God. Their meaning within those traditions is quite different from what it might be for outsiders, or for scholars using only modern literary and historical resources for making sense of them.

Is there a danger of misreading biblical texts if we read them as literature rather than as Scripture? Smith suggests an analogy: we can read poetry as if it were prose, but we would, in the process, miss a crucial dimension of its meaning; similarly, we can read the Bible as if it were merely literature, but we would miss the crucial dimension of its meaning as Scripture.

It is sometimes suggested that in teaching the Bible as literature rather than as Scripture we can stand on common ground, for we need not deal with all those theological interpretations that divide us. This, we believe, is a naive notion. If students are to make educated judgments about the meaning of a text, they must have some sense of the major alternative readings of it. To ignore systematically the profoundly influential theological interpretations, insisting that the only relevant resources for interpreting the text are those provided by secular scholarship, is to take sides in matters of considerable controversy. Perhaps even worse, by excluding the religious interpretations, teachers keep students ignorant of the controversy.

Consider, for example, how the teacher's edition of Prentice-Hall's *Literature: World Masterpieces* handles the Creation narratives from Genesis. It urges teachers to ask questions such as: What does the text mean when it says that "God created man in his own image"? Explain what the fruit of the tree of the knowledge of good and evil symbolizes. To whom is God referring when He says that Adam has become "one of us"? What are the differences between the two Creation narratives in Genesis? All of these questions are, of course, theologically loaded—and deeply controversial. Never, however, does the teacher's edition appeal to any theological reading of the text to answer its own questions (1992, pp. 38–45). Rather, it cites the Hebrew language, narratives from other cultural traditions in the ancient Near East, archetypes—and students' own intuitions about the text. Nowhere is there any suggestion that the religious traditions that adopted this text as Scripture, reflected on its meaning for millennia, and developed rich theological resources for interpreting it might be relevant to the discussion.

What does the text mean? Well, we disagree, deeply—often on theological grounds. As we described it in Chapter 2, our governing educational framework requires that when we disagree, students must learn something of the alternatives if they are to be liberally educated. Moreover, the ideal of religious neutrality requires that we include in the discussion the major, relevant religious readings; public education can't nurture an uncritical secularity.

Of course, not all biblical texts are so controversial as Genesis 1. Students can read some parts of the Bible simply for the story or the poetry. Moreover, literary criticism is often invaluable in enabling students to see the many ways in which language is used in biblical texts. We would miss the revelatory power of many texts (including the Song of Songs and the Creation narratives of Genesis) if we ignored their significance as art. But teachers must be sophisticated enough to appreciate when theological readings must be included in the discussion—and students must appreciate the Bible's status as Scripture.

Obviously, teachers and texts can't insist on one correct interpretation, but they should, at least in the most important cases, inform students of the major alternatives. Chapter 8 provides further discussion of how to teach about the Bible and Scriptures from other traditions.

Performances

It may be helpful to explore the distinction between studying and practicing religion, particularly as it is related to artistic performances.

As we have seen, it is unconstitutional to read the Bible *devotionally*, for this would be a religious exercise; it is not, however, unconstitutional to study the Bible—when done "objectively" or neutrally. As we suggested in Chapter 4, visits to art museums can be wonderful ways of providing students with insight into religion. One reason that art museums are safe, of course, is that museum culture is quite different from church culture. The context of a religious painting, hanging on the wall of a museum, is not religious, but detached, secular. The appropriate response is not worship or reverence, but aesthetic reflection. (This is not to say that art museums don't create their own, somewhat more secular, sense of reverence before great works of art.) Of course, students should appreciate the fact that religious art has often been wrenched from its intended religious context when they encounter it in museums.

Sacred music, like sacred art and Scripture, can be studied. But what about *performing* sacred music? Although the Supreme Court hasn't ruled in this area, lower courts have made it clear that context and purpose are all-important. A Christmas concert at which students perform only Christian music might well be perceived as a religious exercise. Similarly, a Christmas pageant is little more than a Christian catechism, especially when performed in December. By contrast, it is not a religious exercise when students present a winter concert at which they perform Christmas music, secular music, and music from other religious traditions.

Yet we might wonder whether performing religious music might not be more like praying—a religious act—than observing sacred art in a museum or studying the Bible in a literature class in that it requires a religious affirmation (to sing "And he shall reign forever and ever" seems to affirm the Christian gospel) and an attitude of reverence. Of course, conventions allow us to assume that sacred music can be performed without imputing to the musician any religious convictions. It would be naive to assume that a professional musician who performed Handel's *Messiah* must be a Christian—or that actors (even if students) must believe the lines they say in plays. Of course, not everyone is comfortable with this distinction between "mere" performance and worship, particularly when children are the performers, and choral and band directors should be sensitive to this. If it offends a student's religious convictions to participate in a performance that he or she takes to be religious, that should be sufficient to warrant an excuse. At the same time, the fact that we can and commonly do draw distinctions between secular and religious contexts and performances does mean that students can perform religious music, just as they can view religious art and study religious Scriptures, as part of the public school curriculum.

The Educational Implications

We can draw a number of implications regarding the role of religion in the teaching of literature and the arts.

• Most important, schools should teach literature and the arts as subjects, open to various kinds of interpretation, rather than as disciplines, narrowly limited to the prevailing (secular) orthodoxies of literary and artistic criticism. As recent battles in our culture wars over the canon show, we disagree deeply about what is good literature and art—indeed, we disagree about what is to count as literature or art at all. What is important, once again, is that (mature) students understand the disagreements; they should hear the various voices, secular *and* religious, in our cultural conversation about literature and art.

• The study of literature and art is invaluable in conveying the many ways in which language and images can be used, combating the authority of literalism in a scientific age. An appreciation for narrative, symbolism, metaphor, analogy, and drama provides ways of making sense of religious texts and the claim that they reveal the truth and the mystery and the heart of reality.

• Literature and art achieve greatness and warrant study for both their aesthetic qualities *and* their religious or "existential" depth. Teachers should include the religious significance of literature and art among their criteria for choosing texts to study. This is particularly important in the absence of required religion courses.

• Schools should require students to read literature from a variety of religious traditions, and teachers should have some sense of the different ways in which those traditions understand art.

• Because of its extraordinary literary influence and religious significance, students should be required to study the Bible in world literature classes. Teachers should choose the selections for their religious as well as their literary significance and should include religious as well as secular interpretations in the discussion when the interpretation of the text is controversial.

• Students should understand that the historical secularization of literature and art is one of the major themes of Western cultural history. They should appreciate how modern art and literature are part of an ongoing cultural conversation about God and the human condition. Of course, they should also understand that there continue to be writers and artists who can only be appreciated in the context of the religious traditions they work within or react to, and students should read contemporary religious literature—which textbooks are likely to slight. They shouldn't learn that the only contemporary literature worth studying, and the only ways in which writers now approach the existential questions of life, are secular.

• Students should learn to think critically—morally, politically, and religiously—about *popular* literature, music, art, and the media, and their role in shaping the youth culture.

• As we argued in Chapter 2, literature and the arts provide marvelous ways of coming to understand religion from the "inside." Just as it is one thing to read about music, and another to listen to it, practice it, or in some way experience it, so it is one thing to read about the basic teachings of religions in a history course and something else to experience the world religiously. Of course teachers can't require students to practice religion or worship God, but through literature and the arts students can imaginatively and vicariously experience something of what it means to be religious. Reading Chaim Potok's *The Chosen* will do more than any historical narrative to convey what it meant to be a Jew at a particular time and place.

• Teachers must understand that the study of literature and the arts is central to *moral education*. At an elementary level, stories and pictures have morals; they convey images of good and evil. At a more sophisticated level, literature and the arts explore those "existential" themes of compassion and suffering, guilt, anxiety, death, identity, duty, hope, and despair that deepen and shape our moral understanding and response to the world. In the end, there are no hard and fast lines to draw between literature, art, religion, and morality, each of which illuminates and shapes the others.

• Finally, because what we ask of teachers requires some sophistication, prospective English and arts teachers should take an undergraduate course in religion and literature, or religion and the arts.

....

Suggested Readings
and Resources

Part One of William Barrett's *Irrational Man* (1962) is a concise and wonderfully insightful account of the secularization of modern art and literature. (Parts Two and Three provide an account of the major existential philosophers). M.H. Abrams provides a classic account of romanticism, perhaps the most important movement in redefining the relationship among religion, literature, and the arts, in *Natural Supernaturalism* (1971). Alfred Kazin's *God and the American Writer* (1997) is a study of a number of the major American writers of the 19th and 20th centuries by one of our greatest literary critics. In *The Death of Satan: How Americans Have Lost the Sense of Evil* (1995) Andrew Delbanco explores the secularization of American culture and literature by focusing on our increasing inability to make sense of evil.

The current state of literary criticism and the implications for religion are explored with clarity and insight in T.R. Wright's *Theology and Literature* (1988). *Literature Through the Eyes of Faith* (1989), by Susan Gallagher and Roger Lundin, is an introduction to literature from the perspective of traditional Christianity. For those who appreciate a challenge, in *Real Presences* (1989), the distinguished literary critic George Steiner critiques current literary criticism and argues for a conception of the arts informed by the presence of God. Though now two decades old, *Religion and Modern Literature: Essays in Theory and Criticism* (1975), edited by G. B. Tennyson and Edward E. Ericson Jr., is an excellent collection of essays on the relationship of religion and literature.

Art, Creativity, and the Sacred (1995), edited by Diane Apostolos-Cappadona, is an excellent collection of essays on the relationship of religion and art. George Pattison's *Art, Modernity and Faith* (1991) is a good, brief introduction to religion and art. John Dixon's *Images of Truth: Religion and the Art of Seeing* (1996) is a fascinating study of religious and aesthetic ways of seeing the world. In their stunningly illustrated *Sacred Architecture* (1997) Caroline Humphrey and Piers Vitebsky describe and show the symbolism of sacred space—how faith is translated into architecture. The *Dictionary of Christian Art* (1998), edited by Diane Apostolos-Cappadona, is an extremely helpful reference work. For a good short account of Islamic approaches to art and literature, see *Seven Doors to Islam: Spirituality and the Religious Life of Muslims*

(1996), by John Renard. *Islamic Arts* (1997), by Jonathan Bloom and Sheila Blair, is the most complete survey of the arts in Muslim countries.

We have relied heavily on Wilfred Cantwell Smith's superb study of Scripture in the major religious traditions, *What Is Scripture?* (1993) in our discussion of teaching the Bible as literature. For a good literary introduction to the Bible, see John A. Gabel and Charles B. Wheeler, *The Bible as Literature: An Introduction* (1990). *The Literary Guide to the Bible* (1987), edited by Robert Alter and Frank Kermode, includes a wealth of essays on the major books of the Bible as well as on more general themes. Most of Robert Alter's many books illuminate the Bible through the use of literary criticism; see especially, his *The Art of Biblical Narrative* (1983) and *The Art of Biblical Poetry* (1987). *The Bible As/In Literature* (2nd edition, 1995), edited by Thayer Warshaw and James Ackerman, is currently the only high school textbook available; it includes biblical texts as well as a wide variety of later literary texts influenced by the Bible.

Additional works on the Bible and sacred Scriptures appear at the end of Chapter 8.

7

The Sciences

THE PROBLEM OF RELIGION AND SCIENCE CUTS MUCH DEEPER than the (often superficial) debate about evolution. Indeed, the nature of this relationship has been one of the major intellectual problems of the modern world, and a vast literature of works by scientists, theologians, and philosophers addresses it—though the national science standards and science textbooks all but completely ignore it. Contrary to much of the conventional wisdom, this discussion has not become passé, but is, if anything, becoming more lively in light of recent developments in both science and theology.

We begin with a few historical generalizations about the impact of the scientific revolution on religion before discussing four ways of relating science and religion. We will take evolution as our major case study because it has generated the most heated battles in our curricular culture wars, but we will also consider several other areas in the science curriculum where religion is relevant, before drawing a number of educational implications.

The Scientific Revolution

In Chapter 2 we retold Arthur Eddington's parable of the fisherman who, after a lifetime of fishing with a three-inch mesh net and never catching any fish shorter than three inches, concluded there were no fish in the ocean shorter than three inches. Just as his fishing net determined what he caught, so our conceptual nets determine what we catch in the ocean of reality. Beginning with physics in the 17th century, then in chemistry in the 18th century and biology in the 19th century, scientists discarded older theological and philosophical nets for those of the modern scientific method—and worked a revolution in the process.

All cultures other than modern Western culture have conceived of reality as having a spiritual dimension that could be known through religious experience. In the Western religions, God was understood to be the creator of the world, and believers could understand nature only by seeing it as God's handiwork, designed to fulfill God's purposes. Because nature was the creation of God, it was good; indeed, it was infused by the spirit of God. Reality was understood to have the structure of a cosmic drama, and as actors in that drama, persons were responsible agents.

Not surprisingly, scientists find in reality only what the conceptual net of modern scientific method allows them to catch—what is measurable, what can be discerned through sense perception and scientific instruments, and what is replicable in scientific experiments. The physicists of the 17th century believed that the ultimate constituents of the world were (quantitatively distinguishable) atoms, and that change was the result of their (quantitatively distinguishable) rearrangement in accord with universal causal laws. Matter was inert, dead. Qualitative colors and sounds were exiled from "objective" nature to the "subjective" minds of observers. The real world is matter in motion, a realm of pure factuality with no inherent moral structure; nature is not purposeful. Science is "value free." Although 20th century quantum mechanics discerns a level of indeterminacy in nature, classical science was deterministic. Indeed, much science continues to hold that our character and our actions are determined by our genes and biochemistry, our environment and various contingencies of reinforcement.

Science has radically extended our conception of the universe in terms of both time and space. Ours is not the cozy world of traditional religion, in which the earth was created to be our home a few thousand years ago. According to modern science, the earth came into being some 4.6 billion years ago, an incidental by-product of the cosmic evolution that began with the big bang some 10 or 20 billion years earlier. And from the time Copernicus displaced our world from the center of a divinely created universe, the earth and its inhabitants have seemed increasingly insignificant in the overall scheme of things. As Carl Sagan once put it,

> there are cataclysms and catastrophes occurring regularly in the universe and on the most awesome scale. . . . It seems likely that every time a quasar explodes, more than a million worlds are obliterated and countless forms of life, some of them intelligent, are utterly destroyed. This is not the traditional benign universe of conventional religiosity in the West, constructed for the benefit of living and especially of human beings. Indeed, the very scale of the universe—more than a hundred billion galaxies, each containing more than a hundred billion stars—speaks to us of the inconsequentiality of human events in the cosmic context. (1974, pp. 290–292)

Because science is willing to question the old "truths," we discover new truths and *progress* becomes possible—both in knowledge and, through technology, in our physical well-being. But if science makes progress possible in human affairs, it appears to deny progress in cosmic affairs. The forces of nature are indifferent to good and evil; science offers no assurance that all things work toward what is good. Evolution, as biologists understand it, has no moral or spiritual purpose, and the second law of thermodynamics tells us that in the long run the universe will run out of energy and die in the cold darkness of space.

One goal of traditional religion was to structure and sustain an understanding of reality as trustworthy; religions provided people with moral and spiritual guidance in living their lives. Science makes no such claims. Rather, its goal is to provide the kind of knowledge that gives us predictive power and, through technology, control over our environment. The philosopher E.M. Adams puts it this way: Before the scientific revolution, humankind faced reality asking, What is demanded of me? How do I set myself right with reality? From within the modern scientific worldview, by contrast, we ask: How do I impose my will on the world? How can I control it (1993, chap. 3)? Arguably, this has been the most profound revolution in human history.

Of course, the great scientists of the scientific revolution were not atheists, and, as we shall see, there are ways of reconciling science and religion. As it is practiced, however, science assumes that God is irrelevant to understanding nature, for scientific method prohibits appeal to miracles, divine purposes, religious experience, or Scripture in its explanations. And, at least implicitly, science has become the arbiter of intellectual respectability; the modern scientific worldview pervades the curriculum.

Yet, students might well wonder whether there is more to reality than scientific nets can catch. Indeed, might our understanding of nature be distorted if we rely on scientific method only? Of course, theologians, using different nets, claim to catch other dimensions of reality.

The Relationship of Science and Religion

Individuals often take one of four different positions on the relationship of science and religion.

1. *Conflict: Religion Trumps Science.* Science and religion sometimes make conflicting claims about reality; when there is conflict, only religion provides reliable knowledge. It is through inerrant Scripture or religious tradition that we come to know the ultimate truth about nature. No doubt good science would always agree with Scripture or religious tradition; but, unhappily, not all science is good science. Religion trumps science.

Most "creation-scientists," for example, begin from the assumption that the truth about nature is to be found in Scripture, and they work to find scientific evidence to confirm what they already know to be true. To be a member of the Creation Research Society, a scientist must affirm the divine inspiration of the Bible, the creative acts of God during the Creation week, the historicity of the Great Flood, and Jesus Christ as savior.

2. *Conflict: Science Trumps Religion.* Science and religion sometimes make conflicting claims about reality, but only science provides reliable knowledge. It is through scientific method that we come to know the ultimate truth about nature. If the scientific net doesn't catch something, it's because it doesn't exist. Science trumps religion.

Sometimes this position is called scient*ism* or natural*ism* or scientific material*ism*—the "ism" suggesting that a philosophical claim about ultimate reality is being made. On this account, religion possesses no competence to make claims about nature, and scientists need not consider religious claims in constructing their picture of nature.

3. *Independence.* Science and religion cannot conflict because they are incommensurable, autonomous endeavors, each with its own methods, each with its own domain. (This is sometimes called the "two-worlds" approach.) One common expression of this view is that science asks objective "how" questions, whereas religion asks personal "why" questions. Their conceptual nets capture aspects of reality so different that they stand in no logical relationship. Science and religion can each be true (or false) in their own terms; they are conceptual apples and oranges. While working in their own domains, neither scientists nor theologians need consider the conclusions of the other; religion and science can be intellectually compartmentalized.

This position is widely held by both theologians and scientists. Adopting it was, at first, a defensive move made by 19th century theologians who believed that science was able to give a complete account of physical reality. As a result, religion must be about a different world, a different dimension of reality. For these liberals, religion was never meant to be a science textbook; its claims about nature simply reflected the fallible prescientific understanding of ancient cultures. What is central to Scripture is its account of the encounters of people with God. Religion is about our existential situation, not physical reality; it is about the meaning of life, not its chemical composition.

Many scientists have also adopted this view. For example, according to a 1981 resolution of the National Academy of Sciences, "religion and science are *separate and mutually exclusive* [emphasis added] realms of human thought whose presentation in the same context leads to a misunderstanding of both scientific theory and religious belief" (1984, pp. 5–6).

4. *Integration.* Science and religion are commensurable endeavors; they can conflict and they can reinforce each other, for they make claims about the same world. Neither can ignore the other, and neither automatically trumps the other; they provide, in effect, complementary methods for rationally pursuing truth. Because science and religion are each competent to illuminate aspects of the same reality, a fully adequate picture of reality must draw on—and integrate—both.

For integrationists, scriptural passages about nature should not be taken literally, but they must still be taken seriously. There is, of course, a theological risk in the integrationist position, for it leaves theological claims subject to revision, or even falsification, by modern science. Still, theological integrationists would hold with Arthur Peacocke, the distinguished biochemist and theologian, that religion and science are "ultimately converging" in that "the scientific and theological enterprises" are "interacting and mutually illuminating approaches to reality" (1984, p. 51).

Roughly a third of Americans believe that the Bible is inerrant and would presumably adopt the view (if asked) that religion trumps science. Very few scientists take this position; it is, after all, utterly at odds with the normal practice of science. No doubt many scientists believe that science always trumps religion; some say so (often in response to creationists), though most scientists simply don't go on record about such things. Because many scientists believe in God yet make no effort to integrate science and religion, instead compartmentalizing them, we suspect that most religious scientists take the independence position. Most liberal theologians, influenced by the intellectual authority of modern science, have adopted some version of either the independence or integrationist positions.

Over the last several decades a shift from the independence to the integrationist position appears to have occurred among both theologians and scientists. Certainly a literature of dialogue has grown rapidly. Why? There are several reasons. First, some scholars argue that recent developments in science—particularly in quantum mechanics, cosmology, chaos theory, and ecology—have provided openings for religious analyses: the world of 20th century science appears to be more hospitable to religion than the classical scientific world of atoms and determinism. Second, recent work in the history, philosophy, and sociology of science has convinced a good number of scholars that science is culturally shaped rather than pristinely "objective." At the same time, many theologians have argued that (liberal) theology can be "rational" or "objective" in some sense; theological claims can be testable—though not in quite the same way as scientific claims. That is, theology and science are not nearly so different as has often been believed, and integration has become a possibility.

Standards and Textbooks

No discussion of the relationship of science and religion appears in the 262 pages of the national science standards, though the standards do claim that "explanations on [sic] how the natural world changes based on myths, personal beliefs, religious values, mystical inspiration, superstition, or authority may be personally useful and socially relevant, but they are not scientific" (National Research Council [NRC], 1996, p. 201). The standards also acknowledge that "science is only one way of answering questions and explaining the natural world"—but they ignore any of the alternatives (p. 138). Presumably, science and religion are distinct domains. At only one point is there any mention of the relevance of religion to science classes; it is a fleeting suggestion that we will consider in due course.

Of the 12 high school science textbooks we reviewed (in biology, earth sciences, and physics) only 2 discussed the relationship of science and religion.[1] The first, a biology text, devoted three pages to reviewing Galileo's troubles with the church, the bogus claims of "creation-science," and Darwin's statement, in the last paragraph of the *Origin of Species,* that "the powers of life" have been "breathed by the Creator" into nature—from which the text concludes that evolution need not be incompatible with religion *(Biological Science,* 1996, p. 16). (It is doubtful that, in the end, Darwin actually believed this; more important, why should we accept Darwin as having settled this question?) The second, a physics text, asserted that religion "has to do not with nature, but with meaning and its implications for personal and communal life." Hence "science and religion are as different as apples and oranges" and "unless one has a shallow understanding of either or both, there is no contradiction in being religious and being scientific in one's thinking" (*Conceptual Physics,* 1992, p. 12). Unfortunately, the discussion is only two paragraphs long and does little to discourage shallow thinking.

What can we conclude? The standards and the texts completely ignore one of the most momentous questions of modern intellectual and cultural history: the relationship of science and religion. Of course, the nature of this relationship is deeply controversial, but

---

[1] The biology texts we reviewed are *Biology: Living Systems* (Glencoe 1994); *Biology* (Prentice-Hall 1995); *Modern Biology* (HBJ/HRW 1993); *Biology* (Addison-Wesley 1993); and *Biological Science* (D.C. Heath 1996). The earth science texts are *Exploring Earth Science* (Prentice-Hall 1995); *Earth Science* (HBJ/HRW 1994); *Earth Science* (Merrill 1995); and *Earth Science* (D.C. Heath 1994). The physics texts are *Physics: Principles with Applications* (Prentice-Hall 1995); *Physics: Principles and Problems* (Glencoe 1995); and *Conceptual Physics* (HarperCollins 1993).

that would seem to be a reason for discussing rather than ignoring it. Indeed, by ignoring the controversy, and by ignoring religion, science education *implicitly* takes sides, teaching students *uncritically* to believe either that science always trumps religion or that they are independent endeavors. Although one or the other of these views might be correct, surely students are not *educated* about the relationship of science and religion, or the possible limitations of science, if they are taught this uncritically.

In fact, one can argue that conventional science and science education are committed in fact, if not necessarily in principle, to scientism or philosophical naturalism, for scientific method and science education allow religion no philosophical room to make claims or provide evidence about nature. Religion is discredited a priori.

Evolution and Biology

Although theologians put up some resistance to evolution after the publication of Darwin's *Origin of Species* in 1859, it is striking how quickly mainline theologians came to accept evolution as God's way of doing things. Indeed, evolution did not become a major issue for most religious conservatives until the 1920s. Those conservatives who read the first chapter of Genesis as "literally" true concluded that evolution is problematic for several reasons. It took too much time: after all, God created humankind (and perhaps the world) within the last six thousand years. More important, God created each species specially, "after its own kind." Species don't evolve. Many conservatives also held that evolution "reduces" people to animals by blurring the lines between them. For some religious conservatives—such as William Jennings Bryan—the major issue was social Darwinism, which used scientific theory to sanction (animal-like) brutality in business and warfare. Finally, some religious conservatives came to believe that there is scientific evidence against evolution and for the special creation (or the "abrupt appearance") of species.

Liberal theologians, by contrast, have accepted evolution, reading Genesis mythically or symbolically rather than literally. In the 19th century, many theologians in Reform Judaism and the mainline Protestant denominations began to argue that religions can be *progressive* by drawing on modern science and liberal social and political ideas to reform their traditions. The human condition should be understood not in terms of a *fall* from grace, but in terms of "evolutionary" progress. For these liberals, biological evolution was not a problem; indeed, it appeared to fit the progressive pattern of existence.

Still, evolution presents a problem for some liberals—though it is not much acknowledged in our culture wars—for as contemporary neo-Darwinism understands it, evolution is inherently *purposeless*. Evolutionary change is the result of natural selection working on the random mutation and recombination of genes. The genius of Darwin's account of evolution (as Darwin well knew) lay in denying divine design and giving a fully "naturalistic" explanation of evolution. The human eye is no longer to be explained in terms of design and God's purposes, but in terms of the incremental survival value that mutations producing slightly greater light sensitivity give to individuals. It makes no scientific sense to say that evolution is the transition from morally or spiritually lower to higher forms of life; human beings are not the end (or purpose) of evolution, but an "accidental" result. Or, as Stephen Jay Gould puts it, we are but a minor species in the Age of Bacteria (1997, chap. 14).[2]

Nonetheless, most Jewish, Catholic, and mainline Protestant theologians accept evolution, reconciling it with their religious commitments in one or the other of several ways. Many theologians have adopted the *independence position* outlined above: science and religion are conceptually different endeavors; the Bible isn't about how nature works, and evolution has no implications for what is central to religion—its account of the meaning of life. This also appears to be the position of the National Association of Biology Teachers: "evolutionary theory, indeed all of science, is necessarily silent on religion and neither refutes nor supports the existence of a deity or deities" (n.d., p. 1).

There are a variety of ways of integrating religion and evolution. Catholicism, for example, accepts evolution but claims that, as the *Catechism* of the Church puts it, "the Universe was created 'in a state

---

[2] In their "Statement on Teaching Evolution" the National Association of Biology Teachers define evolution as an "unpredictable and natural process" that is "affected by natural selection, chance, historical contingencies and changing environment." The statement asserts that natural selection has "no specific direction or goal," and stipulates that nonnaturalistic and supernatural causes have no role to play in science. Until the fall of 1997, the NABT statement also characterized evolution as an "unsupervised" and "impersonal" process, but these terms were removed after objections from two scholars in religious studies convinced the NABT that they were gratuitously hostile to religion. It is not obvious that dropping these terms alters the thrust of the statement, however.

of journeying' toward an ultimate perfection yet to be attained, to which God has destined it. We call 'divine providence' the dispositions by which God guides his creation toward this perfection" (1994, p. 80). Evolution *is* purposeful, though God has chosen to work through the "secondary" causes of nature. Moreover, God is a personal God who, on occasion, intervenes in the affairs of this world by way of miracles. And, as Pope John Paul II recently affirmed, God directly intervened in evolution to create a break between animals and humankind: Adam and Eve were real people; God created them and their descendants—unlike animals—with immortal souls (1996a, p. 352).

Liberal theologians often reject the traditional conception of a transcendent, creator God, arguing instead that God is *immanent,* a creative and purposeful force working *within* us and all of nature, moving us to higher moral and spiritual planes of existence through evolution. Variations on this view are held by "Process" theologians (drawing on the influential work of Alfred North Whitehead), some feminist theologians, and some New Age thinkers.

Typically, theologians who argue for integrationist positions draw on the commitments and resources of their religious traditions (Scripture, history, and religious experience) to develop a more adequate, inclusive understanding of reality than either science or theology can provide by itself. In the process, the claims of both science and religion may need to be modified or reformulated.

Some advocates of "intelligent design theory" forego theological commitments, however, and argue that God is the best possible scientific explanation available for the evolutionary evidence. So, for example, gaps in the fossil record, or complex, interrelated changes in cellular development are best explained in terms of coordinated design in nature.

In the end, there are *several* alternatives to orthodox neo-Darwinism and fundamentalist creationism, and yet almost all discussions of evolution are framed in terms of these two polarized positions. In fact, surveys suggest that a significant minority of Americans take some kind of middle position. According to a 1991 Gallup Poll, while 47 percent of Americans believe that God created humankind within the last 10,000 years and 9 percent believe that God had no part in evolution, 40 percent of the respondents believe that God directs evolution. The remaining 4 percent believe something else or claim no opinion (1991, p. 231).

Standards and Textbooks

The *National Science Education Standards* emphasize that evolution is central to modern biology and recommend that the curriculum include it in grades 5 through 8 as well as in high school biology courses (National Research Council [NRC], 1996, pp. 158, 181–187). The standards say nothing about creation-science or religious interpretations of nature.

Each of the biology texts we reviewed includes long accounts, covering several chapters, of biological and human evolution; indeed, two of the five texts begin with evolution as the central organizing theory of modern biology. Each text presents all of the usual geological, fossil, physiological, genetic, and biochemical evidence for evolution. One text includes a fairly substantial discussion of biology and its relationship to natural theology before Darwin, and concludes that Darwin "subverted" the traditional religious understanding of the world (*Biology*, 1993, p. 422). No text mentions any scientific arguments against evolution or discusses the possibility of design in nature.

We must also note, however, that a growing number of science teachers, fearing controversy, are not discussing evolution. Moreover, at least some teachers include creationism of one kind or another in biology courses even though it is not in the texts and is not part of their official curriculum.

The Big Bang and Cosmology

For several decades now most cosmologists and physicists have agreed that the origins of the universe can be traced back 10 or 20 billion years to a "big bang." Whereas many people have perceived evolution as a threat to religion, some theologians and scientists have taken the big bang to corroborate the idea of creation. In his 1951 address to the Pontifical Academy of Science, Pope Pius XII declared that the big bang bears witness to "the primordial Fiat lux," confirming "the contingency of the universe" and "the epoch when the cosmos came from the Hands of the Creator" (quoted in Jastrow, 1978, p. 142). The astronomer Robert Jastrow ended his popular book *God and the Astronomers* by describing the modern cosmologist who has finally "scaled the mountains of ignorance" and "is about to conquer the highest peak; as he pulls himself over the final rock, he is greeted by a band of theologians who have been sitting there for centuries" (1978, pp. 105–106).

If Pius and Jastrow were saying that the big bang *confirms* theological accounts, most scientists and theologians would disagree. The "hands of the Creator" are not, after all, detectable by scientific method. In fact, science may not be able to say anything about what caused the big bang. No doubt some cosmologists believe that they can get very close to the big bang—to within a fraction of a second of it—but because the laws of nature are themselves the *product* of the big bang those laws cannot be used to explain it. As the astrophysicist William Stoeger puts it,

> [the big bang cannot] be considered as a beginning either of the universe or of time . . . much less of creation in the theological sense of that word. Rather, it underscores the fact that our universe . . . was once dominated by such extreme conditions that none of the categories we now rely upon to describe physical reality would have been applicable, including those of space and time, matter, and particle. (1996, p. 193)

If the cause of the big bang is of some theological interest, so is its immediate aftermath. Over the past decade some scientists, philosophers, and theologians have argued that there is cosmological evidence that the universe was *fine-tuned* to produce life, for the odds against life in the wake of a big bang are almost infintesimal *and yet there is life.* (Such claims often go under the label the "Anthropic Principle.") For example, had the expansion rate one second after the big bang been smaller by one part in a hundred thousand million million, the universe would have collapsed; had it been one part in a million stronger, it would have expanded too quickly for life to form. If the strong nuclear force were slightly weaker, only hydrogen would exist; if it were slightly stronger, all hydrogen would have converted to helium and stable stars could not have existed. And these coincidences could be multiplied many times (Barbour, 1990, pp. 136–137). According to Stephen Hawking, "The odds against a universe like ours emerging out of something like the Big Bang are enormous" (quoted in Boslough, 1985, p. 121). What is the most reasonable explanation for such coincidences? Arguably, that the universe was *designed* to support life.

Creation

Not all religious traditions include the idea of creation. Followers within some traditions believe the universe to be eternal. Some Hindu texts tell of vast cycles of creation and dissolution: "The Himalayas, it is said, are made of solid granite. Once every thousand years a bird flies over them with a scarf in its beak that brushes the ranges as it passes. When by this process the Himalayas have been worn away, one day of a cosmic cycle will have collapsed." The gods themselves are created and then die as ultimate reality—Brahman—oscillates between the fullness of being and pure potentiality: "Just as the spider pours forth its thread from itself and takes it back again . . . even so the universe grows from [and dissolves back into] the Imperishable" (Smith, 1991, p. 68).

Other religious traditions are agnostic about creation. When the Buddha was asked whether the world was eternal, he responded with the parable of a foolish man who had been shot with an arrow but would not consent to be treated until he learned all of the details about who had shot him. The religious life does not depend on dogmas of creation: whether the world is eternal or not "there still remain birth, old age, death, sorrow, lamentation, misery, grief, and despair" (Burtt, 1955, p. 35). What is religiously important is escape from suffering and the wheel of rebirths, not metaphysical speculation.

In contrast to the Eastern religions, creation is part of the Western Scriptural traditions: In the beginning God created the heavens and the earth. Unlike Christianity, Judaism has placed rather more emphasis on how to live—and the Law—than on what to believe; it has been open to a variety of ways of reading Genesis, and has made "no systematic attempt" to define "an orthodox cosmology" (Katz, 1978, p. 148). The idea of creation was written into the Christian creeds, however, and acquired considerable theological importance. There are, of course, a number of Creation narratives in the Bible (Genesis 1:1–2:3, 2:4–3:24, Job 38–41, Psalms 74, Isaiah 40–48, and John 1), though Genesis 1 has become the most prominent. Although scholars differ on the translation and meaning of Genesis, the orthodox Christian tradition is *not* that God created order out of existing chaos (one reading of Genesis 1:1) but that God created all that is, the world and perhaps time as well, out of nothing: *creation ex nihilo.*

The alternative—and a secondary theme in much theology—has been God's *continuing creation,* which might be understood in either of two ways. In the first, God continually sustains creation ontologically: creation is not an event in time, but the continuing dependence of the world on God for its existence at any time. As the physicist and theologian John Polkinghorne once put it, "God is not a God of the edges, with a vested interest in beginnings. God is the God of all times and all places" (1993, p. 18). In the second, God continually brings new and higher forms of being into existence. This latter view is, at one and the same time, evolutionary and creationist. These several forms of creation need not be incompatible, but may simply reflect different emphases. What is important in any of these "creationist" accounts is that the existence of the world depends on, and is ultimately explainable in terms of, God; scientific accounts are, at best, incomplete.

As we've seen, for many theologians and scientists, science and religion are radically different kinds of endeavors; the Genesis narrative should not be read as historical fact—and the big bang can neither falsify nor verify Biblical or theological claims about the world. Yet, for an increasing number of theologians and scientists, the big bang *does* have theological relevance. If the big bang does not *confirm* creation *ex nihilo,* it is at least *consonant* with it, and the evidence from cosmology of a "fine-tuned" universe may be evidence for a creator God. Needless to say, the God of the big bang is not obviously the personal God of much traditional religion. What is important for those who take the integrationist position is the apparent convergence of science and (liberal) theology, each providing evidence for the role of God in creating the universe.

Standards and Textbooks

According to the national science standards "the origin of the universe remains one of the greatest questions in science," and the standards recommend that students learn about the big bang theory (NRC, 1996, p. 190). The standards also note that "the age of the universe and its evolution into galaxies, stars, and planets—and eventually life on earth—fascinates and challenges students" (NRC, 1996, p. 188). The standards say nothing, however, about relating the big bang to religion; nor do they make any reference to the anthropic principle. Two of the three physics texts we reviewed discussed the big bang theory and cosmological evolution; none mentioned any other account of the origins of the universe. One text devoted five sentences to the cosmological evidence for a "fine-tuned" universe, but did not relate the evidence to God or provide any context for making sense of it religiously.

Nature and Ecology

Environmentalists and scholars often claim that Western culture has been singularly destructive and bears special responsibility for our environmental crisis. Many of them attribute to modern science an intellectual framework that is particularly congenial to the exploitation of nature. Of course, science provides the know-how to create the technology that has been so destructive, but at a deeper level it conceives of nature as inert, dead, and value free; because science discerns only quantitative distinctions in reality, it can make no sense of the idea that nature is sacred or that it imposes moral or spiritual requirements on us. Indeed, a goal of science is to provide precisely that kind of knowledge of causal laws that allows us to manipulate and exploit nature for our own purposes—whatever they might be.

Others have argued, however, that Western religious traditions are complicit in this responsibility. One reason modern science developed in the West was that the Bible long ago laid the groundwork for "disenchanting the world." By emphasizing a single, transcendent creator-God, the Bible began to secularize nature. Arguably, this was a point of the Creation narrative in Genesis 1: God created the sun and moon, the plants and animals; they were not themselves deities, but lifeless objects. God is the only deity.

The religious sources of our environmental crisis may cut deeper still, however. People often argue that the Bible is anthropocentric in the sense that God gave humankind *dominion* over nature (Genesis 1:26–29, Genesis 9:1–3, Psalms 8:5–8): the plants and animals are to serve our purposes. Moreover, many theologians draw a sharp distinction between spirit and matter, elevating the former and devaluing the latter. Only persons are immortal and of value; this world, nature, is of only passing value as our temporary home.

Eco-Theology

We can argue on secular grounds that it is in our long-term self-interest to protect the environment. Of course, what is in our long-term self-interest doesn't always move us to act in the here and now; moreover, the long term is often "discounted" in the cost-benefit analyses done by policymakers. Theologians have argued, in response, that only a religious understanding of nature can ground an adequate environmental ethic.

Over the past several decades, many Jewish and Christian theologians have mined the Bible for examples of God's care for nature: after the flood, God covenanted not just with Noah and his human family, but with "every living thing" never to destroy the world again (Genesis 9:8–17); God declared that the Sabbath is for animals (as well as for people) to rest, and even the land shall rest by lying fallow every seventh year (Exodus 23:10–12, Leviticus 25:1–5); the Psalms celebrate the beauty and goodness of nature (e.g., Psalm 104); and in the New Testament, Jesus affirmed God's care for the sparrows and the lilies of the field (Matthew 6:26–29). Of course, in the first chapter of Genesis, God declares creation to be good *before* the creation of Adam and Eve; nature is good in and of itself, not simply in serving human purposes.

As a result of reflection on these and other passages, theologians have argued that the "dominion" that God gave humankind over nature is best understood as *stewardship.* The world belongs to God: "The earth is the Lord's and the fullness hereof" (Psalms 24:1). We are obligated to care for nature not simply because it is in our long-term self-interest, but because God requires it of us. God's creation must be treated with reverence.

Some Christian theologians have recently resurrected an incarnational or sacramental theology in which the idea of God as trinity bridges the gulf between the transcendent Creator and nature. Christ was the incarnation of God in human flesh. Moreover, through Christ as "Logos" all things were created (John 1), and through Christ all things in heaven and on earth are redeemed (Colossians 1:15–20) that, in the end, "God may be all in all" (I Corinthians 15:25). As God is present in the wine and bread, so God is present in the working of the world: nature isn't inert but is animated by the spirit of God.

Some liberal theologians have gone well beyond Biblical texts to reshape traditional interpretations of God and nature. As we saw in our discussion of evolution, many theologians appeal to an *immanent* God who works through evolution, transforming the world. The work of Alfred North Whitehead and the process theologians who follow him have been particularly influential, as have been various forms of "creation spirituality" developed by Matthew Fox and Thomas Berry. These theologians have extended our conception of God's action from a largely historical to a broadly cosmic context; the story of God is not simply that of a brief span of time on the earth; it is the story of the evolving universe understood spiritually.

Ecofeminist theologians have argued that the transcendent creator-God of the Bible, who is disembodied mind and who speaks with power and authority, is conceived in narrowly masculine terms, and they would replace this male God with an immanent God who speaks to us from within and, in Rosemary Radford Ruether's words, "beckons us into communion" with all of nature (1992, p. 254). Reality isn't dualistic, split between mind and matter, God and creation. Sallie McFague (1993) has suggested that we think of God as a creator-mother who gives birth to the universe, or that we reconceive nature as God's body.

Many eco-theologians have been influenced by non-Western religions that place a much greater emphasis on the divinity of nature than do Judaism and Christianity. Within Native American and African religious traditions, nature embodies those spirits and divinities that the monotheistic traditions exorcised, and within Eastern religions—particularly Hinduism, Buddhism, and Taoism—all of reality is understood as being in some sense one with God or the Divine (Brahman, Nirvana, the Tao). These traditions have been much less anthropocentric than have the Western traditions. Human beings are but a small part of reality, not its masters, and we are intimately related to all of nature, with which we must live in harmony.

An impressive body of denominational and ecumenical responses to the environmental crisis now exists. In fact, a broad consensus cuts across conservative and liberal traditions regarding theological conceptions of stewardship. For example, after a 1993 "summit" on the environment, an ecumenical group of Jewish, Christian, and Native American religious leaders concluded that

> a consensus now exists, at the highest level of leadership across a significant spectrum of religious traditions, that the cause of environmental integrity and justice must occupy a position of utmost priority for people of faith. . . . We pledge to take the initiative in interpreting and communicating theological foundations for the stewardship of Creation. ("Statement," 1991, p. 637)

Many eco-theologians emphasize the relationship between ecology and economics. The combination of consumerism and technology has been particularly destructive, and, therefore, the solution to the crisis is, in part, a matter of social justice: placing environmental constraints on the marketplace, adopting more modest lifestyles, and encouraging globally coordinated redistribution of the earth's resources. It is "manifestly unjust," Pope John Paul II has said,

> that the privileged few should continue to accumulate excess goods, squandering available resources, while masses of people are living in conditions of misery. Today, the dramatic threat of ecological breakdown is teaching us the extent to which greed and selfishness—both individual and collective—are contrary to the order of creation, an order which is characterized by mutual interdependence. . . . (1989/1996b, p. 233)

Some liberation theologians have begun to extend the concept of justice beyond humankind to include nature. According to the authors of a report to the World Council of Churches: "People across the earth are fighting for liberation from the pain of oppression. . . . Liberation [now] needs to be extended to animals, plants, and to the very earth itself, which sustains all life" (*Liberating Life*, 1990, p. 252).

Standards and Textbooks

The national science standards emphasize the importance of understanding ecosystems and the threat to their survival when "humans modify ecosystems as a result of population growth, technology, and consumption" (NRC, 1996, p. 186). In their sole recommendation to include some study of religion in science courses (the one exception to the silence on religion we mentioned earlier), the standards suggest that students might investigate various factors affecting environmental quality, including "the role of economic, political, and religious views" (NRC, 1996, p. 198). Each of the biology and earth science texts we reviewed includes one or several chapters on ecosystems and brief discussions of pollution and the ecological crisis, but none mentions religious interpretations of the problem or, more generally, of nature.

Other Issues

We suggest, all too briefly, a few more places where questions about the adequacy—or correctness—of science might be raised on religious grounds.

• *Technology.* Particular forms of technology—nuclear weapons, for example—may be intrinsically problematic on religious grounds, but the primary religious problem with technology is, arguably, the *technological ethos* our culture has developed. From within that ethos we tend to reconceptualize moral and spiritual problems as technological problems: health is a matter of high-tech medicine rather than prayer or living well; sexual responsibility is a matter of condoms and birth control pills rather than chastity and virtue; environmental protection is a matter of clean energy rather than simpler lifestyles and social justice. As we begin to think technologically we naturally reconceive the world—and its people—as objects to be manipulated, and, in Martin Buber's terms, the "I-Thou" language of personal relationships gives way to the "I-It" language of "objective" detachment (1958). Our sense of the sacred has withered, and we no longer feel reverence toward nature. Not only is there no moral compass built into technology or the science that shapes it, but the omnipresent "technological imperative" demands that we think and act technologically.

• *Genetic engineering.* Some forms of gene therapy involve only the individuals who are treated and are relatively uncontroversial, but "germ-line" therapy that affects genetic inheritance opens the door to social engineering and raises major moral and theological questions. The recent successful cloning of mammals makes these issues particularly urgent. Some theologians reject out-of-hand the idea of "playing God" by tampering with divinely created human nature, while some more liberal theologians argue that because God works through us and through evolution we can be "coworkers" with God, using judicious genetic interventions to help fulfill the divine potential in human nature.

• *Health and healing.* All religious traditions have provided spiritual explanations for sickness and health and have used prayer, meditation, and other spiritual means to restore health. Within modern Western civilization scientific accounts of sickness and health gradually undermined these religious interpretations. In the last several decades, however, something of a cultural shift has taken place as various forms of holistic medicine have acquired a measure of respectability even within the medical establishment, and as people have more fully appreciated the role of the mind (or soul) in healing. Indeed, there are now some efforts under way to test scientifically the efficacy of prayer and other spiritual practices in healing. All of this is deeply controversial. What does seem clear is that traditional scientific accounts of health and healing can no longer be *assumed* to be adequate. Neither the science standards nor the national health education standards discuss religious interpretations of any of these issues.

Constitutional Constraints

Before we can draw out the educational implications of our discussion, we must be clear about the constitutional constraints within which science education must proceed. Three Supreme Court rulings are particularly relevant.

As we have seen, in *Abington v. Schempp* (1963) the Court made it clear that it is *permissible* to teach students about the Bible and religion in public schools when this is done "objectively as part of a secular program of education."[3] It is undoubtedly constitutional to teach students about religious accounts of origins and nature. Of course, the purpose of such teaching cannot be to proselytize or indoctrinate students.

In *Epperson v. Arkansas* (1968) the Supreme Court struck down an Arkansas law that prohibited the teaching of evolution. The First Amendment, Justice Abe Fortas wrote, "mandates governmental neutrality between religion and religion, and between religion and nonreligion."[4] The purpose of the Arkansas law, however, was "to blot out a particular theory because of its supposed conflict with the Biblical account, literally read."[5] Because its purpose was to protect Christian fundamentalism, it was not religiously neutral.

If the teaching of evolution could not be prohibited, then perhaps teaching creation-science could be required; but in *Edwards v. Aguillard* (1987) the Court struck down Louisiana's "balanced treatment" act. Citing a paper trail of comments by the legislators who passed the act, Justice William Brennan concluded its purpose was to shore up fundamentalist Christianity and discredit evolution "by counterbalancing its teaching at every turn with the teaching of creation science."[6]

---

[3] See School District of Abington v. Schempp, 374 U.S. 203, 225 (1963).

[4] Epperson v. Arkansas, 393 U.S. 97, 104 (1968).

[5] Epperson v. Arkansas, 393 U.S. 97, 109 (1968).

[6] Edwards v. Aguillard, 482 U.S. 578, 589 (1987).

Because the *purpose* of both the Arkansas and Louisiana laws was religious, they ran afoul of the neutrality required by the Establishment Clause. The Court has also repeatedly held, however, that a religious purpose need not invalidate a law or policy if there is *also* a *secular* purpose for it. Justice Fortas found none for the Arkansas law; nor could Justice Brennan for the Louisiana act. But surely there is at least one powerful secular reason for requiring students to study religious accounts of origins and nature: a good liberal education requires it. If students are to think in an informed and critical way about matters of controversy and importance (like the origins of life), they must understand religious as well as secular points of view.

Indeed, as we argued in Chapter 1, there may be a *constitutional* reason for *requiring*, not just permitting, students to learn about religious accounts of origins. Because the Establishment Clause requires public schools (as governmental agencies) to be religiously neutral, and because the only way to make sense of neutrality is in terms of fairness to the contending alternatives, schools must teach students about religion if they teach ways of thinking about the world that are critical of religion.

As we have seen, there are ways of reconciling modern science and much liberal religion; it is not at all clear, however, how conservative religious claims about origins and nature can be reconciled with science. Should our position be that it is permissible to teach scientific ways of understanding origins and nature that conflict with conservative religion so long as they can be reconciled with liberal religion? Is this neutral among religions—as the Establishment Clause requires? Obviously not.

But is it clear that science—as it is commonly practiced and taught—is neutral regarding even liberal religion? As we have seen, neo-Darwinian accounts of evolution conflict with the teleological accounts of evolution found in some versions of liberal theology, and it is hard to reconcile ecofeminist theology with conventional scientific interpretations of nature. Indeed, a good deal of liberal theology makes claims about nature that modern science either ignores or considers false.

Perhaps most troublesome, however, is that by ignoring religion in teaching science, we teach students *uncritically* to conceive of nature in exclusively secular terms. By systematically allowing students to remain ignorant not just of creationism and conservative religion, but of liberal ways of integrating science and religion, science education profoundly biases the thinking of students.

Clearly the solution cannot be to censor science; this would be to provide religion with a curricular veto—hardly a neutral scheme. A true neutrality would require two things. First, students must learn about *various* alternative religious ways of conceiving nature—both conservative and liberal. Second, they must learn about the various ways of relating science and religion; they must understand the controversy over whether science and religion conflict, are conceptually independent, or need to be integrated.

It is important to keep in mind that schools can't privilege fundamentalism as the only alternative to science. As we have seen, the Establishment Clause requires neutrality among religions. The discussion must include all of the major religious ways of understanding nature. No doubt there is a practical problem here that stems from the number of religious views that are available, but there are not so many *types* of accounts. In any case, when neutrality is hard to come by, it would seem incumbent on us constitutionally to try to approximate rather than ignore it.

Where in the curriculum we teach about religious accounts of nature is, of course, crucial. Some have argued that Justice Brennan's ruling in *Aguillard* prohibited teaching about religious accounts of origins in science classes, but (carefully read) Brennan ruled the Louisiana act unconstitutional because it had a religious *purpose,* leaving open the possibility that a properly secular purpose could justify teaching *about* religion in science courses. With the proper purposes, then, where we teach about religion is an educational rather than a constitutional question—and as we shall see shortly, we can read even the national science standards as providing secular reasons for including some discussion of religion in science classes.

The Educational Implications

The relationship between science and religion has at least the following implications for education.

• *The secularization of Western civilization* is one of the major trends of modern history, and certainly one of the major reasons for this has been the growing cultural authority of modern science. Indeed, the scientific revolution was, perhaps, the most important of all revolutions in human history because it has so radically changed our understanding of the universe, of what it means to be a person, of what it means to be rational, of what is important and ultimately meaningful. Intellectual respectability in the modern world (and in the curriculum) is now largely a matter of scientific respectability. The history of science, therefore, is not just about science; it is about modern culture. One task of a liberal education is to locate students historically in the most important ongoing cultural conversations. The scientific revolution and its cultural impact should be a major theme of both history and science courses.

• *Science as a discipline.* We don't teach the "subject" of nature—which might be open to various scientific and religious interpretations—but rather the "discipline" of science, as defined by scientific method. Although science textbooks include perfunctory chapters on scientific method, they rarely include any discussion of the relationship of science to religion; nor do they include any discussion of religious alternatives to scientific theories in the body of the texts. The effect of this is that we *implicitly* teach students either that science always trumps religion or that the two are incommensurable endeavors. Both positions are deeply controversial among theologians—and even among some scientists.

Arguably, the a priori refusal of scientists to consider religious evidence, theological arguments, or design explanations for cosmic or biological evolution suggests that scientific method and the practice of science are dictated by philosophical or ideological convictions about reality that cannot themselves be scientifically verified. Indeed, one might argue that science proceeds on the *faith* that scientific conceptual nets will prove adequate, in the end, to catch everything. But how do we know that now?

A good liberal education requires that when we disagree about matters of great importance, we teach students the conflicts; we teach them about the contending alternatives. Indeed, if students are to think *critically* about science and its relationship to other domains of knowledge, their education can't be limited to scientific perspectives on these relationships. Of course, a part of what is at issue is what counts as an *other* domain of knowledge; some believe that science and religion share an overlapping domain.

• *Fairness.* We do not advocate "balanced treatment" or "equal time" for religion in science classes. We do recommend that science texts and courses provide some context for understanding connections and conflicts with religion by putting them into historical and philosophical perspective. Texts should acknowledge that these relationships are controversial and can be understood in various ways; they must show some sophistication.

All science texts and courses should include some discussion of the relationship of science and religion in an opening chapter or in opening lectures, as part of a broader review of the history and philosophy of science and scientific method. Sections of texts and courses dealing with evolution, the big bang, ecology, and other religiously important and controversial issues should provide some context for understanding what is at issue religiously. For example, biology texts and courses should explain why religious conservatives reject evolution *and* why religious liberals accept it (but may still have problems with neo-Darwinism).

This is what we called, in Chapter 2, a *minimal* fairness. A *robust* fairness would require a course in religious studies that treats religious interpretations of nature in greater depth in the context of the study of various religious traditions, taught by teachers certified in religious studies. By their very nature science courses can't be robustly fair; but the curriculum as a whole can be. Science teachers aren't prepared to deal with religious perspectives on nature. We do recommend that all prospective science teachers take an undergraduate course in science and religion.

- *Theory and fact.* Some religious conservatives argue that evolution should only be taught as theory—meaning by this, as *speculation*—rather than as fact. This argument has a point, though it is often misunderstood. In science, a theory is not a hypothesis or (mere) speculation, but a comprehensive conceptual scheme that relates a broad range of phenomena in a way that provides explanatory power. Theories can be confirmed. No doubt some aspects of evolution remain controversial among scientists (gradualism versus punctuated equilibrium, for example), but most scientists take evolution and neo-Darwinian accounts of it to be confirmed; these matters aren't mere speculation.

But it is one thing to teach students that neo-Darwinism is good science; it is another thing to teach them that they are justified in believing it to be true, *all things considered.* Whether neo-Darwinism is either true or an adequate account of evolution is, in part, a philosophical question, and answers depend on how we assess the relationship of science and religion. As we know, this relationship is controversial.

It is not the proper task of public schools to encourage, much less *uncritically* encourage, students to accept secular rather than religious interpretations of nature. It is their task to enable students to understand both and to think in informed ways about their relationship. Students must learn what scientists take to be good science; they must also learn that what is true, *all things considered,* may be something else. One purpose of a liberal education is to make sure that students are in a position to make "all things considered" judgments, rather than accepting uncritically the conventional wisdom of any discipline, science included.

If we take religious neutrality seriously we have to "bracket" truth claims regarding matters of religious controversy. Just as teachers and texts cannot teach that religious creationism is true or false, so they cannot teach that theories that conflict with it are true or false.

• *Creation-science and intelligent design.* To the extent that creation-science assumes a particular reading of Scripture as its starting point, it has no claim for inclusion in the science curriculum *as science*—though, obviously, any truly *scientific* evidence put forward by creation-scientists may have a legitimate claim to be taken seriously. Advocates of "intelligent design" theories often distinguish their approach sharply from that of creation-scientists, arguing that they do not start from (a literal reading of) Genesis, but from scientific evidence for levels of complexity and interdependence in nature that can only be plausibly explained in terms of design. Because mainstream science is committed to *philosophical naturalism,* they argue, it doesn't allow design arguments to be considered. Indeed, intelligent-design theorists sometimes claim that they are more truly scientific in their approach, because they don't rule out explanations on philosophical grounds.

Of course, if we take either intelligent design theory (or creation-science, for that matter) to be *nothing more than* science, there is no argument to be made for including either one in the curriculum as a matter of *religious neutrality.* If they are science, the argument for including them should be made in terms of good science education. We believe that scientists should be free to determine both what counts as good science and what range of alternative scientific theories should be included in the curriculum when scientists disagree among themselves. Given the number of its advocates, there may be no more obligation to include intelligent design in the science curriculum than any scientific theory held by a relatively small minority of scientists.

Having said this, we also note that science changes, and scientists have, on occasion, come to realize they have been overly dogmatic in their criteria for determining what counts as good science. Some design theories in both cosmic and biological evolution are grounded in sophisticated analyses of evidence and strike us as warranting discussion. Moreover, the ideal of a liberal education is always to be inclusive rather than narrow.

We would add that legislators are not likely to be competent to determine what counts as good science; the balanced-treatment laws were heavy-handed and misguided efforts from the beginning. We believe that it *does* fall within the competence of legislatures to require that students study religion—and religious conceptions of nature and origins—as part of a good liberal education, however. Obviously such study must be done in a way that has educational integrity, does not privilege a particular religious tradition, and does not proselytize but maintains religious neutrality.

• *The principle of cultural location and weight.* Although a good liberal education provides students with alternative ways of understanding controversial issues, it will not present those alternatives in the abstract, but in context. Creation-science, theories of intelligent design, theological accounts of evolution, and neo-Darwinism aren't simply alternative items on a cafeteria line that students should be free to choose depending on their tastes. If they are to make educated judgments about the alternatives, they should understand how widely held the different views are and within which scientific and religious traditions. Which are consensus views, which are controversial views, and for whom? And what can each view say in defense of itself or in criticism of its competitors?

• *Primary sources.* As is always the case in dealing with controversial issues, it is important to use primary sources and let advocates of the contending alternatives speak for themselves. This is particularly important when textbooks are not at all open to some of those alternatives. Again, we are not advocating equal time, but science education must take place in the context of liberal education, and on particularly important and controversial issues, it must expose students to a wider range of voices than they now hear.

• *Teachers' responsibilities.* Needless to say, neither the ideal curriculum nor ideal textbooks are just around the corner. This being the case, we recommend (1) that science teachers familiarize themselves with the basic issues regarding the relationship of science and religion, particularly in their own discipline(s); (2) that when they have an informed understanding of the basic issues, they provide students with some sense of what is at issue religiously at appropriate points in their classes, using such supplementary readings, from several religious traditions, as are available; and (3) that they remain neutral on questions of ultimate truth (as opposed to what counts as good science).

• *The science standards again.* Although the standards say virtually nothing about religion, we take our recommendations to be in their spirit. Consider the following statements from the standards. *In science courses* students should learn "the difference between scientific and other questions" and "appreciate what science and technology can reasonably contribute to society and what they cannot do" (NRC, 1996, pp. 169–170). In studying science "students need to understand that science reflects its history and is an ongoing, changing enterprise." Students should learn about "the role that science has played in the development of various cultures" (NRC, 1996, p. 107). Most important, *students should learn how scientific knowledge "connects to larger ideas, other domains, and the world beyond"* [emphasis added] (NRC, 1996, p. 36). This being the case, teachers need to be able to make "conceptual connections" to "other school subjects" and be able to use "scientific understanding and ability when dealing with personal and societal issues" (NRC, 1996, p. 59). Finally, we've noted that the standards suggest that students might study religious views of the environment (NRC, 1996, p. 198). That is, the standards conceive of science education as requiring some understanding of the development and influence of science in history, and its relevance to social issues, other subjects in the curriculum, decision making, "larger ideas," and "other domains." So even though the standards say virtually nothing explicit about religion, they seem implicitly to require some discussion of religion nonetheless.

• *Shifting boundaries.* Finally, it is important to remember that the conventional disciplinary boundaries have been challenged from a variety of directions over the past several decades. Many *secular* postmodernist scholars have attacked the "objectivity" of modern science, arguing that it is culturally biased, reflecting the interests and ideology of its time, place, and class. Some scientists argue that recent developments in cosmology, chaos theory, and quantum mechanics make the world of late-20th-century science a rather more mysterious world, one more open to religious interpretation, than the old deterministic billiard-ball world of classical science. And, finally, liberal theologians have turned more and more to integrationist approaches in developing new theological interpretations of nature. As culturally significant as they are, all of these developments (and others) should be mirrored in some way in science education.

We want to be very clear about what we are *not* arguing in this chapter. We are not arguing that any particular scientific claims are false, that scientific method is inadequate for understanding reality, or that any particular religious claims about nature are true. (Indeed, we are inclined to think that modern science is the greatest of all human intellectual achievements.) But the relationship of science and religion, and the truth of various scientific and religious claims about nature, are deeply controversial. If students are to be liberally educated, they must be initiated into a discussion in which they hear a *variety* of voices, not just those of scientists. And it is unfortunate that the usual way of framing the discussion makes Christian fundamentalism the sole alternative to modern science, when there are various moderate, liberal, and non-Christian theological alternatives as well.

To some considerable extent, modern science has come to define what it is reasonable to believe—not just about nature, but about all of life. For many educators, scientific method defines what it means to be rational. Hence, it is tremendously important that students acquire some critical distance on the claims of science. Unfortunately, educators do nothing to give students the resources to judge the adequacy of science *all things considered*. This is no small matter; it plays a major role in marginalizing religion and *uncritically* constricting our sense of what is reasonable.

Suggested Readings and Resources

The recent literature on science and religion is enormous; we can hardly scratch the surface. For those who need a good introduction to the major issues, the place to start is the work of Ian Barbour, whose encyclopedic understanding of science, theology, and philosophy makes him a superb guide. In *Science and Religion* (1997) Barbour provides both a historical overview of the developing relationship of science and religion and a deeply informed analysis of current science and theology and various ways of understanding their relationship. We have drawn heavily on Barbour and on the philosopher E. M. Adams, whose *Religion and Cultural Freedom* is an illuminating and challenging philosophical study of the relationship of science, religion, and modernity.

Several anthologies provide excellent introductions to the relationship of science and religion generally, as well as to particular issues. See, for example, *Religion and Science* (1996), edited by W. Mark Richardson and Wesley J. Wildman; *Physics, Philosophy, and Theology: A Common Quest for Understanding* (1988), edited by Robert J. Russell and colleagues; *Science and Theology* (1998), edited by Ted Peters; and *Evidence of Purpose* (1994), edited by Sir John Templeton.

Steven Katz's "Judaism, God, and the Astronomers," in Robert Jastrow's *God and the Astronomers* (1980), is a superb account of how Jewish and Christian thinking about creation and evolution differ. Two of George Marsden's essays provide excellent accounts of conservative Protestant views of science: "Evangelicals and the Scientific Culture," in *Religion and Twentieth Century American Intellectual Life* (1989), edited by Michael J. Lacey; and "Understanding Fundamentalist Views of Science," in *Science and Creationism* (1984), edited by Ashley Montagu.

The historian of science Ronald Numbers has written a superb history of creation-science called *The Creationists* (1992). In a series of books Berkeley law professor Philip Johnson has argued that Darwinism is, essentially, a closed philosophical theory that rules much of the relevant evidence out of bounds a priori; see his *Darwin on Trial* (1991), and *Reason in the Balance: The Case Against Naturalism in Science, Law, and Education* (1995). In *Darwin's Black Box* (1997), the biochemist Michael Behe provides a sophisticated argument for intelligent design in dealing with evolution. *Pandas and People* (1989) is a short, low-key, but controversial textbook supplement designed to inform students about intelligent design theory as an alternative to conventional evolutionary theory.

Teilhard de Chardin's *The Phenomenon of Man* is a classic (if difficult) statement of divinely guided evolution. For a good, more recent and readable theological exploration of evolution, see Philip Hefner's *The Human Factor: Evolution, Culture, and Religion* (1993). Conrad Hyers provides an interesting and thoughtful reading of the Genesis Creation narratives and their relationship to science in *The Meaning of Creation* (1984). Several highly respected scientists with considerable theological sophistication have argued forcefully for integrating science and religion. See, for example, biochemist Arthur Peacocke's *Creation in a World of Science* (1979) and *Theology for a Scientific Age* (1990), or any of the many works of physicists Paul Davies and John Polkinghorne. The theologian Langdon Gilkey's *Maker of Heaven and Earth* (1959) has been the classic statement of what we have called the "independence" position, but also see his more recent "integrationist" study *Nature, Reality, and the Sacred* (1993). In *Religion and Creation* (1996) Keith Ward looks at Hindu, Muslim, Jewish, and Christian thinking about creation, focusing primarily on the 20th century.

Worldviews and Ecology (1994), edited by Mary Tucker and John Grim, is a good collection of essays on ecology from the perspectives of the major world religions. For a more comprehensive anthology, see *This Sacred Earth: Religion, Nature, Environment* (1996), edited by Roger Gottlieb, a superb collection of documents and essays from various Western religious traditions. In *Religion and the Order of Nature* (1996) Seyyed Hossein Nasr explores how nature has been understood in the world's religions, describes the secularization of nature by modern science, and argues for returning to the idea that nature is sacred. In *The Universe Story* (1992) the physicist Brian Swimme and theologian Thomas Berry offer a spiritual interpretation of the universe from the Big Bang to the present day.

Two of the most influential ecofeminist theologies of nature are Rosemary Radford Ruether's *Gaia and God: An Ecofeminist Theology of Earth Healing* (1992) and Sallie McFague's *The Body of God: An Ecological Theology* (1993).

The theologian David Ray Griffin has written extensively about the theological implications of *postmodern* ways of thinking science and religion; see especially his introduction to *The Reenchantment of Science* (1988). Also see Nancy Murphey's insightful works, especially *Anglo-American Postmodernity: Philosophical Perspectives on Science, Religion, and Ethics* (1997).

Darwin, by Adrian Desmond and James Moore is a superb biography, a good read, and especially helpful on Darwin and religion. For critiques of religious interpretations of evolution see Jacques Monod's *Chance and Necessity* (1971), Richard Dawkins' *The Blind Watchmaker* (1986), and most of the many works of Stephen Jay Gould. In *Dreams of a Final Theory* (1992) the distinguished physicist Stephen Weinberg rejects accounts of a "fine-tuned" universe, arguing that a "chilling impersonality" is characteristic of the laws of nature (p. 245).

8

The Bible and World Religions

IF RELIGION IS TO BE TAUGHT *ACROSS THE CURRICULUM*—AS WE have argued—then the Bible and world religions will properly come in for some discussion in many courses, and the themes of this chapter will be relevant to most teachers.

We have argued not just for the *natural inclusion* of religion in existing courses, however, but for *courses in religion*. If educators are to take religion seriously, if they are to treat it with a robust fairness, then there must be *required courses* in religious studies taught by teachers competent (and certified) to teach them. We have acknowledged that neither certified teachers nor required courses are likely prospects in the foreseeable future—but it is important to keep the ideal in mind if we are to move in the right direction.

Of course *elective* courses in the Bible and world religions, if not quite common, are not uncommon either—and there should be more of them. In this chapter we discuss the educational and constitutional issues relating to such courses—and propose what we take to be important in any introductory course in religious studies.

The Constitutional Framework

The Supreme Court has never ruled on the constitutionality of courses in religion, though lower courts have approved both elective and required religion courses when conducted in accord with the Supreme Court's ruling in *Abington v. Schempp* (1963). As we have seen, in his majority opinion Justice Tom Clark distinguished between *devotional* Bible reading, which is unconstitutional, and study of the Bible that, when conducted *"objectively as part of a secular program of education,"* is constitutional.[1] In a concurring opinion, Justice William Brennan, the strictest "separationist" on the Court in recent decades, agreed that the prohibition on devotional Bible reading "plainly does not foreclose teaching *about* the Holy Scriptures" or religion more generally.[2] It is permissible to teach about the Bible and religion in public schools; this is not controversial.

But it must be done properly. What does it mean to teach about the Bible or religion "objectively, as part of a secular program of education"? Both Justices Clark and Brennan grounded their opinions in the Court's reading of the Establishment Clause as requiring religious *neutrality*. To teach objectively is to teach neutrally. As we have seen, two kinds of neutrality are required: neutrality among religions, and neutrality between religion and nonreligion. Schools can't privilege any particular religious tradition or any particular religious interpretation of the Bible. When we disagree—as we do about religion in general, and the Bible in particular—the only way to be neutral is to be fair to the contending parties, include them in the discussion, and refrain from taking sides.

The Court's claim that the Bible and religion must be studied as part of a "secular program of education" should not be taken to mean that the Bible must be read as secular scholars or scientists do (for that would privilege nonreligious over religious approaches and violate the neutrality between religion and nonreligion also required by the Establishment Clause); rather, the *purpose* of studying the Bible or religion must be educational, not religious. Religion courses cannot be used to proselytize or indoctrinate students.

Although lower courts have held that private funds may be used to pay a Bible teacher, it is clear that those funds must come with no strings attached; Bible courses must be completely under the control of the school system. Teachers cannot be required to pass any religious test.

---

[1] Abington v. Schempp, 374 U.S. 203, 225 (1963).

[2] Ibid., 300.

The Educational Framework

Why is religion important enough to be included in the curriculum? In Chapter 2 we suggested three secular, educational reasons. First, religion has been a powerful influence historically on literature and art, politics and war, morality and our intellectual life. Students must understand a good deal about religion if they are to understand what we already require them to study in history and literature courses. Second, religions continue to offer widely accepted answers to those existential questions about the meaning of life—suffering and death, tradition and identity, reason and faith, happiness and justice—that we inevitably ask as human beings. Students can't be educated persons without understanding something about how religions have answered these questions.[3] Third, a liberal education should introduce students to the major ways people have devised for making sense of the world, enabling them to think in an informed and critical way about the alternatives. We now teach students to think in exclusively secular ways about every subject in the curriculum; the study of religion provides critical perspective on students' secular studies.

Because religions are embedded in worldviews that make sense of reality in terms that are sometimes foreign to modern science and our secular disciplines, religions are difficult to understand. Moreover, religions differ from one another in ways that complicate their study. We have argued that students cannot learn enough about religions by way of "natural inclusion" to get "inside" religious ways of making sense of the world. Consequently, we have argued, high school students should be required to take at least one yearlong course in religion, and if that course is to serve the purposes of a liberal education, it must include the study of several religious traditions.

Finally, it is important to note, yet again, the congruence between our civic and educational frameworks. The purpose of studying religion in a public school is not to initiate students into a religious tradition (as is proper in a church, synagogue, mosque, or temple); rather, it is to inform students about various religions, the different ways they have been understood, their relationships to one another, and their implications for how to make sense of the world,

---

[3] Some religious conservatives make a related argument—that study of the Bible should be part of moral education in the schools. We will consider the relationship of religion and moral education in Chapter 9.

fairly. This is what both the constitution and a good liberal education require.

Bible Courses

Schools rightly require virtually all students to read a Shakespeare play at some point; yet they usually ignore the Bible although it has been immeasurably more influential than all of Shakespeare's plays together. No book has been so influential in the history of the world as the Bible. Indeed, for millions of Americans the Bible continues to be the source of their deepest convictions and commitments. If any book merits inclusion in the curriculum, it is the Bible.

Bible courses might take a number of shapes.

• *The Bible as Literature.* Students might study the Bible in terms of aesthetic categories, as an anthology of narratives, stories, and poetry, exploring its language, symbolism, motifs, and archetypes.

• *The Bible in Literature.* Students might study the ways in which later writers have used Biblical stories, language, symbols, motifs, and archetypes. We've already discussed these two alternatives in Chapter 6.

• *The Bible as History.* Students might study the Bible for the light it throws on ancient history. As we argued in Chapter 4, the *sacred history* found in the Bible is quite different from the secular history of academic historians. What we can learn about history from the Bible depends on how we interpret it and the criteria we use to assess the validity of historical claims—both matters of considerable controversy.

• *The Bible in History.* Students might study how people of various religious traditions have understood the Bible, and how it has influenced our social and cultural institutions, our beliefs and values.

However important the Bible is as literature or history, however great its influence has been on later literature and history, its primary importance has clearly been as a religious text, *as Scripture;* indeed, this is the source of the Bible's literary and historical importance. To read the Bible simply as literature or history would be a little like reading poetry as if it were no more than prose; it would be to miss a dimension of meaning that is in Scripture. It is through the Biblical account of the Creation, God's covenant with Abraham, the moral radicalism of the Hebrew Prophets, Jesus' teaching of love and the coming Kingdom of God, and his death and resurrection, that Jews and Christians have acquired their understanding of reality. To not appreciate the *religious* roots of civilization with all of the theological, moral, social, political, and scientific branches that are nourished by them, is to remain uneducated. And so we add a fifth possibility.

• *The Bible as Scripture.* Students might consider the central *religious* claims made in the Bible, how various religious traditions have interpreted those claims, and how those claims have influenced our history and culture. Of course, to study the Bible as Scripture, as we propose it, is not a matter of reading it devotionally, but learning *about* how the Bible has been understood as Scripture within various traditions.

The Major Issues

Whatever the rubric, we must address several major issues if we are to adopt a neutral and educational approach.

• *Whose Bible?* We've talked so far as if there were a single Bible, when, in fact, there is a Jewish Bible (the Hebrew Scriptures, or *Tanakh),* and various Christian Bibles—Catholic, Protestant, and Orthodox—each composed of different books, arranged in different orders. These differences are significant. Needless to say, it makes a great deal of difference if the New Testament is part of the Bible. (Of course, Judaism is a religion of the Talmud as well as of the Hebrew Bible.) Even the arrangement of books is of significance: for example, the Hebrew Bible ends with Cyrus's admonition to the Jews in II Chronicles to go to Jerusalem; the Christian Old Testament ends with Malachi's prophecy of the coming of the Messiah.

To adopt any particular Bible will suggest to students that it is normative, the best Bible. It will be the Bible of some students and will be foreign to others. Arguably, public schools should use an inclusive Biblical sourcebook that is different from but includes the key texts of each of these Bibles (though such a textbook would not itself be a Bible). If a single Bible is to be used, it must, inevitably, be the most inclusive; hence, teachers should remind students at various crucial points in the course that their Bible is different from other Bibles and the significance of this. Students should, of course, study how the various Bibles came to be.

- *Whose translation?* Traditions and denominations often have their own authorized translations. Whatever its literary merits or religious authority for conservative Protestants, the language of the King James Bible is difficult—it was archaic even when it was translated in the 17th century—and a modern translation is essential. Many scholars prefer the New Revised Standard Version, but many conservatives object to its use of gender-inclusive language. What is important educationally is for students to understand these controversies, read from several translations, and reflect on their theological significance.

- *Whose interpretation?* Horace Mann and his successors in the common school movement of the 19th century argued that the King James Bible should be read in school without comment or theological gloss as a way of maintaining doctrinal neutrality. Mann's approach continues to have its advocates. The manual for the widely used curriculum of the National Council on Bible Curriculum in Public Schools rightly states that study of the Bible must be free of sectarian biases, but it takes this to mean that the King James Bible (which it recommends) should be read without commentary: "Study about the Bible should center on the biblical text itself rather than the extraneous material and theories which might express a particular theological position rather than the historical presentation found in the Bible." Indeed, this approach is "consistent with the teaching found within [the Bible]" (1996, pp. 62, 73).

Of course, this was—and is—a peculiarly Protestant (indeed, conservative Protestant) approach to the Protestant King James Bible. Jews have always read the Hebrew Bible through rabbinic commentary, and Catholics have always insisted that the Catholic Bible requires the authoritative interpretation of the church. Why? Because the meaning of the Bible isn't obvious; it requires interpretation. That is, *just* to read the Bible doesn't avoid sectarian bias; rather, it adopts a particular sectarian approach.

But couldn't one argue that reading the Bible without commentary is not simply a Protestant approach, it is a *secular* approach and, as such, is appropriate for public schools? There are two problems with this. First, the Establishment Clause requires neutrality between religion and nonreligion as well as neutrality among religions; that is, schools can't privilege a secular over a religious reading of the Bible any more than they can privilege a particular religious interpretation. The other problem is that any good secular reading of the

Bible (or Homer or Plato or any secular text) requires the use of modern historical and literary criticism; that is, it requires scholarly commentary to make sense of the text.

Beginning in the 19th century the resources of modern secular scholarship (in history, philology, and archaeology) were brought to bear in developing a new understanding of Biblical texts. For example, scholars argued that the Torah, or Pentateuch, was not the work of Moses but the "redaction" of at least four quite different sources. Biblical texts (such as the Noah narrative) were variations on non-biblical stories common in the ancient Near East. The Gospels were written 30 to 90 years after Jesus' death by men who did not know him but drew on various sources to develop somewhat different—and conflicting—portraits of him.

In our century, liberal Jewish and Christian theologians have drawn heavily on this scholarship to interpret the Bible and rethink their traditions, while conservative Christians and Orthodox Jews have typically reaffirmed that the Bible is inerrant—at least in its essential teachings. (It is important to note that there is a difference between holding the Bible to be *inerrant,* and holding that it should be read *literally;* theologians have often held, for example, that the true or intended meaning of a passage is allegorical, or metaphorical, and requires interpretation.)

And then, of course, there are the fundamental differences between Jewish and Christian readings of Scripture. Does the "suffering servant" passage in Isaiah 53 refer to Jesus or to Israel? Is the serpent of Genesis 3 Satan? Do we read the Hebrew Bible, the Christian Old Testament, in terms of the New Testament? Not if we're Jewish.

Teachers must maintain some sense of tension between letting the text (like any primary source) speak for itself and drawing on the resources of different (secular and religious) interpretative traditions for understanding it. If we are to educate students about the Bible, if it is to be studied neutrally, we must expose students to the major different ways of reading the Bible in our religious and scholarly traditions. To do this effectively requires the use of secondary sources that deal with various approaches to the Bible.

• *Whose selections?* Individuals often argue that the Bible can be quoted in support of any cause. This is an exaggeration, but there is a point to it. Some biblical texts were quoted by slave holders, others by abolitionists. Different religious traditions have valued (and sometimes denigrated) different portions of the Bible. Students should read enough of the Bible to acquire some sense of its recurring themes, but if they can't read all of the Bible (and it's unlikely that they can), teachers must be careful in selecting the parts they assign.

• *The Bible and history.* One of the problems with *just* reading the Bible is that this wrenches it out of its historical context, throwing students on their own, typically meager, resources for making sense of texts written in different languages and cultures. Students should learn about the Bible in the context of the ancient Near East, in part to understand what was common to the times and what was distinctive about the Bible. Even more important, students must study the Bible in the context of the various major historical interpretative traditions that have shaped its meaning as Scripture. Indeed, because the Bible has been the most influential of all books, students should learn something about its historical influence on a wide variety of cultural institutions and controversies—and on people's most basic beliefs and values *here and now.*

• *Required Bible courses?* Given its importance and influence, schools should require all students to study the Bible in some depth, but we do not favor required Bible courses as the way of accomplishing this end, in part because this comes a little too close to privileging the Jewish and Christian traditions. Educators should incorporate some study of the Bible into appropriate world history and literature courses (at contextually appropriate places)—though, as we've argued, natural inclusion doesn't get us very far. The ideal, once again, is to incorporate the Bible into a religion course in which it would be studied with other sacred scriptures. When the Wake County schools in Raleigh, North Carolina, began offering high school Bible courses several years ago, they required that each of the high schools also offer world religions courses. We find considerable merit in *elective* Bible courses but believe they should be supplemented in the curriculum by courses in other world religions that give all students the opportunity to study their own traditions—and convey to them the sense that their religions are taken seriously.

World Religions Courses

As important as it is for students to understand the Bible, a course on the Bible and its influence will not educate them about religion generally. Just as there is more to history than American history, so there is more to religion than the Bible, Judaism, and Christianity. Schools must take seriously other religious traditions, and one way to do this is through a course in world religions.

The Major Issues

• *Diversity and depth.* There is, of course, an inevitable neutrality problem with any world religions course, for there is not time in the school day to be fair to *all* religions. There are also educational tensions here. The "fairer" the course—the more religions studied—the more superficial it will be. The religions of the world are not minor variations on a theme, easily captured in short lists of basic beliefs or values. Moreover, some religions have been—and continue to be—more influential than others and, as a result, are more important to study on educational grounds.

Neutrality and breadth must be balanced with relevance and depth. We suggest that in a year-long course students should explore a few religious traditions in some depth—with, perhaps, a cursory survey of other religions to give them some sense of breadth. No doubt Christianity should be one of the religions studied because of its deep influence on American institutions and on the beliefs and values of many students. Neutrality requires that it not be privileged, however, in at least two senses. First, Christianity cannot be assumed or argued to be the "true" religion. Second, schools must teach students about several religions that contrast in marked ways to Christianity. Schools should include at least one non-Western religion in the course, and if a substantial number of students come from a particular minority tradition, it would be good to include that religion in the mix. Indeed, it is important to acknowledge and study the exploding religious diversity of American culture; most urban schools will have students who are members of many of the world's religions.

• *The many dimensions of religion.* In Chapter 2 we cited Ninian Smart's taxonomy of the seven dimensions of religion: doctrine; myth or narrative; moral and legal teachings; ritual; religious experience; social institutions; and art. Different religious traditions give different weight to these various dimensions of religion. For many Christians, especially conservative Protestants, salvation hinges on what one believes. Indeed, from the beginning, Christianity defined itself in terms of creeds, and required *orthodoxy,* or right belief. Some religions—Judaism, Islam, and Confucianism, for example—place less emphasis on belief, however, and more on practice—and are often called "orthoprax" religions. So, for example, Jews are to keep the commandments, observe the rituals, and sustain tradition. It is often said that one is a believing Christian, a practicing Jew. In other religious traditions, ritual, mystical encounters with the Transcendent, philosophical reflection, art and the experience of beauty, or living in harmony with nature may be central.

It is important both that students appreciate these differences and that teachers not impose their own conception of what is or should be normative in religion on other traditions, but convey to students *each religion's own conception of what is normative.*

• *Internal diversity.* Of course, every religious tradition comes in different varieties. We need only think of the differences between Pentecostals and Presbyterians, Russian Orthodoxy and Roman Catholicism, African and Anglican versions of Christianity. For some Christians salvation hinges on what one believes; for others it is found in mystical union with God; for yet others, in liberating the oppressed. The term *Hinduism* suggests a unity that obscures a bewildering diversity of myths and rituals, beliefs and values, institutions and theologies. (Indeed, *Hinduism* is a Western term used for the first time in the 19th century to categorize the various "religions" of India; Hinduism is simply the religions of the Hindus.) Although one can trace the legacy of distinguishable Confucian, Taoist, and Buddhist traditions in China, Chinese religion has long been an amalgam of them. And, of course, the rubrics "African religion" and "Native American religion" mask a great deal of diversity.

Acknowledging these differences is important, in part because students will sometimes not recognize their own traditions in the simplified versions of them they will encounter in the classroom.

• *Scripture.* All religions have sacred scriptures—texts that members of those traditions have found to reveal the nature of God and ultimate reality—and it is important that students read scripture, learning about religions from the "inside" through their primary sources. As we saw in our discussion of the Bible, students must also appreciate something of the diversity of meaning that scriptures have in different traditions.

Of course, not all religions have *written* scriptures; much African and Native American religion does not—though many of these traditions have stories and myths, orally transmitted, that function as scripture. (In most religious traditions, "scripture" was conveyed orally for centuries before it was written down.) Whereas Western religions have a closed canon, most Eastern religions (Hinduism, Mahayana Buddhism, Chinese and Japanese religions) do not, but draw on a wide array of scriptures of varying degrees of influence at different times and places. The authority of canonical scriptures has given a measure of unity to Judaism, Christianity, and Islam that is not typical of other traditions.

Even among Western religions, there are significant differences in how scripture is understood, however. For example, within Islam the Qur'an is understood much as Christ is understood in the Christian tradition—as the immediate revelation of God. By contrast, Christians typically understand the New Testament as being once removed from God, bearing witness to the revelation of God in Christ. The word *Qur'an* in Arabic means "recitation," and Islam places an emphasis on reciting scripture that is absent in Christianity. Moreover, the Qur'an is not to be translated, but read and recited in Arabic; again Christianity has no parallel.

It is important to remember, of course, that sacred texts are not as central to all religions as they are to Western religions. Other religions may better be approached through art or ritual or tradition.

• *Development and progress.* Another danger of fixating on sacred texts and the origins or "classical" forms of religions comes from the fact that religions develop. Historically, one can't understand Christianity apart from its development through the church fathers, the medieval synthesis of theology and Greek philosophy, the Reformation, and the development of modern liberal Christianity and conservative reassertions of orthodoxy. Christians often regard Judaism primarily as a precursor to Christianity, which ignores the transforming impact of rabbinic teaching (canonized in the Talmud), and its development in response to Greek philosophy and modernity. Indeed, every religion develops in response both to the larger world and to internal social and intellectual movements—while, no doubt, maintaining traditions and sacred texts that are, relatively speaking, more revered by "conservatives" than "liberals" within those traditions.

Of course, when the question of development is posed as a question of *progress,* it becomes controversial—and very important for students to understand. Religious liberals accept the idea of religious progress: through experience, reflection, and scholarship we can acquire greater insight into God and reality and reform our religious traditions. Conservatives often believe, by contrast, the truth was given once and for all in the past, and the only kind of reformation that is possible is dispensing with later accretions and distortions and returning to the original revelation.

• *God.* Needless to say, different traditions have understood God in very different ways. There is the obvious difference between monotheistic, animistic, and polytheistic conceptions of divinity. Whereas the Western religions have traditionally understood God as personal, Eastern religions have more commonly held an impersonal or mystical conception of God (as Nirvana, Brahman, the Tao). Consequently Western scriptures are often understood as the "Word" of God, for God, like persons, reveals "Himself" in language. Of course, mysticism is not utterly foreign to the West, and constant debate has occurred over the extent to which personal language can be applied to God. Some religious liberals argue that the idea of God as a person should be recognized as myth that, if taken literally (as conservatives often do) is a kind of idolatry; it confuses an image of God with the "ineffable" reality of God. Conservatives, by contrast, often find liberal demythologizing of God-talk to be dangerously unscriptural. How literally we take scriptural language about God determines whether it is appropriate to use masculine pronouns for God—another matter of some controversy.

Again, the point is that conceptions of God are quite different in different traditions; it won't do to say (as teachers sometimes do) that deep down all religions worship the same God. They don't—or, at least, the claim that they do is deeply controversial.

• *Religion from the outside and the inside.* It is important, once again, to sustain some kind of balance in approaching religion. We've argued that scripture must be put in historical and linguistic context, using the resources of secular scholarship. Some comparative study of what is common to religions and what is distinctive about each, in turn, is both interesting and important. What can be said about how religions come into existence, develop, and relate to one another?

But, of course, one major purpose of studying religion is to acquire some sense of how the world looks from *within* those traditions. Here, as we argued in Chapter 2, the goal is to nurture an *informed empathy*, an imaginative understanding of the world as seen through the eyes of people in different religious traditions. In such study, they should be allowed to speak for themselves, using the conceptual resources of their own traditions, to make sense of their own religion, lives, and the world.

Consequently, a good course in world religions should use—and balance—both primary sources (scripture, theology, art, film, and literature) drawn from within religious traditions, and secondary sources (perhaps textbooks) that approach various religious traditions from the outside.

Live Religions

A well-constructed course in world religions may serve as an excellent introduction to religion, but if educators focus all of the attention on sacred texts and the classical, historical forms of religions, they will not adequately address one major educational problem that concerns us: the relationship of *live* religions to various "subjects" of the curriculum. The importance of religion lies not just in its historical influence but in the implications of living religion for how *we* think about the world and live our lives.

As we noted in Chapter 2, for most of history religion pervaded all of life. People in other times and cultures haven't divided the world up as we do. Indeed, *religion* is a modern Western word that *we* have come to use to categorize ideas and institutions in strikingly new and different ways (Smith, 1963). Beginning in the 17th century, Western intellectuals gradually distinguished religion from politics, economics, history, morality, and science, secularizing our ways of conceiving these disciplines. Contemporary public education teaches students that secular ways of experiencing the world are normative, that the modern secular worldview goes without saying. Of course, in cases in which the logic of arguments and evidence is exclusively secular (and is often defined by scientific method), students come to understand religious claims as matters of seemingly blind faith. This is a peculiarly modern, Western view, and one point of a good religion course should be to examine this claim. After all, in all cultures, and for most of human history, it was *reasonable* to understand the world religiously.

There are many ways of defining faith and reason, but we might put the problem this way: because we teach students so little about religion, we teach them, in effect, to accept the adequacy of secular ways of thinking about life and the world *uncritically, as a matter of faith* (Nord, 1995, pp. 179–186). We have argued that it is essential to enlarge the curricular discussion to include religious voices if students are to be truly educated—that is, if they are to be able to think critically or *reasonably* about their lives and what they learn elsewhere in their coursework.

To teach students about every "subject" in the curriculum in secular terms only is neither neutral, nor does it constitute a good liberal education. We would have students learn something about several different religious ways of making sense of the major, religiously contested issues addressed in the curriculum: the origins of the world; the meaning of history; the meaning of America; justice; sexuality and the family; abortion; and morality—that is, those issues we address in Chapters 3 through 9 of this book. Students should learn enough about religion to enable them to understand, and participate in, our ongoing cultural discussion of these issues.

One task of a religion course must be to explore the relationship between religious and secular ways of making sense of the world. Where are the tensions and conflicts, the points of agreement and compatibility? Such "worldview analysis," as Ninian Smart calls it (1987, chap. 1), is neither an easy nor uncontroversial task. What is important is that students understand something of our ongoing cultural discussion about these matters and not (blindly) accept the current conventional wisdom.

Of course, this agenda requires time—at least a year—and the ideal would be a two-year sequence in which students studied world religions in their classical forms and historic development the first year, and the relevance of religion to contemporary issues and the other "subjects" of the curriculum the second.

Reminders

Because religion is a complicated subject, and because courses in religion have the potential to be controversial, we end this chapter with a few pointed reminders.

• *Age-appropriateness.* We have argued that educators can do much to develop the religious literacy of elementary school students, but the complexity of religion and the potential for controversy require that students in Bible and religion classes possess a good deal of maturity. Such courses should be taught only in high schools.

- *Excusal.* If schools require religion courses, we suggest that they have an excusal policy allowing students to be exempted if taking the course would burden their consciences. As we saw in Chapter 1, an argument for excusal policies can be made on "free exercise" grounds, but there are also reasons of sensitivity and political self-interest for having such a policy; indeed, such a policy would likely make required courses politically feasible.

- *Clear policies.* Because religion courses are controversial, it is important that school systems have clear religion policies that have grown out of successful efforts to find common ground and establish trust in a community before they are planned or put into place. Parents, teachers, and administrators all need to understand the constitutional and educational frameworks that must shape such courses. Students might read and discuss excerpts from *Abington v. Schempp* and other court rulings as part of the introduction to any religion course.

- *Teacher preparation.* As we've seen, religion courses require a great deal of sophistication on the part of teachers. We do not favor religion courses unless there are teachers competent to teach them. Religion teachers need to be certified, and certification should require a least an undergraduate minor in religious studies. That is, the field of "religious studies" needs to be developed in public education as it has been in higher education. Scholars in religious studies and education must think carefully about what mix of courses should be required to prepare teachers to teach about religion in public schools—and then make sure that such courses are offered.

Suggested Readings and Resources

Wilfred Cantwell Smith's *What Is Scripture?* (1993) is an extraordinarily helpful account of the idea of scripture in the major world religions. *Sacred Writings* (1994), edited by Jean Holm with John Bowker, provides good overviews of the origins, translations, interpretations, and use of scriptural texts in the major world religions. In *The Bible As Literature* (1990), John Gabel and Charles Wheeler provide historical and literary background on the composition of the Biblical texts, the formation of the canon, and translations of the Bible. Jeremy Daniel Silver's *The Story of Scripture* (1990) and Samuel Sandmel's *The Hebrew Scriptures:*

An Introduction to Their Literature and Religious Ideas (1978) are helpful studies of the Jewish Scriptures from within the Jewish tradition.

For background on the all-important split in the late 19th and early 20th centuries between liberals and conservatives over modern historical study of the Bible, see Martin Marty's *Modern American Religion: Vol. 1 (The Irony of It All, 1893–1919)* and *Vol. II (The Noise of Conflict, 1919–1941)*. William R. Hutchison's, *The Modernist Impulse in American Protestantism* (1976) and George M. Marsden's *Fundamentalism and American Culture* (1980) are classic studies of liberalism and fundamentalism during this crucial period. For a good historical survey of how the Bible has been interpreted from the Church Fathers through the present day, see *A Short History of the Interpretation of the Bible* (1984), by Robert M. Grant with David Tracy. Donald McKim's *What Christians Believe About the Bible* (1985) provides historical background but focuses on recent interpretations ranging from fundamentalism to feminism. See James Barr's *The Bible in the Modern World* (1990) for a good account of the Bible's encounter with modernity, and *Scripture in the Jewish and Christian Traditions: Authority, Interpretation, Relevance* (1982), edited by Frederick E. Greenspahn, for essays written from Protestant, Catholic, and Jewish perspectives. In *The Bible in Translation: An Essential Guide* (1997), Steven M. Sheeley and Robert N. Nash provide brief but helpful accounts of the major English translations of the Bible.

There is, of course, a truly vast literature on world religions. Huston Smith's *The World's Religions* (1958, 1991) is justifiably considered a classic; his newer *Illustrated World's Religions* (1995) adds pictures. Also Ninian Smart has written a number of excellent studies of the world's religion: see his *Religious Experience of Mankind* (1976), with chapters devoted to each of the major religions, or his *Dimensions of the Sacred: An Anatomy of the World's Beliefs* (1996), with chapters devoted to the different dimensions of religion (myth, morality, art, etc.), each illustrated with examples from the different religions. Smart was also the chief consultant for *The Long Search*, an excellent 13-part videotape series on the world's religions. Karen Armstrong's *A History of God* (1993)—deservedly a bestseller—traces the development of ways in which God has been understood in the Jewish, Christian, and Islamic traditions from the beginning to the present day. *The Story of the World Religions* (1988), by John Tully Carmody and Denise Lardner Carmody, is a textbook that might be used with bright high school students. For the primary sources, see *Sacred Texts of the World: A Universal Anthology* (1984), edited by Ninian Smart and Richard B. Hecht; *The World Religions Reader* (1998), edited by Gwilym Beckerlegge; and *Readings in Judaism, Christianity, and Islam* (1998), by John Corrigan (Contributor), Frederick M. Denny (Editor), and Martin S. Jaffee.

Jacob Neusner has edited an excellent set of essays dealing with religious pluralism in the United States: *World Religions in America* (1994). In Chapter 4 we described at some length the CD-ROM *On Common Ground: World Religions in America* (1997) produced by the Harvard Divinity School's Pluralism Project, and the 17-volume series *Religion and American Life* (forthcoming) for use in high school classrooms. The *World Religions & Cultures* catalog of the Social Studies School Service lists many of these and other resources (books, videos, and CD-ROMS); call 1-800-421-4246 for a copy.

While it was prepared for college teachers, *Teaching the Introductory Course in Religious Studies: A Source Book* (1991), edited by Mark Juergensmeyer, provides a wealth of helpful essays for high school teachers (including essays on teaching the major world religions). All teachers would benefit greatly from access to the authoritative essays in the 13-volume *Encyclopedia of Religion* (1987), edited by Mircea Eliade. The *HarperCollins Dictionary of Religion* (1995), edited by Jonathan Z. Smith, includes charts, pictures, short essays on innumerable topics, and longer essays on the major world religions.

Michael J. Buckley explains the development of modern atheism through the French Enlightenment in *At the Origins of Modern Atheism* (1987). In *Without God, Without Creed* (1985) James Turner shows how modern "unbelief" came to characterize much of American intellectual life by the end of the 19th century. (Also see the books by Marsden and Reuben in the Suggested Readings and Resources for the Introduction.) For defenses of contemporary atheism, see Paul Kurtz, *In Defense of Secular Humanism* (1983), and Anthony Flew's *Atheistic Humanism* (1993).

9

Moral Education

THE PRECEDING FIVE CHAPTERS HAVE DEALT WITH THE
proper place of religion in particular courses. Moral education, however, is generally understood to cut across the curriculum and is
appropriately integrated into all courses as well as into the extracurricular activities and ethos of schools. So our focus shifts somewhat in this last chapter.

There is not a lot of agreement about what moral education
should be, and there is no "discipline" of moral education corre-
sponding to the disciplines that define the courses we have discussed
so far. We will argue that "moral education" is an umbrella term for
two quite different tasks and approaches. The first, which might better be called moral "socialization" or "training," is the task of nurturing in children those virtues and values that make them good people.
Of course, good people can make bad judgments; it's often not easy
to know what is morally right. The second task of moral education is
to provide students with the intellectual resources that enable them
to make informed and responsible judgments about difficult matters
of moral importance. Both are proper and important tasks of schools—
and both cut across the curriculum.

The inevitable question, of course, is, whose morality will be
taught? We will offer our answer by way of a sketch of a theory of
moral education. Given this theory—and the civic and educational

181

frameworks we outlined in Chapters 1 and 2—we will draw out the implications for the role of religion in moral education. To put a little flesh on these theoretical bones, we will take sex education as a case study.

Education as a Moral Enterprise

We trust that it is uncontroversial to say that schooling is unavoidably a moral enterprise. Indeed, schools teach morality in a number of ways, both implicit and explicit.

Schools have a moral ethos embodied in rules, rewards and punishments, dress codes, honor codes, student government, relationships, styles of teaching, extracurricular emphases, art, and in the kinds of respect accorded students and teachers. Schools convey to children what is expected of them, what is normal, what is right and wrong. It is often claimed that values are *caught* rather than *taught;* through their ethos, schools socialize children into patterns of moral behavior.

Textbooks and courses often address moral questions and take moral positions. Literature inevitably explores moral issues, and writers take positions on those issues—as do publishers who decide which literature goes in the anthologies. In teaching history we initiate students into particular cultural traditions and identities. Although economics courses and texts typically avoid overt moral language and claim to be "value free," their accounts of human nature, decision making, and the economic world have moral implications, as we have seen.

The overall shape of the curriculum is morally loaded by virtue of what it requires, what it makes available as electives, and what it ignores. For example, for more than a century (but especially since *A Nation at Risk* and the reform reports of the 1980s), there has been a powerful movement to make schooling and the curriculum serve economic purposes. Religion and art, by contrast, have been largely ignored (and are not even elective possibilities in many schools). As a result, schooling encourages a rather more materialistic and less spiritual culture—a matter of some moral significance.

Educators have devised a variety of approaches to values and morality embodied in self-esteem, community service, civic education, sex education, drug education, Holocaust education, multicultural education, values clarification, and character education programs—to name but a few. We might consider two of the most influential of these approaches briefly.

For the past several decades values clarification programs have been widely used in public schools. In this approach, teachers help students "clarify" their values by having them reflect on moral dilemmas and think through the consequences of the options open to them, choosing that action that maximizes their deepest values. It is unjustifiable for a teacher to "impose" his or her values on students; this would be an act of oppression that denies the individuality and autonomy of students. Values are ultimately personal; indeed, the implicit message is that there are no right or wrong values. Needless to say, this is a deeply controversial approach—and is now widely rejected.

The character education movement of the last decade has been a response, in part, to the perceived relativism of values clarification. According to the "Character Education Manifesto," "all schools have the obligation to foster in their students personal and civic virtues such as integrity, courage, responsibility, diligence, service, and respect for the dignity of all persons" (Boston University, 1996). The goal is the development of character or virtue, not correct views on "ideologically charged issues." Schools must become "communities of virtue" in which "responsibility, hard work, honesty, and kindness are modeled, taught, expected, celebrated, and continually practiced." An important resource is the "reservoir of moral wisdom" that can be found in "great stories, works of art, literature, history, and biography." Education is a moral enterprise in which "we need to re-engage the hearts, minds, and hands of our children in forming their own characters, helping them 'to know the good, love the good, and do the good'" (Boston University, 1996).

Finally, we note what is conspicuous by its absence: although all universities offer courses in ethics, usually in departments of philosophy or religious studies, very few public schools have such courses. Unlike either values clarification or character education programs, the major purpose of ethics courses is usually to provide students with intellectual resources drawn from a variety of traditions and schools of thought that might orient them in the world and help them think through difficult moral problems. As important as we all agree morality to be, it is striking that schools do not consider ethics courses an option worth offering.

Training and Education

In Chapter 2 we distinguished between socialization, training, and indoctrination on the one hand, and education on the other. Socialization, we suggested, is the uncritical initiation of students into a tradition, a way of thinking and acting. Education, by contrast, requires critical distance from tradition, exposure to alternatives, informed and reflective deliberation about how to think and live.

Not all, but much character education might better be called *character training or socialization,* for the point is not so much to teach virtue and values by way of critical reflection on contending points of view, but to structure the moral ethos of schooling to nurturing the development of those moral habits and virtues that we agree to be good and important, that are part of our moral consensus. This is not a criticism of character education. Children *must* be morally trained. But there are limitations to character education as a general theory of moral education; it was not designed to address critical thinking about those "ideologically charged" debates that divide us. Character education does appeal, as the Manifesto makes clear, to a heritage of stories, literature, art, and biography to inform and deepen students' understanding of, and appreciation for, moral virtue. Often such literature will reveal the moral ambiguities of life, and discussion of it will encourage critical reflection on what is right and wrong. But if the literature is chosen to nurture the development of the *right* virtues and values, it may not be well suited to nurture an appreciation of moral ambiguity or informed and critical thinking about contending values and ways of thinking and living. (Of course, character education programs often nurture the virtues of tolerance, respect, and civility that play major roles in enabling educational discussion of controversial issues.)

One of the supposed virtues of the values clarification movement, by contrast, was its use of moral dilemmas and divisive issues; moreover, in asking students to consider the consequences of their actions, it required them to think critically about them. But the values clarification movement never required students to develop an *educated* understanding of moral frameworks of thought that could inform their thinking and provide them with critical distance on their personal desires and moral intuitions; it left them to their own inner resources (which might be meager).

Let us put it this way. Character education is an essential aspect of moral education, but a fully adequate theory of moral education must also address those morally divisive ("ideologically charged") issues that are sufficiently important so that students must be educated about them. Of course, one of these issues is the nature of morality itself; after all, we disagree about how to justify and ground those values and virtues that the character education movement nurtures.

If students are to be morally educated—and educated about morality—they must have some understanding of the moral frameworks civilization provides for making sense of the moral dimension of life. After all, morality is not intellectually free-floating, a matter of arbitrary choices and merely personal values. Morality is bound up with our place in a community or tradition, our understanding of nature and human nature, our convictions about the afterlife, our experiences of the sacred, our assumptions about what the mind can know, and our understanding of what makes life meaningful. We make sense of what we ought to do, of what kind of a person we should be, in light of all of these aspects of life—at least if we are reflective.

A Theory of Moral Education

We have space here to offer only the briefest sketch of a theory of moral education.

- For any society (or school) to exist, its members (students, teachers, and administrators) must share a number of *moral virtues:* they must be honest, responsible, and respectful of one another's well-being. We agree about this. Public schools have a vital role to play in nurturing these consensus virtues and values, as the character education movement rightly emphasizes; indeed, a major purpose of schooling is to help develop good persons.

- If we are to live together peacefully in a pluralistic society, we must also nurture those *civic virtues and values* that are part of our constitutional tradition: we must acknowledge responsibility for protecting one another's rights; we must debate our differences in a civil manner; we must keep informed. A major purpose of schooling is to nurture good citizenship.

- But when we *disagree* about important moral and civic issues, including the nature of morality itself, then, for both the civic and educational reasons we discussed in Chapter 2, students must learn about the alternatives, and teachers and schools should not take official positions on where the truth lies. The purpose of a *liberal education* should be to nurture an informed and reflective understanding of the conflicts.

• What shape moral education should take depends on the maturity of students. We might think of a K–12 continuum in which character education begins immediately with the socialization of children into those consensus values and virtues that sustain our communities. As children grow older and more mature they should gradually be initiated into a liberal education in which they are taught to think in informed and reflective ways about important, but controversial, moral issues.

• Character education and liberal education cannot be isolated in single courses but should be integrated into the curriculum as a whole. We also believe, however, that the curriculum should include room for a moral capstone course that high school seniors might take, in which they learn about the most important moral frameworks of thought—secular and religious, historical and contemporary—and how such frameworks might shape their thinking about the most urgent moral controversies they face.

Whose Values?

This is, of course, the inevitable question: If we are going to teach values, whose values are we going to teach? The answer is simple, at least in principle: We teach everyone's values. When we agree with each other we teach the importance and rightness of those consensus values. When we disagree, we teach *about* the alternatives and withhold judgment.

For example, we agree about democracy; it is proper, indeed important, to convey to students the value of democracy and the democratic virtues. We disagree deeply about the values of the Republican and Democratic parties, however. We can't leave politics out of the curriculum simply because it is controversial. If students are to be *educated*, if they are to make informed political decisions, they must learn something about the values and policies of the two parties. In *public* schools, teachers and texts should not take sides when the public is deeply divided; there should be no *established* political party. Schools should teach students about the alternatives fairly.

And so it should be with every other major moral or civic issue that divides us—including religion.

Liberal Education as Moral Education

A good liberal education will provide students with a basic cultural literacy about those aspects of the human condition sufficiently important to warrant a place in the curriculum. We have argued in earlier chapters that a major purpose for studying history and literature is the understanding and insight they provide into the human condition. History is a record of social, political, moral, and religious experiments; it provides interpretations of the suffering and flourishing of humankind. The study of literature gives students imaginative insights into how people have thought and felt about the world in different times and places. History and literature provide students with a multitude of vicarious experiences so that they are not at the mercy of their limited and inevitably inadequate personal insights and experiences. So, for example, it is impossible to understand matters of racial justice (and so specific a policy issue as affirmative action) without understanding a good deal of history, and the insights gained from imaginative literature (art, drama, and film) will be immensely valuable in making that history come alive. Indeed, one major criterion for choosing the history and literature we teach should be its relevance to deepening students' understanding of what is central to the suffering and flourishing of humankind.

As we suggested in Chapter 2, a liberal education has both conservative and liberating aspects. A good liberal education will initiate students into cultural traditions, shaping their moral identities in the process. We are not social atoms, but inheritors of languages, cultures, institutions, and moral traditions. From the beginning it has been a purpose of public education to make students into good citizens, good Americans. In teaching history we provide students with a past, a sense of identity, a role in developing stories, a set of obligations.

But a good liberal education will also teach students that disagreements among us run deep: we often disagree deeply about the meaning and lessons of history—as the debate over identity and multiculturalism makes clear. We often disagree about the justice and goodness of different cultures and subcultures. We disagree about how to make sense of the world, about how to interpret it. Indeed, we often disagree about what the relevant facts are—or, even more basically, what counts as a fact, as evidence, as a good argument. We have quite different worldviews. *A good liberal education will initiate students into a discussion of the major ways civilization has devised for talking about morality and the human condition.*

Religion and Moral Education

Most proposals for moral education are alike in employing vocabularies sterilized of religious language. The net effect, yet again, is the marginalization of religion. The implicit message is that religion is irrelevant to the development of virtue, moral judgment, and the search for moral truth. But if students are to be liberally educated and not just trained or socialized, if schools are not to disenfranchise religious subcultures, and if they are to be neutral in matters of religion, then we must include religious voices in the discussion.

• The character education movement is grounded in the conviction that there are *consensus* virtues and values. The consensus must be local, but it may also be broader; indeed, its advocates sometimes claim (rightly) that virtues such as honesty and integrity are universal and are found in all the world's religions. Nonetheless, because religion can't be practiced in public schools and because it is often controversial, the character education movement avoids it. Religion is mentioned only once in the "Character Education Manifesto"—in the claim that character education is a joint responsibility of schools, families, communities, *and churches* (as well, presumably, as non-Christian religious institutions) (Boston University, 1996).

Clearly the moral ethos of *public* schools must be secular rather than religious; character education cannot use religious exercises to nurture the development of character. But character education cannot implicitly convey the idea that religion is irrelevant to morality. We have noted that character education employs literature and history to convey moral messages. Some of those stories and some of that history should make clear that people's moral convictions are often grounded in religious traditions.

• When teachers and students in the higher grades discuss controversial moral issues—abortion, sexuality, and social justice, for example—they must include religious perspectives on them in the discussion. For constitutional reasons those religious interpretations cannot be disparaged or advocated.

• As we've noted many times, one reason we disagree in our moral judgments is that we are committed to strikingly different worldviews. Some of us ground our moral judgments in Scripture, others in cost-benefit analyses, yet others in conscience (and there are many other alternatives). Even when we agree—about honesty, for example—we may disagree about why we should be honest. Long-term self-interest and love of humanity may both prescribe honesty as the best policy—though one's attitude and motivation, the kind of person one is, may be quite different; and, of course, there will be occasions when the requirements of love and (even long-term) self-interest will diverge. Just as in math, it is not enough that we agree about the right answer (but we must get it in the right way), so in any domain of the curriculum a good education requires more than a shallow agreement about conclusions. To be educated requires an understanding of the deep reasons for belief and values.

Historically, religions have provided the categories, the narratives, the worldviews, that provided the deep justifications for morality. From within almost any religious worldview, conservative or liberal, people must set themselves right with God, reconciling themselves to the basic moral structure of reality. They are to act in love and justice and community, being mindful of those less fortunate than themselves. The conventional wisdom now, however, is that we can teach morality without reference to religion. Indeed, the deep justifications have changed (and often become more shallow in the process). Health and home economics texts often ground their account of values in Abraham Maslow's humanistic psychology, whereas the economics standards and texts appeal to neoclassical economic theory and modern social science. Modern science (at least implicitly) teaches students there is no moral structure to nature. Our whole moral vocabulary has changed: like modern culture generally, modern education often emphasizes rights over duties, individualism over community, autonomy over authority, happiness over salvation, self-esteem over self-sacrifice, and cost-benefit analysis over conscience. Indeed, students may learn that there are no right or wrong answers when moral judgments are the issue.

The problem is not just that educators ignore religious accounts of morality; it is that the secular worldview that pervades modern education renders religion suspect.

How do we make sense of religious accounts of morality? A little "natural inclusion" here and there will help. A yearlong course in religious studies will help more. We also find merit in the idea of a senior capstone course in ethics in which students would study various secular and religious ways of understanding morality and several of the most pressing moral problems of our time.

Moral Education and the Bible

Conservative religious parents sometimes ask that Bible courses be offered in public schools as a way of addressing the moral development of children. As we have seen, the courts have made it clear that public schools cannot teach students that the Bible is true, or that children should act in accord with Biblical morality.

Nonetheless, there is a constitutional way in which study of the Bible is relevant to moral education. By studying the Bible (or any religious text), students will encounter a vocabulary and framework for thinking about morality and the human condition that will quite properly provide them with critical distance on the secular ideas and ideals they acquire from elsewhere in the curriculum—and from popular culture.

Morality is at the heart of all religion, and, as we've argued, one important reason for studying religion is to acquire some sense of the answers that have been given to the fundamental existential questions of life. Teachers and texts can't endorse religious answers to those questions, but they can and should expose students to them fairly as part of a good liberal—and moral—education. Students may find those answers compelling even if their teachers and texts don't require them to.

Religion and Sex Education

It may be helpful to sketch the relevance of religion to one particularly troublesome part of the curriculum: sex education.

It is important for students (at some age) to understand the biology of sexuality; but, of course, the purpose of sex education has always been something more than simple science education. Its primary purpose has been to guide students' behavior, addressing major social problems such as unwanted pregnancies and the spread of sexually transmitted diseases (STDs).

One way to address these problems is to teach students sexual abstinence. Another is to provide them with a little technological know-how regarding birth control and condoms. Not surprisingly, many parents (including many religious conservatives) view the condom approach as a legitimation of sexual promiscuity and favor "abstinence only." Many educators respond that it is naive to teach abstinence only because many adolescents will inevitably engage in sexual behavior and they must learn how to protect themselves and others. The pragmatic middle ground has become "abstinence but": teach students abstinence but include something about condoms as well.

Whichever position we take requires that we give students reasons for using condoms or foregoing the pleasures of sexuality. Three kinds of answers are common. First, it can be argued that either approach is in one's long-term self-interest, and much sex education focuses on the unhappy consequences of unplanned pregnancies and STDs. Some students will recognize the risks and alter their behavior accordingly—though adolescents are not typically strong on long-term self-interest and deferred gratification. Perhaps more important, if it is to be truly *educational,* sex education must make students aware of the fact that sexual behavior is universally held to be subject to moral as well as prudential judgments. To be ignorant of this is to be uneducated.

So, how do we introduce morality into sex education? A second approach—that taken in each of the four high school health texts we reviewed—is a variation on values clarification.[1] Students should act responsibly: they should survey their options, consider the consequences (on themselves and on others), and then act in a way that maximizes whatever it is that they value most. Each of the health texts concludes that responsible individuals will practice abstinence. The problem, of course, is that this conclusion requires a considerable act of faith, for what students value most is up to them. The books offer no grounds for assessing the values of students as morally right or wrong; values are ultimately personal.

Health, home economics, and sex education texts and materials often use the language of *values* rather than that of *morality.* One reason is that for many educators "morality" has become synonymous either with what is "moralistic" (and hence narrow and intol-

---

[1] The four health texts we reviewed are *Perspectives on Health* (D.C. Heath 1994); *Glencoe Health* (Glencoe 1994); *Health: Skills for Wellness* (Prentice-Hall 1994); and *Holt Health* (Holt 1994).

erant) or what is religious. But, of course, this is an extraordinarily narrow view of morality. Indeed, no philosophers (in whose domain the field of ethics is usually taken to reside) use "morality" in such narrow ways. We suspect that the deeper problem is that much social science can't make sense of morality and so must translate it into talk of choices and personal values. Virtually all the health and home economics texts we reviewed start from the position of humanistic psychology. But if the authors can't cast their conceptual nets wider than this, it is not surprising that they don't catch morality in them.

One irony in all of this is that virtually everyone still believes that some actions *are* morally right and other actions *are* morally wrong. Pedophilia is morally wrong. Not telling the person with whom one proposes to have sex that he or she has an STD is morally wrong. Honesty isn't just a matter of cost-benefit analysis and personal values; it is *morally binding*. If people don't understand this, they are ignorant, and if we don't teach students this, we are irresponsible.

As we have argued, the character education movement has been a widely accepted (and much needed) antidote to the relativistic tendencies of values clarification, and it offers another approach to sex education. Sexual relationships, like all relationships, should be characterized by honesty, loyalty, and respect for the feelings, privacy, and well-being of others—and broad consensus supports this. Prudence, self-control, and a willingness to defer gratification are virtues of unquestionable importance in all aspects of life, but particularly in matters of sexuality. (Whereas the values clarification approach typically highlights dilemmas and choices, character education emphasizes habit; self-control can't just be the result of decisions made as we go along.) We agree that it is wrong for children to have sexual relationships. We might even agree that sexual modesty in dress and demeanor is an important virtue, at least for children. The moral consensus on sexuality is, no doubt, limited and fragile. Still, because there is a consensus, schools should constantly emphasize these moral virtues and principles by means of their ethos, dress codes, stories told and read, and, of course, in health, home economics, and sex education courses. Sex education must also be moral education.

Is this sufficient? What about religion?

We have argued that character education cannot (implicitly) give the impression that religion is irrelevant to morality. Children's stories about love and romance and marriage and the family should include religious literature.

Character education builds on moral consensus, but obviously there is also a good deal of (often strong) disagreement on matters relating to sexuality—abstinence and birth control, abortion and homosexuality, for example. Not surprisingly, we also disagree about what to teach students about these things; indeed, we often disagree about *whether* to teach about such things. Our claim is this: *if* we are to include controversial issues in the sex education curriculum, then, as always, students must hear the different voices—secular and religious, conservative and liberal—that are part of our cultural conversation. Given the importance of religion in our culture, to remain ignorant of religious ways of thinking about sexuality is to remain uneducated. Indeed, the term "sex education" is something of a misnomer; as it is usually taught, sex education is far from being truly educational, for it limits the range of voices allowed into the discussion.

Older students should learn about religious as well as secular arguments for abstinence, and they should learn how different religious traditions regard birth control. (Although all of the health books we reviewed discussed condoms, none mentioned that Roman Catholic teaching forbids artificial birth control.) Indeed, they should learn something about the relevant Scriptural sources (in different traditions) for sexual morality, marriage, and the family. They should know, for example, that within religions, marriage is a "holy" or sacramental (and not just a legal) institution. They should understand the policy positions on controversial sexual issues taken by contemporary religious organizations and theologians. Students are *illiberally* "educated" if they learn to think about sexuality in only secular categories.

Or consider abortion. For many religious people, abortion is *the* most important moral issue of our time; for them, it is *the* most important consequence of unwanted pregnancies and sexual promiscuity. Yet most sex education ignores abortion. Of the health texts we reviewed only one mentioned it—devoting a single paragraph to explaining that it is a medically safe alternative to adoption. That paragraph concludes: "This procedure has sparked a great deal of controversy" (*Perspectives on Health*, 1994, p. 163). Well, yes. We suggest that to be an educated human being in the United States at the end of the 20th century one must understand the abortion controversy; indeed, its relevance to sex education is immediate and tremendously important.

So what does it mean to be educated about abortion? Certainly students should understand the point of view of the Roman Catholic Church and those religious conservatives who believe that abortion is murder. They should also understand the point of view of those religious liberals (from various traditions) who are pro-choice. They should understand feminist positions on abortion. They should learn about the key Supreme Court rulings and different ways of interpreting the implications of political liberty for the abortion debate. Students should read primary source documents written from within each of these traditions. And, of course, teachers and texts should not take positions on where truth lies when we are so deeply divided.

Or consider homosexuality. The health texts we reviewed each mentioned that some people are heterosexual and others are homosexual (though not everyone would agree with this way of putting it) and that we don't quite know what accounts for the difference. That's it. Like abortion, however, the issue of homosexuality (and gay rights) is one that is tremendously important for students to understand if they are to be informed citizens and *educated* about sexuality.

One approach is for educators to decide what is right (when we disagree) and then teach *their* views to children. New York City's *Children of the Rainbow* multicultural curriculum is a rather notorious example; it would have taught elementary school children the acceptability of homosexuality and nontraditional families had not a coalition of religious conservatives rebelled, ultimately forcing the departure of the system's chancellor. Our objection to this curriculum is not its position on homosexuality; it is that it takes a position at all. It is proper and important to teach children to respect the rights of others; name calling and gay bashing are not permissible—and there is broad consensus about this. But we disagree deeply about homosexuality on moral and religious grounds. Given our *civic* framework, it is not permissible for a public school to institutionalize a moral or religious position on a divisive issue and teach it to children uncritically. Given our *educational* framework, students must learn about the alternative positions when we disagree; all the major voices must be included in the discussion. Of course, the New York City case was particularly troubling because the children were so young.

What then would an adequate sex education curriculum look like? It must, of course, be age appropriate. Lessons and courses for young children should adopt the character education model, and we must take great care to ensure that we don't encourage premature sexual behavior; character education continues to be appropriate for high school students—so long as it deals with matters about which we agree. Indeed, we are inclined to think that adolescents need moral guidance in matters of sexual morality rather more than they need freedom. They must learn to think about sexuality in moral terms.[2]

We have also argued, however, that we need to educate mature students regarding some matters of great importance about which we disagree deeply. When we do this, however, we must educate them liberally, including all of the major voices—religious as well as secular—in the discussion.

We have already noted that one disagreement is over whether to teach abstinence only. Unhappily, our differences here appear to be irreconcilable. We do believe that some of the controversy would dissipate if sex education were truly liberal. If it would take seriously moral and religious ways of thinking about sexuality, then discussion of condoms would be less likely to be understood as legitimizing promiscuity. Still, if schools require such courses, they should include opt-out (or opt-in) provisions. We suspect that if parents were convinced that educators took their moral and religious views seriously, fewer would have their children opt out.

We recognize that adequate materials are lacking and most teachers are not prepared to include religious perspectives on sexuality in their classes. It is no easy task to make sense of the soul when discussing abortion in a health class, sacramental understandings of marriage in a home economics class, or the sinfulness of promiscuity in a sex education class. Sex education teachers usually have backgrounds in health education, psychology, and the social sciences rather than the humanities or religious studies, and they may have no background in religious studies to help them make sense of religious perspectives on sex education. This is, once again, reason for a required course in religious studies (or a moral capstone course) that provides a sufficiently deep understanding of religion to enable students to make sense of religious interpretations of morality and sexuality. Still, for both civic and educational reasons, some attention to religion in sex education courses is absolutely essential.

---

[2] See, for example, Character Education Partnership's *Character-Based Sex Education in Public Schools: A Position Statement* (geninfo@character.org).

Finally, we note that other teachers will sometimes find themselves drawn into both sex education and moral education. Much fiction, for example, deals with sexuality—dating, love, marriage, integrity, adultery, homosexuality, and the family. As we argued in Chapter 6, the study of literature is important for the insight and perspective it provides on the inescapable existential questions of life—a good number of which bear on sexuality. Moreover, it is tremendously important that teachers in a variety of courses provide students the moral resources for thinking critically about the portrayal of sexuality in popular culture.

Reminders

Finally, a few reminders.

• *Pluralism and relativism.* In Chapter 2 we noted that one of the most difficult tasks for teachers is to convey to students the difference between pluralism and relativism. The civic ground rules of our democracy and the ideal of liberal education require that we respect the pluralistic nature of our society and take seriously the various participants in our cultural conversation about what is morally required of us. But teachers must not take this to mean that all moral positions are equally good or true. For the most part, moral disagreements are about what *the truth* is, what justice truly requires. It is true, of course, that within some important intellectual traditions the idea of moral truth makes no sense, and older students should be introduced to such traditions too—though even here there is often a *pragmatic* moral consensus about some important basic virtues and values. The fact that we disagree about the nature of morality doesn't mean there are not better and worse ways of thinking about it.

• *Absolutism.* People sometimes claim that because religious accounts of morality are *absolutist,* religion, by its nature, cannot tolerate dissent. This has, of course, been a common religious position; it has also been a common *secular* position in the 20th century (among Nazis and communists, for example). Some religious traditions have placed considerable emphasis on free conscience, however, and if some religions have claimed to know God's law with considerable certainty, others have emphasized humility. Just as scientists can believe in objective truth and yet favor an open society in which we debate what that truth is, so religious folk can believe in moral truth and yet favor an open society in which we pursue it openly, with humility.

• *Religious diversity.* If there are shared moral values that cut across religions, we also need to remember that there are also differences among religions, and it won't do to say that they all agree about morality. As we've just suggested, some traditions favor religious establishments and are intolerant of dissent, while others value freedom of conscience and the separation of church and state; some religions have required nonviolence, others have called for holy wars; some have emphasized love and mercy, and others justice and retribution; some have required chastity and poverty, yet others have sanctified marriage and wealth. Some religions have understood morality in terms of God's law, others in terms of love, or grace, or tradition, or liberating the oppressed. Religious conservatives have often grounded morality in Scripture, whereas religious liberals have often held that through continuing moral and religious experience, reason and reflection, we can progressively acquire deeper insight into morality and reform our traditions. Some conservatives believe that people are so sinful that only the threat of hell or the experience of divine grace can move them. Liberals often have a somewhat more optimistic view of human nature in which we have at least a significant potential for doing good apart from supernatural intervention. Teachers must be aware of the complexity of their subject.

• *Suffering.* We often think of morality in terms of personal virtues such as honesty, responsibility, and integrity—in part, perhaps, because such virtues are relatively uncontroversial, in part because they are congenial to an individualistic society. But there are dangers in uncritically conceiving of morality as a matter primarily of *personal* virtue. Historically, morality has been intimately tied to visions of justice, social institutions, and ways of thinking about human suffering and flourishing. Indeed, given the ubiquity of suffering and injustice, it is hard to think of a more important task for schools than moral education *broadly conceived.* Of course, much that students study in history and literature classes *does* address the nature of suffering, injustice, and the human condition.

Conclusions

One purpose of moral education is to help make children virtuous—honest, responsible, and compassionate. Another is to make mature students informed and reflective about important and controversial moral issues. Both purposes are embedded in a yet larger project— making sense of life. On most accounts, morality isn't intellectually free-floating, a matter of personal choices and subjective values. Moralities are embedded in traditions, in conceptions of what it means to be human, in worldviews.

How we ground and justify moral claims is tremendously important. It makes a huge difference if we think, for example, in terms of neoclassical economic theory and cost-benefit analyses, humanistic psychology and self-actualization, or moral theology. In spite of religious diversity and the great differences between liberals and conservatives within religious traditions, the vast majority of religious folk agree that reality has a God-given moral structure, and this distinguishes them from most secular folk.

In their influential study of American culture *Habits of the Heart,* Robert Bellah and his colleagues (1985) argued that most Americans speak two quite different moral languages: an older, now "secondary" language derived from our civic and religious traditions; and a newer, "first" language of "utilitarian" and "expressive" individualism that is reinforced over and over again by modern culture. Unfortunately, they argue, this language of individualism is not nearly rich enough to allow us to make sense of those moral virtues and vices that are part of our civic and religious traditions. If we haven't already become completely preoccupied with liberty and rights, self-interest and self-esteem, autonomy and individualism, we are in danger of this happening; we are losing our ability to speak meaningfully about virtue and duty, love and self-sacrifice, community and justice. The tendency is to forget the older languages, particularly when the everyday language of culture and the marketplace, schooling and scholarship are secular.

We agree. Too much education is relentlessly fixated on economic and technological development—both of which are important, of course. But, *in the end,* one of the things most people learn is that the greatest sources of meaning in life come not from wealth and technological wizardry but from altogether different realms of experience. We suggest that if students are to be adequately oriented in life, they should be educated somewhat less about its material dimensions and somewhat more about morality and those forms of community that bind us together with our fellow human beings, with the past, with our posterity, and, perhaps also with God.

Suggested Readings
and Resources

It is important at the outset to remember that morality acquires its meaning and its force by virtue of its location within a worldview; there is a danger in abstracting moral principles and values from the contexts that make sense of them. Religious morality must be studied in religious context, paying attention to the theological and institutional webs of meaning that shape and sustain morality.

For a basic introduction to how morality is understood in world religions, see *How to Live Well: Ethics in World Religions* (1988), by Denise Lardner Carmody and John Tully Carmody. See *Readings in Christian Ethics: A Historical Sourcebook* (1996), edited by J. Phillip Wogaman and Douglas M. Strong, for a good collection of excerpts from major Christian writers arranged chronologically, and *From Christ to the World: Introductory Readings in Christian Ethics* (1994), edited by Wayne G. Boulton, for a rich collection of biblical texts, articles, and documents, arranged topically, with an emphasis on recent texts. For a short narrative account see *Christian Ethics: An Introduction Through History and Current Issues* (1993), by Denise Lardner Carmody and John Tully Carmody. *Contemporary Jewish Ethics and Morality: A Reader* (1995), edited by Elliot Dorff and Louis Newman, is a superb collection of articles covering a wide range of moral issues. For morality in the Islamic tradition, see John Renard, *Seven Doors to Islam: Spirituality and the Religious Life of Muslims* (1996).

Sexuality: A Reader (1998), edited by Karen Lebacqz and David Sinacore-Guinn, includes an array of essays and official statements on sexuality from the major religious traditions. *Homosexuality and World Religions* (1993), edited by Arlene Swidler, includes essays on how homosexuality has been understood in the major religions. *Homosexuality in the Church: Both Sides of the Debate* (1994), edited by Jeffrey S. Siker, includes essays written from conservative and liberal positions, and the texts of a number of denominational statements on homosexuality. *Abortion: A Reader* (1996), edited by Lloyd Steffens, is a superb collection of 45 essays and documents from a wide variety of religious perspectives. See Pope John Paul II's encyclical *The Gospel of Life (Evangelium Vitae)* (1995) for the Roman Catholic position on abortion and the sanctity of life.

In perhaps the most influential critique of American culture of the past several decades, *Habits of the Heart: Individualism and Community in American Life* (1985), Robert Bellah and his colleagues show how traditional civic and religious ways of thinking about morality and community have been undermined by American individualism. For books dealing with the relationship of religion to politics and social justice, we refer the reader to "Suggested Readings and Resources" following Chapter 5.

To give some sense of the range of recent work in moral theology, we suggest the following: Martin Buber, *I and Thou* (1923); Reinhold Niebuhr, *Moral*

Man and Immoral Society (1932) and An Interpretation of Christian Ethics (1935); C. S. Lewis, The Abolition of Man (1947); Abraham Joshua Heschel, Man Is Not Alone (1951) and God in Search of Man (1956); H. Richard Niebuhr, The Responsible Self (1963); Richard Rubenstein, After Auschwitz: Radical Theology and Contemporary Judaism (1966); James Cone, A Black Theology of Liberation (1970); Rosemary Radford Ruether, Sexism and God-Talk (1973); Gustavo Gutierrez, A Theology of Liberation (1973); Stanley Hauerwas, The Peaceable Kingdom: A Primer in Christian Ethics (1983); and Pope John Paul II, The Splendor of Truth (1993).

Three very good (if often challenging) books by philosophers trace the historical development of moral theory and its relationship to religion: Ethics After Babel (1988), by Jeffrey Stout; The Sources of the Self: The Making of the Modern Identity (1989), by Charles Taylor; and Whose Justice, Whose Rationality? (1988), by Alasdair MacIntyre. Religion and Morality (1973), edited by Gene Outka and John P. Reeder Jr., is a good collection of philosophical essays dealing with the relationship of religion and morality.

The Character Education Partnership provides advice and assistance for schools and communities interested in developing character education programs. For more information, write to the CEP at 918 16th St., NW, Suite 501, Washington, DC 20006, call 800-988-8081, or visit their web site (www.character.org).

Some of the themes in this chapter are explored at greater length in Warren A. Nord's Religion and American Education: Rethinking a National Dilemma (1995), Chapter 11.

Conclusions

WE DON'T TAKE RELIGION SERIOUSLY IN THE PUBLIC SCHOOL curriculum.

We ignore it—not completely, of course, but we do relegate it to distant times and places (in history and literature courses). The curriculum all but completely ignores religion as a *live* way of making sense of the world in the here and now. We trust that over the course of Chapters 3 through 9 this has become graphically clear: in course after course we teach students to think about matters that are religiously controversial in exclusively and uncritically secular ways. The implicit message is that students can learn everything they need to know about whatever they study (other than history and historical literature) without learning anything about religion: religion is irrelevant in the search for truth.

There are many reasons for this: religion is controversial; there are fears about church-state conflicts; teachers are insecure teaching about something they don't understand themselves. But the roots of the problem are largely philosophical, a matter of worldview. Educators have come to adopt the view that our intellectual disciplines must be scientific, or at least secular. We don't teach *subjects* (which might be interpreted in religious as well as secular categories); we teach *disciplines:* we teach students to think about the world in exclusively secular ways. This marginalizes religion intellectually.

It is not the conscious intention of educators to marginalize religion—and there certainly is no conspiracy to undermine the religious convictions of students. Most educators have themselves been illiberally educated. The problem is rooted in the parochial nature of our intellectual life, in our uncritical secularism, in religious naivete.

We have argued that the failure to take religion seriously is problematic for three major reasons. First, it means that public education doesn't take the public seriously; we have educationally disenfranchised members of religious traditions. Second, public education is not religiously neutral as the First Amendment and the courts require it to be. Finally, in failing to take religion seriously we educate our children parochially or illiberally; we uncritically teach them to make sense of the world in exclusively secular ways; indeed, we come close to indoctrinating them.

Religion must be incorporated into the curriculum for three correlative reasons:

1. The civic argument. *Public schools must be built on common ground.* If we are to live together we must take each other seriously; we must respect each other. This certainly doesn't mean that we must agree with each other. It does mean we should listen to each other. The curriculum must be inclusive, teaching students about religious as well as secular ways of living and thinking.

2. The constitutional argument. *Public schools must be religiously neutral—neutral among religions, and neutral between religion and nonreligion.* We have noted that educators no longer think it fair or neutral to ignore black history and women's literature. It should be just as obvious that religious voices must be included in the curriculum. Of course the First Amendment *requires* neutrality in matters of religion—and, as we've argued, neutrality requires fairness. Public schools are not free to ignore religious ways of thinking and living when they teach secular ways of thinking and living that are religiously contested.

3. The educational argument. *Finally, if students are to be liberally educated they must understand a good deal about religion.* We like to think of liberal education as an initiation into a conversation in which students listen to, reflect on, and think critically about the major voices in our world, addressing the most important questions of life. Some of those voices are secular and some are religious. In-

deed, students can't think critically about science or their secular studies unless they understand enough about alternative religious worldviews to acquire some critical distance on them.

These civic, constitutional, and educational arguments for including religion in the curriculum are deeply complementary, for the governing virtue of each approach is fairness. It is also worth noting, once again, that although there are religious arguments for taking religion seriously, we haven't appealed to them. Our arguments are secular arguments.

They are also arguments built on the principles that have shaped what we have called the New Consensus and, as such, they constitute a "middle way" through the minefields of our culture wars, one that we believe has the greatest chance for leading to a peaceful resolution of the conflict.

The New Consensus points beyond the failed models of public education—both the "sacred" public school of our early history, and the "naked" public school of our recent history—to the "civil" public school, where people of all faiths and no faith are treated with fairness and respect. Only when we treat all people with respect, only when we include religious as well as secular voices in the conversation, only when we build public schools on common ground, will we secure the support necessary to sustain public education through the battles in our culture wars.

To many teachers the task of incorporating religion into their courses will be a daunting one. We have argued that religion is relevant to virtually every subject in the curriculum, and often in myriad ways. Indeed, in a book of this length we could, in many cases, just scratch the surface.

There is, of course, a danger in making the task appear too difficult; we would be truly sorry if we discouraged teachers from undertaking it. On the other hand, there is also a danger in failing to acknowledge just how far short most education falls in adequately educating students. We must be aware of the ideal if we are to move in the right direction with an appropriate sense of urgency.

Significant, if incremental, improvements are readily possible. Simply understanding the ground rules—the civic, constitutional, and educational frameworks—is tremendously important, and we trust that our readers will have a good grasp of them after reading this book. Moreover, every teacher can read a few books (in his or her copious free time) to develop a deeper understanding of our religious traditions and their relevance to what is taught.

But, obviously, if we are to approximate the ideal, some significant reforms must take place in our educational system, as we suggested in Chapter 2. Religion is not only controversial, it is complicated, and it is naive to think that we can incorporate it into the curriculum painlessly. *All* teachers need to learn more about religion and its relationship to what they teach—*and* religious studies needs to be developed as a certifiable field in public education.

Finally, we note that our criticisms and reform proposals are not merely academic (as if "merely academic" meant they were not important in the real world). Religion is important. If God exists there are implications. Of course, we don't agree about whether God exists or what the implications might be if God does exist. But, we've argued, educated folk should think about such things. Unfortunately, religion has become so marginalized in the consciousness of most educators that arguments for including it in the curriculum are often dismissed as the special pleading of yet another special interest group wanting its inevitably marginal slice of space and time in an unhappily overextended curriculum. Such objections are, we suggest, symptoms of the problem. Consider the time and effort we put into athletics, or computers, or, indeed, into mathematics. Can it really be true that it is more important for college-bound students to take 12 years of math and no religion, rather than 11 years of math and 1 year of religion?

Our priorities are skewed. We have lost perspective on what is, perhaps, most important of all: understanding our place in the overall scheme of things. One of the ironies of American life is that for all our religiosity, we simply don't take religion seriously in our schools.

References

Adams, E.M. (1993). *Religion and cultural freedom.* Philadelphia: Temple University Press.

Angus Reid Group. (1996). God and society in North America. Presentation (survey).

ASCD Panel. (1988). *Religion in the curriculum.* Alexandria, VA.: Author.

Barbour, I. (1997). *Science and religion: Historical and contemporary issues.* San Francisco: HarperSanFrancisco.

Barrett, W. (1962). *Irrational man.* Garden City, NY: Doubleday Anchor.

Bellah, R., et al. (1985). *Habits of the heart: Individualism and community in American life.* Berkeley: University of California Press.

Boslough, J. (1985). *Stephen Hawking's universe.* New York: William Morrow.

Boston University, Center for the Advanced of Ethics and Character. (1996, March). The character education manifesto. *Character, Vol. IV,* 2: 1, 6.

Buber, M. (1958). *I and thou* (R.G. Smith, Trans.). New York: Charles Scribner's Sons.

Burtt, E.A. (Ed.). (1955). *The teachings of the compassionate Buddha.* New York: New American Library.

Cairney, W., and Winternitz, K., revision coordinators. (1996). *Biological Science.* Lexington, MA: D.C. Heath.

California Department of Education History-Social Science Curriculum Framework and Criteria Committee. (1987, 1997). *History-social science framework for California public schools.* Sacramento: Author.

Campbell, N.E. (1993). *Biology.* Redwood City, CA: Addison-Wesley.

Catechism of the Catholic Church. (1994). Rahway, NJ: Paulist Press.

Center for Civic Education. (1994). *National standards for civics and government.* Calabasis, LA: Author.

Conceptual physics. (1992). San Francisco: HarperCollins.

Consortium of National Arts Education Associations. (1994). *National standards for arts education.* Reston, VA: Music Educators National Conference.

Delbanco, A. (1995). *The death of Satan: How Americans have lost the sense of evil.* New York: Farrar, Straus, and Giroux.

Dixon, J. (1995). Tuscan theology. In D. Apostolos-Cappadona (Ed.), *Art, creativity, and the sacred* (pp. 277–296). New York: Continuum. (Original work published 1984.)

Eliot, T.S. (1932). Religion and literature. In G.B. Tennyson and E.E. Ericson Jr. (Eds.), *Religion and modern literature* (pp. 21–30). Grand Rapids, MI: William B. Eerdmans Publishing Company.

Frank, R.H., Gilovich, T., and Regan, D.T. (1993, Spring). Does studying economics inhibit cooperation? In *Journal of Economic Perspectives, Vol. 7*: 159–71.

Gagnon, P., and the Bradley Commission on History in Schools. (Eds.). (1989). *Historical literacy: The case for history in American education.* New York: Macmillan Publishing Company.

Gallup poll: Public opinion 1991. (1991). Wilmington, DE: Scholarly Resources.

Getchell, L.H., et al. (1994). *Perspectives on health.* Lexington, MA: D.C. Heath.

Gould, S.J. (1997). *Full house.* New York: Random House.

Haynes, C.C. (1990). *Religion in American history: What to teach and how.* Alexandria, VA: ASCD.

Haynes, C.C., and Thomas, O. (Eds.). (1994, 1996). *Finding common ground: A First Amendment guide to religion and public education.* Nashville, TN: First Amendment Center.

Holdren, J., and Hirsch, E.D., Jr. (Eds.). (1996). *Books to build on: A grade-by-grade resource guide for parents and teachers.* New York: Delta Publishing.

Hunter, J.D. (1991). *Culture wars: The struggle to define America.* New York: Basic Books.

International Reading Association and the National Council of Teachers of English. (1996). *Standards for the English language arts.* Newark, DE/ Urbana, IL: Author.

Jastrow, R. (1978). *God and the astronomers.* New York: Warner Books.

John Paul II. (1996a). The ecological crisis: A common responsibility. In R.S. Gottlieb (Ed.), *This sacred earth: Religion, nature, environment* (pp. 230–237). New York: Routledge. (Original work published in 1989.)

John Paul II. (1996b, November 14). Message to pontifical academy of sciences on evolution. *Origins: cns documentary service.*

Katz, S.T. (1978). Judaism, God, and the astronomers. Afterword to R. Jastrow, *God and the astronomers* (pp. 147–161). New York: Warner Books.

Leinwand, G. (1986). *The pageant of world history.* Needham Heights, MA: Allyn and Bacon.

Liberating life: A report to the World Council of Churches. (1990). In R.S. Gottlieb (Ed.), *This sacred earth: Religion, nature, environment* (pp. 251–269). New York: Routledge.

Literature: World masterpieces (Teacher's edition). (1992). Englewood Cliffs, NJ: Prentice-Hall.

McFague, S. (1993). *The body of God: An ecological theology.* Minneapolis, MN: Fortress Press

Mill, J.S. (1965). *On liberty.* In M. Lerner (Ed.), *Essential works of John Stuart Mill* (pp. 249–360). New York: Bantam Books. (Original work published 1859)

National Academy of Sciences. (1984). *Science and creationism.* Washington, DC: National Academy Press.

National Association of Biology Teachers. (n.d.). Statement on teaching evolution. (www.nabt.org/oldsite/evolution.html). Reston, VA: Author.

National Center for History in the Schools. (1996). *National standards for history.* Los Angeles: Author.

National Council for the Social Studies. (1984/1990). Including the study about religion in the social studies curriculum: A position statement and guidelines. Reprinted in *Social education, 54,* 310. (Reprinted from 1984.)

National Council for the Social Studies (1994). *Curriculum standards for the social studies.* Washington DC: Author.

National Council on Bible Curriculum in Public Schools. (1996). *NCBCPS Manual.* Greensboro, NC: Author.

National Council on Economics Education. (1997). *National content standards in economics.* New York: Author.

National Research Council. *National science education standards.* (1996). Washington, DC: National Academy Press.

Neuhaus, R.J. (1984). *The naked public square: Religion and democracy in America.* Grand Rapids, MI: Eerdmans.

Nord, W. (1995). *Religion and American education: Rethinking a national dilemma.* Chapel Hill, NC: University of North Carolina Press.

Peacocke, A. (1984). *Intimations of reality: Critical realism in science and religion.* South Bend, IN: University of Notre Dame Press.

Polkinghorne, J. (1993). *Religion in an age of science.* The McNair Lecture at the University of North Carolina at Chapel Hill.

Religion in the public school curriculum: Questions and answers. (1994). In C.C. Haynes (Ed.), *Finding common ground: A First Amendment guide to religion and public education* (chap. 6, pp. 1–4). Nashville, TN: First Amendment Center. (Original work published 1988.)

Ruether, R.R. (1992). *Gaia and God: An ecofeminist theology of earth healing.* San Francisco: HarperSanFrancisco.

Sagan, C. (1974). *Broca's brain: Reflections on the romance of science.* New York: Random House.

Schumpeter, J. (1972). *Capitalism, socialism and democracy* (3rd ed.). New York: Harper Torchbooks.

Sewall, G.T. (1995). *Religion in the classroom: What the textbooks tell us.* New York: American Textbook Council.

Smart, N. (1996). *Dimensions of the sacred: An anatomy of the world's beliefs.* Berkeley: University of California Press.

Smart, N. (1987). *Religion and the Western mind.* New York: Macmillan.

Smart, N. (1976). *The religious experience of mankind* (2nd ed.). New York: Charles Scribner's Sons.

Smith, H. (1991). *The world's religions.* San Francisco: HarperSanFrancisco.

Smith, W.C. (1993). *What is scripture?* Minneapolis, MN: Fortress.

Smith, W.C. (1963). *The meaning and end of religion.* New York: Mentor Books.

Statement by religious leaders at the summit on the environment. (1991). In R.S. Gottlieb (Ed.), *This sacred earth: Religion, nature, environment* (pp. 636–639). New York: Routledge.

Stoeger, W. (1996). Key developments in physics challenging philosophy and theology. In W.M. Richardson and W.J. Wildman (Eds.), *Religion and science* (pp. 183–200). New York: Routledge.

Tillich, P. (1957). *Dynamics of faith.* New York: Harper and Row.

Vitz, P.C. (1986). *Censorship: Evidence of bias in our children's textbooks.* Ann Arbor, MI: Servant Books.

Winthrop, J. (1956). A model of Christian charity. In P. Miller (Ed.), *The American Puritans: Their prose and poetry* (pp. 79–84). New York: Columbia University Press. (Original work published 1630)

Wordsworth, W. (1950). Lines composed a few miles above Tintern Abbey, on revisiting the banks of the Wye during a tour. In T. Hutchinson (Ed.)/E. De Selincourt (Ed., rev. ed.), *The poetical works of Wordsworth.* New York: Oxford University Press. (Originally published 1798)

Wright, T.R. (1988). *Theology and literature.* New York: Basil Blackwell.

Wuthnow, R. (1993). *Christianity in the 21st century.* New York: Oxford University Press.

Index

Page numbers followed by *n* refer to "Suggested Readings and Resources" at the end of chapters.

About the Authors

Warren A. Nord received his Ph.D. in philosophy from the University of North Carolina at Chapel Hill in 1978. Since 1979 he has taught the philosophy of religion and been director of that university's Program in the Humanities and Human Values. He is the author of *Religion and American Education: Rethinking a National Dilemma* (1995), a comprehensive study of historical, philosophical, constitutional, and pedagogical issues relating to religion and education. He may be reached at the Program in the Humanities and Human Values, Campus Box 3425, University of North Carolina at Chapel Hill, Chapel Hill, NC 27599 (e-mail: wnord@email.unc.edu).

Charles C. Haynes is Senior Scholar for Religious Freedom at the First Amendment Center and serves on the Board of Directors of the Character Education Partnership. He was a principal organizer and drafter of a series of consensus guidelines on religious liberty issues in public schools endorsed by leading religious and educational organizations. Dr. Haynes is the author of *Religion in American History: What to Teach and How* (1990) and *Finding Common Ground: A First Amendment Guide to Religion and Public Education* (1994). He holds a master's degree in religion and education from Harvard Divinity School and a Ph.D. in theological studies from Emory University. He may be contacted at the First Amendment Center, The Freedom Forum, 1101 Wilson Blvd., Arlington, VA 22209. Phone: 703-284-2859, Fax: 703-284-2879. E-mail: chaynes@freedomforum.org

About the First Amendment Center

The Freedom Forum First Amendment Center at Vanderbilt University was founded December 15, 1991, the 200th anniversary of the ratification of the Bill of Rights to the U.S. Constitution.

The Center serves as a forum for dialogue, discussion, and debate on free expression and freedom of information issues.

The Center's mission is to foster a greater public understanding of and appreciation for First Amendment rights and values, including freedom of religion, free speech, and free press, and the right to assemble peaceably and to petition government.

The Center is affiliated with Vanderbilt University in Nashville, Tennessee, through the Vanderbilt Institute for Public Policy Studies.

First Amendment Center
1207 18th Avenue South
Nashville, TN 37212
615-321-9588

www.freedomforum.org

First Amendment Center
Board of Trustees